Read, Writing

Grammar for College Writers

Patricia Porter
San Francisco State University

Deborah vanDommelen
San Francisco State University

HEINLE
CENGAGE Learning

Australia • Brazil • Japan • Korea • Mexico • Singapore • Spain • United Kingdom • United States

HEINLE
CENGAGE Learning™

Read, Write, Edit:
Grammar for College Writers
Patricia Porter, Deborah vanDommelen

Publisher: Patricia A. Coryell

Director of ESL Publishing: Susan Maguire

Senior Development Editor:
  Kathy Sands-Boehmer

Development Manager: Sarah Helyar Smith

Development Editor: Kathleen M. Smith

Editorial Assistant: Evangeline Bermas

Senior Project Editor: Tracy Patruno

Senior Manufacturing Coordinator:
  Marie Barnes

Senior Marketing Manager: Annamarie Rice

Marketing Associate: Laura Hemrika

Compositor: Publishing Services

Cover Image: © Christie's Images/CORBIS

Library of Congress Number: 2001133361

ISBN-13: 978-0-618-14495-2

ISBN-10: 0-618-14495-1

Heinle
25 Thomson Place
Boston, MA 02210
USA

Cengage Learning is a leading provider of customized learning solutions with office locations around the globe, including Singapore, the United Kingdom, Australia, Mexico, Brazil and Japan. Locate our local office at:
international.cengage.com/region

Cengage Learning products are represented in Canada by Nelson Education, Ltd.

Visit Heinle online at **elt.heinle.com**
Visit our corporate website at **cengage.com**

Photo Credits: Page 2: From "When You Shouldn't Tell It Like It Is" by Deborah Tannen, *The Washington Post,* March 1987, copyright Deborah Tannen. Reprinted by permission. This article is adapted from the author's book *That's Not What I Meant!: How Conversational Style Makes or Breaks Relationships* (Ballantine 1986). Page 24: Excerpt from "Return to Vietnam" by Elsa Arnett from *San Jose Mercury News,* April 8, 2001, p. 26A. Copyright © 2002 San Jose Mercury News. All rights reserved. Reproduced with permission. Page 44: "You Say Tomato" by Lalita Khosla from *Forbes,* May 21, 2001, p. 36. Reprinted by permission of Forbes Magazine © 2003 Forbes Inc. Page 65: From R.W. Griffin, *Management,* 4th edition. Boston: Houghton Mifflin Company, 1999, p. 152. Page 68: Excerpts from "Communicating in the Online Workplace" in *Management,* 8th edition by Robert Kreitner. Copyright © 2001 by Houghton Mifflin Company. All rights reserved. Reprinted by permission. Page 86: From P. Delevett, *San Jose Mercury News,* March 1, 2002, p. 1C. Page 94: From *Zen Comments on the Mumonkan* by Zenkei Shibayama. English language translation copyright © 1974 by Zenkei Shibayama. Reprinted by permission of HarperCollins Publishers Inc. Page 124: From *The House on Mango Street.* Copyright © 1984 by Sandra Cisneros. Published by Vintage Books, a division of Random House, Inc., and in hardcover by Alfred A. Knopf in 1994. Reprinted by permission of Susan Bergholz Literary Services, New York. All rights reserved.

Printed in the United States of America
8 9 10   12 11 10

Contents

Chapter 2   Review of Common Structure Problems: Sentence Structure, Subject-Verb Agreement, Verb Tenses   23

Appendix B　Grammar Reference Charts　159

Appendix C　Strategies for Writing　185

Introduction

Read, Write, Edit: Grammar for College Writers is designed for students in universities, community colleges, and intensive language programs—a population that includes international and resident ESL students as well as bilingual students who have attended school in the U.S. most or all of their lives. The primary goal of the book is to help students become successful academic writers by addressing their needs to a) understand grammatical structures fundamental to college writing and b) develop effective editing skills.

Organization of Chapters and Appendixes with Suggestions for Teaching

Read

The short readings and follow-up activities provide context for discussion, writing, and study of selected grammar features.

Before Reading   These questions generate important background information and help students connect their knowledge and experience to what they are about to read. The questions also help students focus their reading.

> *Suggestions:* The questions are designed to promote schema building, not extensive discussions of the topics. Quickly clustering or listing students' ideas on the board is usually sufficient to introduce the topic and engage students in the content of the reading.

Readings The readings are short texts of various genres—narration, description, opinion, and argumentation—both fiction and nonfiction.

> *Suggestions:* The readings are short enough to be read aloud by the teacher following a brief pre-reading discussion. They can also be assigned as homework along with the After Reading questions.

After Reading These questions aid students' comprehension of the reading, make connections between the language of the text and the author's intended meaning, and promote student reflection on the content. Charts, grids, or visuals help students organize material and figure out the meaning of both content and grammar.

> *Suggestions:* Assigning these questions for homework often leads to more productive in-class discussions. Written answers, especially those at the paragraph level, can serve as content for grammar assessment and review, especially when learners put them on the board and then check each others' work for both content and form. This language analysis can be done before the coverage of the grammar sections as a kind of preview of problematic grammar features in the students' writing, or it can be done in connection with the analysis and editing activities in the grammar Practice sections.

Write

Although the focus of *Read, Write, Edit* is on studying grammar in academic contexts, learners have many opportunities for exploring their ideas in writing: in short written responses in After Reading, in extended pieces of more formal writing in Topics for Writing, or in activities in the grammar Practice sections. All this writing provides meaningful material for students to use as they learn to edit their writing accurately. Support is given in Appendix C, Strategies for Writing. (See description below.)

Topics for Writing These writing prompts provide variety and flexibility and may be used as they appear in the text or easily adapted to fit a teacher's specific class or purpose. In addition, many of these topics are designed to elicit and promote the practice of the grammar features in the chapter in an academic context.

> *Suggestions:* Teachers can choose specific topics to encourage the use of the target grammatical features as well as the practice of different genres of writing. Since some topics include built-in "options," teachers can assign written responses that vary in complexity and in the time it requires to complete them. Students should begin writing about these topics immediately after completing the reading so that they can use their writing as the basis for revision and editing activities in the grammar Practice sections.

Using Vocabulary Accurately These lists of key words and collocations related to the readings offer support for academic writers' ongoing need to build vocabulary. The lists also draw students' attention to the importance of word partnerships.

> *Suggestions:* Teachers can encourage students to use these expressions in their responses to After Reading questions and Topics for Writing prompts, and can provide individual or group feedback on students' papers or on board work regarding lexical problems. Teachers can also have students keep lists of word partnerships as described in Appendix A.

Edit: Grammar Previews, Tips, and Practice

In order to be successful editors, students must have sufficient grammatical knowledge of the structures commonly used in academic writing, and must develop appropriate strategies for editing. The grammar sections described below are designed for that purpose. Each chapter contains a Listening/Writing activity related to the reading (Chapter 6 contains two) and three or four grammar topics, each of which has Preview activities, Grammar Tips in chart format, and Practice activities.

Listening/Writing Activities: Dictation/Dictocomp These sections include a short, cohesive text that is based on the content of the reading and that contains the target structures for the chapter. The language generated by these activities is intended to be used for analysis of specific language structures. These activities develop listening skills, raise awareness by helping learners make connections between spoken and written language, and encourage learning through negotiation as peers work together to compare their texts with the original and to help each other focus on accuracy.

> *Suggestions:* Teachers can choose dictation (exact reproduction of the text read aloud by the teacher) or dictocomp (reconstruction of the text for meaning) depending on their students: orally fluent learners tend to respond more positively to dictocomp and reconstruction of the text in pairs or small groups, while less fluent students tend

to benefit from dictation. In either case, it is productive to use the board and review student texts with the whole class for completeness and accuracy. For dictation, one or several students can write on the board while the rest of the class write at their desks; for dictocomp, several reconstructions can be put on the board. Teachers can also use a dictation/dictocomp as a pre-reading activity to introduce a reading or as post-reading comprehension follow up to aid discussion of the reading. They may also use this activity to establish context for grammar teaching without having to assign the reading.

Preview: Assess What You Know These activities inductively introduce the structures and forms that are the focus of the chapter as they require learners to demonstrate what they know in a problem-solving format. Students analyze functions, structures, and/or forms in contexts related to the readings and are asked to formulate their own "rules."
   Suggestions: Teachers can use the grammar Preview activities to activate students' schemata, engage learners in thinking about salient features, diagnose their understanding and proficiency, and help them assess their knowledge of structures. Students who prefer a more deductive approach to learning can study the charts first and then do the Preview activities as follow up.

Grammar Tips: Check Your Work The grammatical information in *Read, Write, Edit* appears in chart format for easy readability. The charts contain succinct explanations of grammar structures, functions, and forms with corresponding examples. The charts also contain examples of typical problems for second language writers as well as tips for avoiding these problems.
   Suggestions: These grammar charts can serve as a resource for teachers as they prepare to teach or review a selected grammar feature. Teachers should direct students to use the charts as they check and modify their work from the Preview sections and encourage them to use the charts as a reference as they work through a chapter, during class discussions of grammar or editing materials, or when writing and editing on their own.

Practice These activities reinforce what students have learned in the Preview and from the grammar charts and provide writing and editing practice at the sentence and discourse levels. Types of activities include text analysis, editing of sentences and texts, sentence and text-level writing, interviews, games, sentence completion, cloze activities, chalkboard composition, and editing of student-written texts. The website for *Read, Write, Edit* has numerous practice activities that supplement these sections.
   Suggestions: Teachers can choose from these many practice activities the ones they find most useful for their classes. They can also have learners work in the format best suited to their learning preferences or the time constraints of the course: individually, in pairs, small groups, or with the whole class. Although many of these editing activities may seem time consuming, they can help to model effective editing procedures, especially when done on overhead transparencies or the board. They can also promote meaningful discussion of students' grammar problems.

Wrap-Up These activities require students to focus on and edit for the specific features of the chapter using their own and their peers' writing. Using the Editing Guides in

Appendix A (see description below), students learn to interact with their writing and to ask appropriate questions to determine if the meaning and form are clear.

>   *Suggestions:* When students put samples of their writing on overhead transparencies or the board and then analyze and edit their work, they reinforce the skills they have been learning. Teachers can individualize learning by helping students figure out which Editing Guides (in addition to those related to a particular chapter) are needed for their writing.

Appendixes

Appendix A: References for Editing This appendix shows students how they can set up their own references for editing. It also includes guides for editing the targeted grammar features for each chapter with a focus on common problems. The step-by-step approach helps students look critically at text: they find and identify structures, figure out forms and meanings, and then correct errors.

>   *Suggestions:* Teachers can use the guides as they appear in the appendix or adapt them to fit their own purposes or the needs of their students.

Appendix B: Grammar Reference Charts These charts supplement the grammar charts in the chapters by offering additional information and examples in an easily accessible format. Some charts provide more detailed coverage of a grammar feature than the charts in the chapters, while other charts provide reference lists for both students and teachers.

>   *Suggestions:* Teachers can refer to these charts as they prepare to teach a chapter or as questions arise in the classroom or in conference. Students can use the charts to check their work or to answer questions they may have when preparing for class, writing a paper, or working on writing assignments for courses in disciplines other than English.

Appendix C: Strategies for Writing This brief guide and reference for students and teachers provides strategies for responding to a writing topic and formulating ideas into essay form. It includes supplementary information and is designed to support student writers at all stages of the writing process.

>   *Suggestions:* If the focus of the course is primarily on grammar instruction and practice, teachers may simply direct students to specific sections of the guide as they work on their writing. If the goals of the course include specific writing instruction, teachers may want to draw extensively on this guide as they plan lessons and project the direction of their courses.

On the Web at elt.heinle.com/readwriteedit

- *An instructor's guide* includes a sample syllabus, additional suggestions for using the materials, assessment suggestions, additional practice activities, and examples to supplement Appendix C.
- *An answer key* for Before Reading and After Reading questions, Preview activities, and Practice activities
- *An appendix of additional readings*, with comprehension questions and writing topics

Acknowledgments

We acknowledge our debt to our major sources of grammatical information: *The Grammar Book: An ESL/EFL Teacher's Course, The Longman Grammar of Spoken and Written English, Using English Your Second Language,* and *The Collins COBUILD English Guides: #3 Articles and #5 Reporting.*

We want to express our appreciation to Natalia Ades, Mark Alberding, Wendy Becktold, Maureen Fitzgerald, Ceci Herrmann, Vicky Holder, John Holland, Kirsten Hilbert, Wendy Levison, Natasha McKeown, Jay Mojica, Barbara Stoops, and numerous reviewers, who gave us valuable feedback and suggestions on pilot versions of the manuscript. We also extend our appreciation to colleagues and friends who contributed to the concept of this book and who supported us through the writing process: Nathalie Destandau, Linda Gajdusek, Lisa Heyer, Peter Ingmire, May Shih, and Karen Wiederholt. We thank Stephen Browning for generously contributing his artistic talent. We thank the students at San Francisco State University for allowing us to use their writing in this book and thank Lilian Tong for her secretarial assistance.

We are especially grateful to Dorothy Danielson for her wise and careful reading of our manuscript and excellent suggestions, and to Kathleen Smith, our wonderful development editor, for her generosity of spirit and perceptive attention to detail. We acknowledge the thorough and attentive work of Cindy Johnson during the book's production phase as well as the thoughtful and creative input of our colleague, Ceci Herrmann, in developing website materials that complement the text. This book could not have come into existence without the encouragement of our editors, Susan Maguire and Kathy Sands-Boehmer, and we thank them for their support and understanding.

Throughout the duration of the project, we have appreciated the patience and liveliness of Evan, Ian, and Nina, and we especially applaud the graciousness and fortitude of Stephen and David.

1

Review of Grammar Basics

Grammar and Writing Goals

- To review the grammar basics of the sentence:
  Parts of speech
  Articles and nouns
  Phrases and clauses
  Verbs and subjects
  Time expressions
  Word forms
- To practice editing:
  Articles and nouns
  Subjects and verbs
  Time expressions
  Word forms

Overview of the Chapter

Read: "When You Shouldn't Tell It Like It Is" with Before Reading and After Reading Questions, p. 2

Write: Topics for Writing, p. 4

Edit: Grammar Previews, Tips, and Practice, p. 5

Read

Before Reading

Respond to these questions to help you think about and understand the reading that follows.

1. What is the difference between directness and indirectness in conversation? What does it mean to *not* "tell something like it is"?

2. Are there times when you think people should not "tell it like it is"? Think of different situations with family, friends, teachers, partners.

Excerpt from **"When You Shouldn't Tell It Like It Is" by Deborah Tannen**

Linguist Deborah Tannen studies and writes about the relationship between language use and human behavior. In the following excerpt, Tannen examines directness and indirectness in everyday language patterns and how these two systems can affect the success or failure of communication.

A woman asked another woman in her office if she would like to have lunch. The colleague said no, she was sorry, she had a report to finish. The woman repeated the invitation the next week. Again her colleague declined, saying she had not been feeling well. The first woman was confused. So she asked her colleague what her refusals meant: Was she really just busy one week and **ailing** the next, or was she trying to say she simply didn't want to have lunch, so stop asking? The response only confused her more: "Well, um, sure, y'know, I really haven't been feeling well and last week really was difficult with that report which, by the way, was about a very interesting case. It was …"

The woman was frustrated. She couldn't understand why her colleague didn't just say what she meant. But the other woman was frustrated too. She couldn't understand why she was being pushed to say no directly, when she had made perfectly clear that she was not interested in pursuing a friendship.

One woman was expecting directness; to her, indirectness is dishonest. The other was expecting her indirectness to be understood; to her, directness is rude, and being direct would mean being a sort of person that she finds **unappealing**. Both felt that their own ways of talking were obviously right. Neither realized that both systems can be right or wrong; each works well with other people who operate on the same system, and both fail with people who do not. They **instinctively** tried to **dispel** the tension by doing more of the same. Neither thought of adopting the other's system.

Many Americans believe that the only purpose of language is to convey information and that information should be stated outright. But there are many reasons why meaning should not be stated outright, why indirectness is useful and even necessary. The study of indirectness and other politeness **phenomena** has received increasing attention in linguistic scholarship. This is a drastic departure from the

1

5

10

15

20

25

---

ailing: sick
unappealing: not attractive
instinctively: without thinking

dispel: (to) get rid of
phenomena: observable events

trend dominant in linguistics in recent decades: formal representation of language not as it is used but as an abstract system. A linguist working in the latter tradition would be concerned with whether a given sentence is grammatical, regardless of whether it might actually be spoken by anyone, let alone how frequently it might be spoken. For linguists concerned with language as it is used in everyday life, sentences that are actually spoken—and often spoken—are the ones of interest, not those that are theoretically possible but never encountered.

30

from *The Washington Post*, March 1, 1987

After Reading

Individually at home, or with a partner or a small group in class, write the answers to these questions to prepare for class discussion. Keep your answers in a notebook or binder to refer to later when you respond to the writing topics, develop your ideas for longer papers, or analyze your writing. Questions marked ¶ are especially suitable for paragraph-length answers that can be used later when you analyze your writing.

1. Summarize the situation and interaction between the two women in the reading. Include the following in your response:

   the two women (their relationship)   how they respond to each other and why
   what they want   how they feel about the situation and why
   what they do

2. Explain the differences between the two women: How do they feel about directness and indirectness in conversation? Why do they feel the way they do? (lines 14–17) Why does their communication fail? When the situation becomes tense, they do "more of the same." (lines 17-20) What could they try doing instead?

3. According to Deborah Tannen, what do many Americans believe that the only purpose of language is? What is her opinion about indirectness in communication? (lines 21–24)

¶ 4. Imagine you are the second woman in the article. How would you respond to the first woman's invitation? What would you do and say? Why?

¶ 5. Do you agree with Deborah Tannen that "indirectness is useful and even necessary"? (lines 23–24) Explain and support your opinion.

Write

Topics for Writing

Respond in writing to one (or more) of the following topics.

1. What is Deborah Tannen's point in "When You Shouldn't Tell It Like It Is"? Using information and examples from the reading, discuss what you think the main idea is.

2. Who do you sympathize with most: the first woman or the second woman? Why?

3. What could the two women do to solve their problems in communicating with each other? Referring to the reading (optional: and your own experience), explain a solution to their problems in communication.

4. Using the reading (and/or your own experience), explain your views on directness and/or indirectness in language. Is indirectness "dishonest"? Is directness "rude"?

5. What role does culture play in directness or indirectness in language? Explain and support your ideas by giving examples from one cultural perspective. Topics to consider: invitations, requests, providing information, discussing personal issues.

6. Write about your experience with a problem in communication: either with directness or indirectness in language or other example. Using detail and description, clearly explain: the people, the situation, the problem with language, the final outcome for you and the other people involved. (Optional: Compare your experience with the situation described in "When You Shouldn't Tell It Like It Is.")

> **Strategies for Writing: Generating and Developing Ideas**
> For a description of ways to generate ideas, such as freewriting, listing, and brainstorming, as well as ways to develop and support your ideas, refer to Strategies for Writing, pp. 185–190.

Using Vocabulary Accurately

As you write about a reading, pay attention to key words and word partnerships, words that occur frequently with each other or that form fixed expressions. For more examples, see Reference Charts 2.1 and 2.2, pp. 172–174. Create your own word partnerships list (see p. 150).

Some key word partnerships for this reading follow. Locate key words in the reading or in Topics for Writing and notice how they are used. For practice, write sentences using some of these expressions.

to say what you mean
to make (*something*) perfectly clear
to state (*something*) outright
to operate on a system
to dispel/relieve the tension
to communicate with someone
to be direct
to be indirect

to be concerned with
to be confused by
to be frustrated by
to be interested in
a drastic departure
a dominant trend
theoretically possible

Edit: Grammar Previews, Tips, and Practice

Listening/Writing Activity: Dictation/Dictocomp

The following dictation/dictocomp text gives information related to the reading "When You Shouldn't Tell It Like It Is," pp. 2–3.

Close your book. As your teacher reads the sentences below (one time all the way through, then by clauses, then all the way through again), do the following:

- For a dictation, try to write exactly what you hear.
- For a dictocomp, take notes on key words and phrases.
- Then, individually or in groups, reconstruct the text, revising and correcting your work and paying attention to problem areas.

1. "To tell it like it is" means to give information clearly and directly.
2. For example, in academic papers, we are expected to "tell it like it is": to write about information and ideas in a straightforward way.
3. In conversation, however, this is not a rule that is necessarily followed.
4. In fact, Americans may disagree about just how much directness is appropriate, especially in social exchanges such as invitations and requests.
5. These disagreements can lead to misunderstandings and confusion.
6. Today linguists are studying the patterns of directness and indirectness in everyday spoken English.
7. Their findings may help us prevent misunderstandings.

1.1 Basic Parts of Speech

Preview: Assess What You Know

This chapter reviews some of the basic components of the sentence. A knowledge of these structures and this terminology will help you in understanding this textbook and, more importantly, in editing your writing.

A. Use the sentences in the dictation in the previous section or the reading "When You Shouldn't Tell It Like It Is," pp. 2–3. To assess what you know about the names of basic parts of speech, find two additional examples of each of the following grammar categories. The first one is done for you.

1. a proper noun (e.g., *Deborah*)   _Tannen_   _The Washington Post_
2. a common noun (e.g., *woman, lunch*)   _____   _____
3. a count noun (e.g., *woman*)   _____   _____
4. a noncount noun (e.g., *directness*)   _____   _____
5. a pronoun (e.g., *she*)   _____   _____
6. a verb (e.g., *asked*)   _____   _____

7. an adjective (e.g., *busy*)   _____   _____

8. an adverb (e.g., *directly*) or adverb
   phrase (e.g., *in recent decades*)   _____   _____

9. a preposition (e.g., *in, to*)   _____   _____

B. Below are the three important categories of common nouns, with an example of each. (Adjectives are in parentheses.) To assess what you know about patterns of nouns and articles (*a, the*), copy the chart below on separate paper and do the following:

- Using the dictation and/or lines 1–10 of the reading, find and list 4 more examples of each type.
- Be sure also to write the articles or determiners that occur with the nouns.
- Figure out which of the three groups always has an article or other determiner or a plural marker (*-s*).

Count Nouns		Noncount Nouns
Singular	*Plural*	
a (straightforward) way	(academic) papers	information

Grammar Tips: Check Your Work

With a partner or a small group, check your answers in the Preview by using the information in Charts 1.1A and 1.1B that follow. Be prepared to explain your answers by referring to specific sections of the charts. Figure out what you still need to learn.

CHART 1.1A **Basic Parts of Speech**[1]		
Part of Speech	**Definition/Description**	**Example**
Noun	A person, place, event, object, or abstraction	woman, Washington, lunch, newspaper, conversation
a. Proper noun[2]	a. The capitalized name of a specific person, place, or thing	a. Deborah Tannen, *The Washington Post*, March, Americans
b. Common noun	b. Some are concrete—something you can see or touch Some are abstract—something you cannot see or touch	b. a woman, a report, papers a refusal, directness, a friendship, the tension
b1. Count noun[3]	b1. Has a singular and a plural form	b1. an answer/answers a system/systems
b2. Noncount noun	b2. Has no plural form and is singular for agreement	b2. information, confusion Directness is rude.

Part of Speech	Definition / Description	Example
Pronoun[4]	Represents a noun or noun phrase	she, her, it, one, the other, both, neither, this, the ones, those, each
Verb	a. Shows an action b. Shows a state of being	a. asked, said, declined, was trying, was being pushed, are spoken b. was (sorry), haven't been feeling, couldn't understand, was expecting, believe, is used
Adjective	Describes a noun and shows how someone or something is	busy, difficult, unappealing, interested, rude, linguistic
Adverb	a. Describes a verb, adjective, or adverb. Shows *how, when, where, how long, how much,* etc. b. Can be a fixed expression	a. she **simply** didn't want, **perfectly** clear, frequently, never, often, actually b. by the way, of course
Preposition	Comes before a noun or pronoun in a phrase to indicate time, space, manner, possession, or some other relationship	**in** her office, **about** a very interesting case, **by** anyone, **with** people

[1]See Reference Chart 1.1, p. 159, for more examples of and information about basic parts of speech.

[2]Proper nouns have special rules regarding the use of the definite article *the*. For example, people's names and languages do not take *the* (Deborah Tannen, English), but names of newspapers do (*The Washington Post*). See Reference Chart 1.5, p. 165.

[3]The categories of count and noncount are important for grammatical choices about articles (*a, the*), and other determiners. (See Reference Charts 1.3 and 1.4, pp.162–164, and Charts 4.2A and 4.2B in Chapter 4, p. 81–83.) The categories of count and noncount are also important for subject-verb agreement. (See Chart 2.2, p. 33, and Reference Chart 2.3, p. 175.)

[4]See Reference Charts 1.2 and 1.3, pp. 161–162, for more information about pronouns and determiners.

CHART 1.1B	Patterns of Articles with Count and Noncount Nouns		
Article	**Count Nouns**		**Noncount Nouns**
	Singular	*Plural*	
Indefinite: *a, an, some, any*	**a** report **an** office	**some/any** reports ___ linguist**s**	**some/any** information ___ indirectness
Definite: *the*	**the** invitation	**the** patterns	**the** tension

CHART 1.1C **Some Problem Areas for Articles and Nouns[5]**		
Problem	**Rule/Tip**	**Examples of Errors and Corrections**
1. Singular count noun *without* an article or determiner	Singular count nouns *must* have an article or other determiner. *Possible corrections:* *Note that for the example sentence, only* a *or* plural *is appropriate.* a. Add an article. b. Add *this/that.* c. Add a possessive pronoun (*my, his, their, ...*) or other determiner. (See Reference Chart 1.3) d. Use the plural.	⊘ Each woman followed **different rule** about being direct. *Corrections:* a. **a** different rule **the** different rule b. **that** different rule c. **her** different rule d. different rule**s**

2. Use of *the*[7]	Use *the* only when you and the reader both know which specific person, thing, or action you are referring to.
	
	 How does the reader know?
	 a. The person, thing, or action has been mentioned earlier in the text.[8]
	  use of *the* previous mention
	  the colleague = a colleague
	  the project = a report
	  the refusal = declining the invitation
	 b. The noun is associated with a person, thing, or action that has been mentioned earlier in the text.
	 In these examples:
	 b1. A question ("she asked her colleague") is generally associated with a response, so we can say "the response."
	 b2. A situation in which two people are frustrated is generally associated with tension, so we can say "the tension."
		⊘ The colleague said that she had **the report** to finish.
		    (The reader probably does not know which report.)
		 Correction: ... she had **a report** ...
		
		 a. One woman extended **a** lunch **invitation** to **a colleague. The colleague** declined **the invitation**, saying she had **a report** to write. She then told her colleague about **the project** she was writing up. The first woman didn't understand what **the refusal** meant.
		
		 b1. She asked her colleague what her refusals meant... **The response** only confused her more.
		 b2. Both women were frustrated. They tried to dispel **the tension** by doing more of the same.

*One helpful rule: Use an indefinite article (**a, some**) the first time you mention a person or thing; then use **the** the second time. Note that the second noun does not have to be the same noun, but it has to refer to or be associated with the person, thing, or action already mentioned.*

[5]See Charts 4.2A and B in Chapter 4, pp. 81–82, for information about nouns used with a general meaning (generically).

[6]The symbol ⊘ indicates that the sentence is not complete or that it contains an error.

[7]See Reference Chart 1.5, p. 165, for additional information about the use of *the* for identified nouns.

[8]Rather than repeating the same noun a second time, writers more often use a pronoun (*she, it*) or use a synonym (a noun that means the same thing).

Practice

Activity 1 • Identify the reference for nouns and pronouns

In the following text, also from "When You Shouldn't Tell It Like It Is," Tannen describes another misunderstanding. Use the text and do the following:

■ Circle the nouns and pronouns.

■ Underline any articles or determiners.

■ Following the rules outlined in Chart 1.1C, draw arrows between the nine nouns and pronouns in bold and the "first mention" of that person or thing. The first sentence is done for you.

A real-estate appraiser[9] complained to a colleague about a client who had called   1
to say that she was leaving for vacation. **His colleague** knew immediately why **the**   2
client had called: She was letting **him** know, indirectly, that she was impatient to re-   3
ceive her appraisal. **The vacation** provided an excuse to remind him. **The appraiser**   4
did not understand **the indirect approach** and didn't realize that **the client** wanted   5
reassurance that her appraisal would be ready by the time she returned.   6

Activity 2 • Identify the reference for pronouns and determiners[10]

Reproduced below are lines 24 through 32 from "When You Shouldn't Tell It Like It Is." Eight pronouns and one determiner (*the latter*) are in **bold**. For each, draw a line back to the noun it refers to; if it doesn't refer to an individual noun, circle the entire expression or idea it refers to. The first one is done for you.

The study of indirectness and other politeness phenomena has received   24
increasing attention in linguistic scholarship. **This** is a drastic departure from the   25
trend dominant in linguistics in recent decades: formal representation of language   26
not as **it** is used but as an abstract system. A linguist working in **the latter** tradition   27
would be concerned with whether a given sentence is grammatical, regardless of   28
whether **it** might actually be spoken by **anyone**, let alone how frequently **it** might be   29
spoken. For linguists concerned with language as **it** is used in everyday life, sentences   30
that are actually spoken—and often spoken—are **the ones** of interest, not **those** that   31
are theoretically possible but never encountered.   32

---

[9]A real-estate *appraiser* is a person who analyzes (*appraises*) land and/or buildings to determine their value in dollars. The value decided on is called an *appraisal*.

[10]For information about pronouns and determiners, see Reference Charts 1.2 and 1.3, pp. 161–162.

Activity 3 • Write sentences using the definite article *the*

Each of these sentences has an underlined noun that is being introduced (mentioned for the first time). On a separate piece of paper, for each item write a related sentence in which you use the noun again (or a synonym) (Chart 1.1C, rule 2a) or an associated noun (Chart 1.1C, rule 2b). Use the definite article. You can use one of the nouns in parentheses or choose your own related noun. The first one is done for you.

1. I read <u>an article</u> about indirectness in spoken English. (article, author, main point)

   Possible related sentences:

   a. *The article said that Americans have different ideas about how direct they should be.*

   b. *The author gave an example of a conflict that arose between two co-workers because one expected directness and the other expected indirectness.*

2. I had <u>a similar experience</u> with a friend. (experience, conflict, problem)

3. My teacher gave us <u>a homework assignment</u> to write about a misunderstanding with a classmate or co-worker. (assignment, paper, composition)

4. Sometimes I have felt <u>tension</u> with my classmates. (tension, problem, difficulty)

5. I found <u>some information</u> about the subject of directness on the Internet. (information, website, article)

6. My classmate found <u>another article</u> about indirectness on the Internet. (article, author, information, main point)

Activity 4 • Edit student writing for article and noun problems

To help you identify errors, (circle) the nouns and <u>underline</u> the articles or plural endings. Refer to Charts 1.1B and C and Reference Chart 1.5, p. 165, for help with making corrections. Note: You will find 13 additional errors. The first sentence is done for you.

Although I was not born in *the* (U.S.) I have had similar (misunderstandings) here   1

with (Americans) and with (non-Americans) too. As soon as I came to the U.S. from

Japan about three years ago, I started to share a house with two Japanese men and

one Japanese-American woman. Before I moved into the house, I signed contract to

live in large room in the house with male roommate.   5

When I moved in, I was surprised to find there was already Japanese-American

woman living by herself in the large room. The man whom I made a contract with

allowed her to live there. Therefore, I had no choice but to live in small room even

though I felt really bad about it.

About one week after I moved in, one of the man realized that I did not feel good   10

about living in the small room, so he had a house meeting with all of roommates to

ask me what I wanted to do. At that time, I could not say, "I do not want to live in the small room." Instead, I just expressed disagreeable feelings about the situation and frowned during discussion. I thought the woman would move out because I showed unpleasant feelings to her. This is indirect Japanese way. However, she continued to 15 stay there because she misunderstood my word and thoughts. She thought that I accepted her staying in the room even though I was not happy about it. After that happened, I could not have good relationship with them because I thought they presumed I was so weak that I couldn't say "No." I ended up leaving there soon without deposit. 20

Activity 5 • Identify and edit nouns, articles, and pronouns in your writing

Look at one paragraph of the writing you did for After Reading or Topics for Writing (pp. 3–4).

- Follow the directions in Editing Guide 1.1, p. 151.
- (Circle) any pronouns and determiners you are uncertain about.
- Exchange papers with a partner. Check each other's analysis and discuss any questions you have about your paper or your partner's paper. Correct the errors.

1.2 Phrases vs. Clauses: Verbs and Subjects

Preview: Assess What You Know

A. Clauses

The basic building block of the sentence is a subject + verb combination. A group of words with a subject + verb combination is a *clause*.

To assess your ability to identify a verb that can be the verb of a clause and its subject, refer to the sentences below and do the following:

- Underline each verb that is the main verb of a clause (complete verbs).
- (Circle) the subject of each complete verb. (The subject is the person or thing that performs the action of the verb.)
- Put a [box] around verb forms that are *not* complete verbs.

The first one is done for you.

1. (Indirectness) can cause people [to misunderstand] each other.

2. In academic papers we are expected to write about information and ideas in a straightforward way.

3. Americans may disagree about just how much directness is appropriate.

4. Linguists, researchers who study language, are investigating the patterns of directness and indirectness in spoken English.

5. Deborah Tannen has presented her ideas and examples in books and articles.

6. The findings of these linguists may help us prevent awkward and frustrating situations.

B. Phrases

A group of words *without* a subject + verb combination is a *phrase*.

Examine the following examples of phrases from the reading. They do not have a subject or a verb (or both).

- On a separate paper write a sentence that includes each phrase. Use correct punctuation and capital letters.
- For each new sentence, underline the complete verb and circle the subject.

The first one is done for you.

1. would like to have lunch
   (The woman) would like to have lunch with her colleague.

2. a report to finish

3. feeling well

4. their own ways of talking

5. about a very interesting case

6. in a friendship

7. operate on the same system

8. to dispel the tension

Grammar Tips: Check Your Work

With a partner or a small group, check your answers in the Preview by using the information in Chart 1.2 that follows. Be prepared to explain your answers by referring to specific sections of the chart. Figure out what you still need to learn.

CHART 1.2 **Phrases[11] vs. Clauses: Finding Verbs and Subjects**	
Tips	**Examples**

1. **Clauses** have subject + verb combinations.
Step One: Find the *complete verb*[12]:
Is there a word (or words) that changes if you change the time reference?
 	
Step Two: Find the *subject*:
Who or what does or did the action of the verb?
	a. One woman <u>was expecting</u> directness. *(in the past)*
	Change to:
	One woman <u>is expecting</u> directness. *(now)*
	   Here, "was expecting" changes to "is expecting" when you change the time reference, so "was expecting" is the verb.
	b1. (One woman) was expecting directness.
	   Who or what "was expecting directness"?
	   The answer is "one woman" so "one woman" is the subject.
	b2. <u>Wanted</u> to be indirect.
	   Who or what "wanted to be indirect"?
	   There is no answer, so there is no subject and the structure is a phrase.

Tips	Examples
2. **Phrases** *do not* have subject + verb combinations.	a. A report to finish *(phrase)* ⊙She⊙ had a report to finish. *(clause)*
***Note:** Prepositional phrases (b) cannot be subjects.*	b. In a friendship *(phrase)* In a friendship, ⊙people⊙ need to be honest. *(clause)*

[11]For examples of types of phrases, see Reference Chart 1.10, p. 170.

[12]To see various verb forms, see Reference Chart 1.6, p. 167. For forms of verb tenses and irregular verb forms, see Reference Charts 1.7, 1.8, and 1.9, pp. 168–169.

Practice

Activity 6 • Identify verbs, subjects, clauses, and phrases

Using this piece of student writing, do the following:

- Underline **verbs** and (circle) **subjects**.
- Find **clauses** and put [brackets] around them.
- List several examples of **phrases** (e.g., *to her, is dishonest, to be understood, with her*).
- Compare your answers with a partner or put examples on the board and discuss.

The first sentence is done for you.

"[⊙One woman⊙ was expecting directness]; [to her, ⊙indirectness⊙ is dishonest]. The   1

other was expecting her indirectness to be understood; to her, directness is rude." I   2

sympathize with the second woman because her indirectness is just a way to be nice.   3

At least she didn't hurt the first woman's feelings by directly telling her she doesn't   4

want to have lunch with her. But I don't understand why she doesn't want to be   5

friends with the first woman. That's strange to me. I don't sympathize with the second   6

woman for missing an opportunity to start a friendship. However, her indirectness   7

should have gotten through to the first woman. I probably would do the same thing if   8

I didn't want to be friends with somebody. I don't blame the second woman for being   9

annoyed.   10

Activity 7 • Analyze and edit your writing for verbs, subjects, clauses, and phrases

Use a paragraph that you wrote for After Reading questions or Topics for Writing on pp. 3–4.

- Follow the same directions as in Activity 6.
- Put a question mark (?) in the margin beside any markings that you are unsure of.
- Exchange papers with a partner. Look at your partner's analysis and discuss any questions you have about your paper or your partner's paper.

1.3   Time Expressions and Verbs

Preview: Assess What You Know

A time expression is a word or phrase that tells *when* something happens or happened and usually signals the tense of the verb. Some time expressions are linked to a definite time and occur with specific verb tenses. Other time expressions are not linked to a definite time and can be used with different verb tenses.

Check your understanding of time expressions by doing the following:

- On a separate piece of paper copy the chart below with the four categories that time expressions can refer to: 1) only the past, 2) only the present, 3) only the future, and 4) different times. (Two examples are given for each.)
- Add as many examples as you can think of for each category.
- For each of those expressions that can be used with different times, write two sentences to show how this is possible.

only past	only present	only future	different times
last week	now	tomorrow	on Sunday
yesterday	at this moment	a month from now	after 6 o'clock

Grammar Tips: Check Your Work

With a partner or a small group, check your lists and your sentences in the Preview by using the information in Charts 1.3A, B, and C that follow. Be prepared to explain your answers by referring to specific sections of the charts. Figure out what you still need to learn.

CHART 1.3A Time Expressions Linked to Definite Times and Tenses	
Time Reference	**Examples**
Past	Deborah Tannen <u>published</u> an article in *The Washington Post* **last week.**
	yesterday.
	a while ago.
	in 1995.
	recently.
	Dr. Tannen <u>has published</u> an article on indirectness **recently.**
	She <u>has been writing</u> another article **since Tuesday.**
Present	She <u>teaches</u> linguistics **these days.**
	She <u>is</u> probably <u>working</u> on a new book **at this moment.**
	now.

Time Reference	Examples	
Future	She <u>will</u> (or <u>is going to</u>) <u>complete</u> her research	**later this week.** **the day after tomorrow.** **this coming Saturday.** **next year.** **tomorrow.**

CHART 1.3B **Expressions Linked to Different Times and Tenses**		
Time Reference	**Examples**	
Past, present, or future	She <u>wrote/is writing/will write</u> the article	**today.** **after six o'clock.** **on Sunday.**
	She <u>was writing/will be writing</u> the article	**for three days.** **at the moment.**

CHART 1.3C **Time Clauses Introduced by Words such as *when, before, after, as, while***	

These time clauses are linked to different times and tenses, depending on the verb in the main clause.

Time Reference	Examples
Past	**After** Tannen <u>wrote</u> "When You Shouldn't Tell It Like It Is," it <u>was published</u> by *The Washington Post.*
Present	**When** she <u>writes</u> an article or a book, she always <u>does</u> extensive research.
Future	**When** she <u>writes</u> about the topic of linguistics **in the future**, she <u>will</u> probably <u>include</u> examples of everyday language use.

Practice

Activity 8 • Identify time expressions and the time reference of verbs

For these sentences do the following:

- Put a wiggly line under the time expressions.
- <u>Underline</u> the verbs.
- Above the verbs, write whether the time reference is past, present, or future.

The first one is done for you.

                     past

1. Deborah Tannen <u>received</u> her Ph.D. from the University of California in 1979.

2. She has published nineteen books in the last twenty years.

3. Currently, she is a Professor at Georgetown University in Washington, D.C.

4. Before she begins a new area of study, she always reviews articles and books on that topic.

5. While appearing on the Oprah Winfrey show some time ago, Tannen talked about her latest book.

6. As Tannen prepares for future writing projects, she will continue to investigate new areas of conversational analysis.

1.4   Word Forms: Nouns, Verbs, Adjectives, Adverbs

Preview: Assess What You Know

To assess what you know about word forms, examine the sentences below, which have form errors. Follow the directions given in each section. The first one in each section is done for you.

A.   *Errors in Noun Forms*

- Underline all the nouns.
- (Circle) and correct the errors in word forms.
- Make notes to explain your corrections.

1. Conversational <u>style</u> has often been the <u>focus</u> of Deborah Tannen's (researches). *research*
   research = noncount noun, no plural

2. I have read three of Tannen's article.

3. She always gives some informations about how problems in conversation can be avoided.

4. It is my believe that the differences she writes about are often cross-cultural, not just American.

5. I have seen these differences result in many bad feeling between peoples. (2 errors)

6. When you are trying hard to communicate successfully, sometimes the greater expectation you have, the greater disappointed you have.

7. The feeling of sad may last for a long time.

B. Errors in Verb Forms

- ■ <u>Underline</u> all the verbs.
- ■ (Circle) and correct the errors in word forms.
- ■ Make notes to explain your corrections.

8. Being too direct <u>can</u> (causes) misunderstanding. *cause*
   modal + simple form

9. My cousin was very upset when his girlfriend told him she had decide not to see him
   anymore.

10. He said he still wanted to going out with her even though she hurted him. (2 errors)

11. He was use to being with her every weekend.

12. Her directness made him felt so sad.

13. In my opinion, they should break up: he has chose the wrong girlfriend.

14. He think that he won't find another girlfriend as great as she is, but I'm sure he can
    success in finding one. (2 errors)

C. Errors in Adjective Forms

- ■ <u>Underline</u> all the adjectives.
- ■ (Circle) and correct the errors in word forms.
- ■ Make notes to explain your corrections.

15. If a speaker prefers directness, the listener might feel (confusing) if *ed*
    he or she prefers indirectness.
    -ed describes the person ("listener") who feels the emotion

16. We all want to avoid misunderstandings in our everydays lives.

17. Having cross-cultural problems is very frustrated for all of us.

18. Increasing communication by e-mail and voice mail can lead to problems because
    we may lose our origin way of communicating with others.

19. Building good communication skills requires one to be patience.

20. Being open-mind also helps with good communication.

D. Errors in Adverb Forms

- <u>Underline</u> all the adverbs.
- (Circle) and correct the errors in word forms.
- Make notes to explain your corrections.

21. In one case, I felt that my sister and I could not talk very ~~comforted.~~ *ably*
    needs adverb to describe the verb "talk"

22. This might have happened because we don't oftenly talk about our personal problems.

23. However, we usually talk very honest about school and our parents.

24. Also, some time we discuss our plans for the future.

25. When we talk about the future, we can speak very direct and open.

 Grammar Tips: Check Your Work

With a partner or a small group, check your answers in the Preview by referring to specific sections in Charts 1.4A, B, C, and D that follow. Figure out what you still need to learn.

CHART 1.4A	**Common Problems with Forms of Nouns**	
Problem / Tip	**Examples of Errors**	**Corrections**
1. Missing -s on plural count nouns	three of Tannen's **article** many bad **feeling** these **difference** one of the **problem**	articles feelings differences problems
2. Putting -s on noncount nouns	**researches** **informations**	research information
3. Putting -s on count nouns that are already plural	**peoples** **medias**	people media
4. Using a verb or adjective instead of a noun (See also Reference Chart 1.11, p. 171.)	my **believe** (verb) his interesting **live** (verb) the greater **disappointed** (adjective) the feeling of **sad** (adjective)	belief life disappointment sadness

CHART 1.4B	Common Problems with Forms of Verbs[13]	
Problem/Tip	**Examples of Errors**	**Corrections**
1. Using the wrong form after a modal or after the infinitive "to" *Always use the simple form.*	can **causes** might **helped** could **to be** found want to **going** happy to **had** learned	can **cause** might **help** could **be** found want to **go** happy to **have** learned
2. Leaving the *-ed* ending off the past tense or past participle	She had **decide**… She **hope** to write…	She had **decided**… She **hoped** to write…
3. Leaving the *-s* ending off the third person singular present tense	He **think**…	He **thinks**…
4. Using the wrong form of an irregular verb (past tense or past participle)	She **hurted** him. He has **chose**. They should have **went**.	She **hurt** him. He has **chosen**. They should have **gone**.
5. Using a noun, adjective, or preposition instead of a verb (See also Reference Chart 1.11, p. 171.)	He can **success**. *(noun)* It will **safe** you a lot of problems. *(adjective)* I can't **against** my culture. *(preposition)*	He can **succeed**. It will **save** you … I can't **go against** …
6. Using the incorrect form after a preposition (other than *"to"*) *Use verb + **ing**.*	By **moved** to the U.S … After **learn** about conversational style …	By **moving** … After **learning** …
7. Confusing structures with: *used to* + simple form *be used to* + verb + *ing* *get used to* + verb + *ing* ***Used to** always has -d.*	He **use to** help us. He **uses to** *writing* articles. He **was use to** being there.	He **used to** help us. He **used to write** articles. He **was used to** being there.
8. Using the wrong form after *make* *Use the simple form or an adjective.*	It made him **felt** sad. It makes him **feels** sad.	It made him **feel** sad. It makes him **feel** sad. It makes him **sad**.

[13]See Reference Chart 1.6 for verb forms, Reference Charts 1.7 and 1.8 for verb tenses and modal combinations (active), and Reference Chart 1.9 for the forms of irregular verbs, pp. 167–169.

CHART 1.4C	**Common Problems with Forms of Adjectives**	
Problem/Tip	**Examples of Errors**	**Corrections**
1. *-ing* vs. *-ed* endings: Using the wrong ending with adjectives describing emotions	She might feel **confusing**. The situation is very **frustrated**.	She might feel **confused**. The situation is very **frustrating**.
a. *-ed* can only describe a person (or animal)—the one who *feels or experiences* the emotion.		a. a **frustrated** listener a **confused** woman a **surprised** audience
b. *-ing* can describe any noun that *causes* the emotion—some other person experiences the emotion.		b. an **exciting** writer *(The writer causes excitement—the reader experiences the excitement.)* a **confusing** conversation *(The conversation causes confusion to someone.)*
2. Using a noun or verb instead of an adjective (See Reference Chart 1.11, p. 171.)	You need to be **patience**. *(noun)* It is a **civilize** way to talk. *(verb)* We may lose our **origin** way to communicate. *(noun)* I felt so **regret** about it. *(noun)*	You need to be **patient**. It is a **civilized** … We may lose our **original** … I felt so **regretful** …
3. Using a plural form before a plural noun *Adjectives and nouns before plural nouns never have an -s ending.*	… in our **everydays** lives … … their two-**hours** lunches	… in our **everyday** lives … their two-**hour** lunches
4. Using the wrong form for comparison *Use -er/-est for adjectives (and adverbs) of one syllable or of two syllables ending in -y. Use more/most for others.*[14]	She is a **more strong** writer. She gave a **distincter** response. She was a **more happy** person.	She is a **stronger** writer. She gave a **more distinct** response. She was a **happier** person.
5. Omitting the *-ed* form in a compound adjective formed with a verb	She is an **open-mind** woman. The **conversation-base** research was a **carefully-plan** study.	She is an **open-minded** woman. The **conversation-based** research was a **carefully-planned** study.

[14]The rules for comparison are actually more complex than this, but this simple rule will work in most cases. When in doubt, consult your dictionary.

CHART 1.4D	**Problems with Forms of Adverbs**	
Problem	**Examples of Errors**	**Corrections**
1. Using an adjective instead of an adverb (See Reference Chart 1.11, p. 171.)	We can speak very **direct** and **open**. We talk **honest** with each other. We speak very **friendly**[15] about school.	We can speak very **directly** and **openly**. We talk **honestly** … We speak **in a very friendly way** …

Problem	Examples of Errors	Corrections
2. Using an invented form	**Some time** we discuss our plans. We **oftenly** talk about the future.	**Sometimes** we … We **often** …

[15]A few adjectives end in *-ly* (e.g., *friendly, lovely, lonely*) and do not have an adverb form. To use these qualities to describe verbs, you need to use expressions such as *in a friendly way*.

Practice

Activity 9 • Identify nouns, verbs, adjectives, and adverbs

Using a paragraph or two of your writing from the Topics for Writing, p. 4:

- Find and <u>underline</u> examples of nouns, verbs, adjectives, and adverbs, and label each.
- Circle any forms you are unsure of.
- Exchange papers with a partner and discuss each other's analysis, making corrections as necessary.

Activity 10 • Edit student writing for word form problems: verbs, nouns, adjectives, and adverbs

The student text below has 10 additional problems with word forms. <u>Underline</u> the errors and write the correct forms above them. Refer to Charts 1.4A through D to help you. The first sentence is done for you.

different

Greeting a business partner in China is a lot <u>difference</u> from greeting a business   1

partner in the U.S. Recently, increasing international trade has made Chinese busi-   2

ness people more awared of cultural differences and has helped them get use to   3

Westerners' frequent use of body gesture. When meeting for the first time, for in-   4

stance, Chinese people evaluate the sincere of prospective business partners by the   5

degree to which the partners meet their expectations about the entire arrangement of   6

the meeting. In other words, if you reserve a nice conference room, prepare some   7

gifts, and pick up your Chinese partners at their convenient, you are more likely to   8

gain their trust. This is a different method from those ignorance foreign investors who   9

just call them up, tell them to come to the hotel they are stay at and don't even bother   10

to see them off at the front door when the meeting is finish. This frustrated way of   11

doing business can causes potential partnerships with Chinese business people to   12

fail.   13

Wrap-Up

Activity 11 • Edit your writing for grammar basics

■ Use your writing for Topics for Writing, p. 4, or for After Reading, questions 4–5, p. 3. Edit for problems with

   Articles and nouns (Use Editing Guide 1.1, p. 151.)

   Word forms (See Charts 1.4A-D and Reference Chart 1.11, p. 171.)

■ For the structures you edit, clearly show on your paper each step described in the Editing Guide. In addition, check your writing to see if you've used any of the word partnerships listed in "Using Vocabulary Accurately," p. 4. Correct any problems you find, and add examples to your word partnerships list. (See p. 150.)

Activity 12 • Class editing workshop: Edit for grammar basics

At home: Follow the directions for Activity 11. In addition, write questions in the margins next to places where you're not sure of your editing choices.

In class: Working with a partner or a small group, trade papers, and talk about each other's questions and writing. Refer to the grammar charts in the chapter and in Appendix B and the Editing Guide in Appendix A to help you. If time permits, put examples from your writing and editing on the board to discuss as a class.

2

Review of Common Structure Problems:

Sentence Structure, Subject-Verb Agreement, Verb Tenses

Overview of the Chapter

Read

Before Reading

Respond to these questions to help you think about and understand the reading that follows.

1. Brainstorm associations with the word "expectation." Think about expectations of parents, siblings, friends, teachers, and yourself. Which ideas are positive? Which are negative?

2. Visualize a time or place that has many memories for you. If you had the opportunity to return to that time or place, what thoughts and/or feelings would you have? Why?

Excerpt from **"Return to Vietnam" by Elsa Arnett**

San Jose Mercury News staff writer Elsa Arnett was born in Vietnam, then moved to the United States in 1971 at age four. The daughter of Pulitzer Prize-winning journalist Peter Arnett and Nina Nguyen Arnett, a Vietnamese librarian, Elsa returned to her birthplace for the first time in the fall of 2000. In the excerpt from her article below, she describes her experience when she first arrives in Hanoi.

Though I spent most of my life in the United States, bits of Vietnamese culture   1
still **seeped** into my American childhood.

I spoke to my mother in Vietnamese. As my schoolmates ate **bologna** sandwiches for lunch, I ate sticky rice and shredded dried pork. Before I got on an airplane, my mother would press her palms together in front of an ivory Buddha to pray for a safe   5
journey.

Beyond that, I felt little connection to my birthplace. Growing up, I **cringed** when I heard **melodramatic** Vietnamese pop music. And I retreated to my room when my mother invited her Vietnamese friends over for dinner.

Will **plugging myself into** Vietnam feel familiar or foreign? The answer comes   10
with rapid force.

First, the heat: **stifling, unrelenting**. I perspire through my shirt in four minutes.

Then, the images along the bumpy highway from the airport to downtown Hanoi: villagers in **conical** hats bent over tender shoots of rice; children perched atop water buffalo; a cluster of schoolgirls pedaling on their bicycles, the tails of their *ao dai*   15
dresses fluttering behind them.

Then the **chaos** of the city: the chatter of Vietnamese voices at the **congested** out-door markets; the fragrance of **anise** from a noodle soup stall; thatched baskets filled with juicy, fist-sized green fruit that resembles **grenades**. And at every corner, the **ubiquitous** cyclos—armies of pedicabs.   20

---

seeped: gradually entered
bologna: lunch meat for sandwiches
cringed: withdrew inside
melodramatic: overly emotional
plugging (oneself) into: putting (*oneself*) into
stifling: extremely hot
unrelenting: without stopping

conical: in the shape of a cone
chaos: extreme disorder
congested: crowded
anise: star-shaped spice
grenades: small explosive devices thrown by hand
ubiquitous: appearing everywhere

I can understand what people are saying. I recognize the exotic fruits. I have experienced all this before. The memories come back, bit by bit. I am comforted.

Down the block, I see a man balancing a wooden pole with a metal canister hanging from each end. I chase him. I ask him to open the lid. Can it be?

Inside the vat is a gleaming, smooth pearly custard made of tofu. This ginger-laced dessert was my childhood favorite. I have thought about it hundreds of times. I have eaten it in the United States, but it never tasted as good.   25

Finally, I will have it again.

The man ladles a generous serving into a bowl, puzzled by my excitement. I cradle the bowl in my palms and take a big gulp.   30

But something isn't right. It is thin, almost tasteless. Too little sugar? Too much water? All I know is that it doesn't measure up to my expectation.

The tofu teaches me a lesson. This place feels like home, but it isn't. Vietnam is a different place; I am a different person. My clothes, my accent, my purchasing power, and my tangled memories set me apart from the country I am standing in. My roots   35
may be here, but they were buried long ago.

from *San Jose Mercury News,* Sunday, April 8, 2001, p. 26A.

After Reading

Individually at home, or with a partner or a small group in class, write the answers to these questions to prepare for class discussion. Keep your answers in a notebook or binder to refer to later when you respond to the writing topics, develop your ideas for longer papers, or analyze your writing. Questions marked ¶ are especially suitable for paragraph-length answers that can be used later when you analyze your own writing.

1. Describe Elsa Arnett's background: her family, place of birth, where she grew up.

2. How does Arnett feel about growing up as a Vietnamese-American? Describe examples of "bits of culture" which "seeped into [her] American childhood." (lines 1–2)

3. Sketch the scene and situation Arnett experiences on her way from the airport. (lines 12–16) Provide as much detail as possible. Be sure to include the following in your sketch: Arnett, the highway, the villagers, the children, the schoolgirls.

4. With as much detail as possible, sketch the scene and situation in Hanoi. (lines 17–26) Be sure to include the following: the marketplace, the people, the baskets, the noodle soup stall, the fruit, the pedicabs, the tofu seller.

5. Compare the sketches you drew in response to questions 3 and 4. Which ones are the most complete? What is difficult to include in your sketches? Describe the sounds, smells, tastes, and memories that Arnett experiences.

6. Describe Arnett's excitement, expectations, and disappointment with the tofu custard she tries.

¶ 7. What is the lesson Arnett learns from her experience with the tofu?

¶ 8. Do you identify with Arnett's experience? Why or why not? Explain.

Write

Topics for Writing

Respond in writing to one (or more) of the following topics.

1. Imagine that you are a reporter interviewing Arnett. You ask her what she means by the quote, "My clothes, my accent, my purchasing power, and my tangled memories set me apart from the country I am standing in. My roots may be here, but they were buried long ago." (lines 34–36) How might she respond to your question? Explain Arnett's possible response by making connections to as much of the article as you can: her past, her trip to Vietnam, her perspective as an American.

2. Discuss the significance of the tofu that Arnett purchases. What lesson does she learn? How does she learn it?

3. "Return to Vietnam" illustrates points about different topics related to the human experience. Choose one of the following topics (or develop an idea of your own) and explain how the article makes a point about the topic you've chosen: *expectations, disappointment, memory, change, roots.*

4. Write about an experience when you learned a lesson about yourself. Compare your experience with Arnett's experience in "Return to Vietnam."

5. Write about your own experience of returning to a place or going to see a person important in your memory. How did this experience compare to your memories or expectations? What did you learn from this experience?

Strategies for Writing: Generating and Developing Ideas

For a description of ways to generate ideas, such as freewriting, listing, and brainstorming, as well as ways to develop and support your ideas, refer to Strategies for Writing, pp. 185–190.

Using Vocabulary Accurately

As you write about a reading, pay attention to key words and word partnerships, words that occur frequently with each other or that form fixed expressions. For more examples, see Reference Charts 2.1 and 2.2, pp. 172–174. Create your own word partnerships list (see p. 150).

Some key word partnerships for this reading follow. Locate key words in the reading or in Topics for Writing and notice how they are used. For practice, write sentences using some of these expressions

to have expectations about (*something*)
to have expectations of (*someone*)
to bring back memories
to have vivid memories of (*someone/ something*)
to feel a connection to (*someone/ something*)
to find one's roots

to learn (*something*) from an experience
to identify with (*something/ someone's experience*)
the significance of (*something*)
to be comforted by (*something/someone*)
to be disappointed by/with (*something/ someone*)

Edit: Grammar Previews, Tips, and Practice

Listening/Writing Activity: Dictation/Dictocomp

The following dictation/dictocomp text gives information related to the reading "Return to Vietnam" on p. 24.

Close your book. As your teacher reads the sentences below (one time all the way through, then by clauses, then all the way through again), do the following:

- For a dictation, try to write exactly what you hear.
- For a dictocomp, take notes on key words and phrases.
- Then, individually or in groups, reconstruct the text, revising and correcting your own work and paying attention to problem areas.

1. Elsa Arnett writes about a memorable experience when she returns to Vietnam, where she was born thirty-three years before.
2. In the beginning, she is unsure about how she will feel when she arrives in Hanoi after so many years.
3. As she travels from the airport, Arnett recognizes familiar images and feels comforted.
4. These images awaken memories from her childhood.
5. Although she understands the language and is excited about the food, she still feels foreign in the country of her birth.
6. Arnett recognizes that she is a different person today and that Vietnam is a different place.

2.1 Independent and Dependent Clauses: Sentences vs. Fragments and Run-on Sentences

Preview: Assess What You Know

A sentence must have one or more independent clauses. To assess your understanding of independent and dependent clauses, do the following:

For each of the following clauses from the reading:

- Write *"I"* on the line for those that are independent clauses (can stand alone as a sentence).
- Write *"D"* on the line for those that are dependent clauses (cannot stand alone as a sentence—fragments).
- For the items marked *"D,"* explain how you know they are not independent clauses.

1. though I spent most of my life in the United States
   D "though" shows this is a D clause

2. as my schoolmates ate bologna sandwiches for lunch

_____

3. my mother would press her palms together

---

4. can it be

---

5. the country I am standing in

---

6. before I got on an airplane

---

7. I can understand what people are saying

Grammar Tips: Check Your Work

With a partner or a small group, check your answers in the Preview by using the information in Charts 2.1A and 2.1B that follow. Be prepared to explain your answers by referring to specific sections of the charts. Figure out what you still need to learn. For a review of clauses, see Chart 1.2 in Chapter 1, p. 12.

CHART 2.1A **Independent and Dependent Clauses; Fragments and Run-on Sentences**	
Information	**Example**
Independent Clause A sentence has at least one independent or main clause (a subject + verb combination) (a, b).	a. Elsa Arnett was born in Vietnam. *(sentence with one clause)* b. Elsa was born in Vietnam, but she left her country as a young child. *(sentence with two main clauses)*
Dependent Clause A dependent clause is generally introduced by a joining word or a signal word such as *when, since, that, where, who*. A dependent clause can't stand alone as a sentence[1] (c, d, e).	c. ... **when** she was a child d. ... **because** her father was a journalist e. ... **whose** mother spoke Vietnamese
Fragment[2] A dependent clause without a main clause (f); a phrase that is missing a subject, a verb, or both a subject and verb, but is punctuated as if it were a sentence (g, h, i).	f. ⃠ Because she understands the language. *(dependent clause, no main clause)* g. ⃠ An image that awakens memories of her childhood *(dependent clause modifies a noun, "image"; no verb for noun "image")* h. ⃠ Is thin, almost tasteless. *(verb phrase only, no subject)* i. ⃠ Growing up in the United States. *(phrase only, no subject or verb)*
Run-on Sentence A sentence with two independent clauses that have no punctuation between them (j) or with only a comma connecting them (k).	j. ⃠ Elsa Arnett writes about a memorable experience she is unsure about how she will feel in Hanoi. k. ⃠ Arnett remembers her past, she writes about those memories.

Information	Example
Order of Clauses The main/independent clause can be first in the sentence (l), or it can sometimes follow the dependent clause (m).	l. **Elsa Arnett writes about a memorable experience** when she returns to Vietnam. m. As she travels from the airport, **Arnett recognizes familiar images and feels comforted.**

[1]See Chapter 5 for types of joining and signal words.

[2]Fragments are generally not acceptable in academic writing, though they are common in other types of writing such as fiction and advertising. Note that Arnett uses fragments in her newspaper article for emphasis.

CHART 2.1B **Finding and Fixing Fragments and Run-on Sentences**	
Problem / Solution	**Examples / Corrections**

Fragments
1. For every group of words punctuated as a sentence, <u>underline</u> the verb and (circle) the subject.
2. Finding a dependent clause:
   If you find both a subject and a verb (a), look for a joining word or signal word that introduces the clause and makes it a dependent clause. <u>Double</u> <u>underline</u> the joining/signal word. If the clause is not connected to an independent clause:
   ■ attach the clause to the independent clause, or
   ■ eliminate the joining/signal word.
 	
3. Finding a phrase:
   If you do not find both a subject and a verb (b):
   ■ add a subject or verb or both, or
   ■ add the fragment to the previous sentence or the following sentence.
	a. (Elsa Arnett) recently <u>went</u> to Vietnam to see her family. ⊘ <u>Because</u> (she) <u>wanted</u> to discover her roots.
	
	(joining word = "because"; dependent clause not attached to an independent clause)
	
	Correction: Elsa Arnett recently went to Vietnam to see her family **because** she wanted to discover her roots.
	Correction: Elsa Arnett recently went to Vietnam to see her family. **She** wanted to discover her roots.
	
	b. ⊘ Traveling from the airport to Hanoi. Arnett was fascinated by what she saw.
	Correction: **Arnett traveled** from the airport to Hanoi. **Along the way, she** was fascinated by what she saw.
	Correction: Traveling from the airport to Hanoi, Arnett was fascinated by what she saw.

Run-on Sentences
1. <u>Underline</u> verbs and (circle) subjects.
2. If you find two or more subject + verb combinations connected by a comma and/or without a joining word or a semicolon (c):
   ■ add a joining word: a coordinator (*and, but,* etc.), a subordinator (*before, after, when, because, although,* etc.), or
   ■ add a period or a semicolon.
	c. ⊘ (Arnett) <u>remembers</u> her experiences in Vietnam, (she) <u>compares</u> them with the reality she finds during a recent visit.
	
	Correction: Arnett remembers her experiences in Vietnam, **and** she compares them with the reality she finds during a recent visit.
	Correction: Arnett remembers her experiences in Vietnam; she compares them with the reality she finds during a recent visit.

Practice

Activity 1 • Identify dependent clauses

Look at the example of student writing below and do the following:

- <u>Underline</u> verbs and (circle) subjects.
- Put [brackets] around any dependent clauses you find. Look for joining/signal words such as *that*, *which*, *because* to help you identify dependent clauses.
- <u>Double</u> <u>underline</u> the joining/signal words.

From the disappointment of the tofu custard, (Arnett) <u>learns</u> [<u>that</u> (Vietnam) <u>is</u> not   1
her home anymore]. What she knows about Vietnam is only from the memories that   2
she has from childhood. Arnett's memories of the tofu custard have led her to believe   3
that Vietnam is a familiar place. Sadly, when the tofu custard does not taste as she ex-   4
pects, she realizes that she has changed. She grew up and has lived her adult life in   5
the United States and that has made Vietnam a foreign land to her.   6

Activity 2 • Identify independent clauses and fragments

For lines 12–22 of the reading (reproduced below):

- Highlight the fragments.
- (Circle) the subject and <u>underline</u> the verb in each independent clause.

First, the heat: stifling, unrelenting. (I) <u>perspire</u> through my shirt in four minutes.   12
Then, the images along the bumpy highway from the airport to downtown Hanoi: 13
villagers in conical hats bent over tender shoots of rice; children perched atop water   14
buffalo; a cluster of schoolgirls pedaling on their bicycles, the tails of their *ao dai*   15
dresses fluttering behind them.   16
Then the chaos of the city: the chatter of Vietnamese voices at the congested out-   17
door markets; the fragrance of anise from a noodle soup stall; thatched baskets filled   18
with juicy, fist-sized green fruit that resembles grenades. And at every corner, the   19
ubiquitous cyclos—armies of pedicabs.   20
I can understand what people are saying. I recognize the exotic fruits. I have ex-   21
perienced all this before. The memories come back, bit by bit. I am comforted.   22

Activity 3 • Edit sentences with fragments and run-on sentences

Items 1–12 below contain problems with punctuation or missing subjects, verbs, or joining words: Use the procedures in Activities 1 and 2, as well as the tips in Charts 2.1A and 2.1B, to help you identify errors and correct them.

Fragments

1. [Since the day [(I)knew [that(I)was going back to China,]]] (I)prayed for the time to go faster.

2. Flying on the airplane. I looked out the window in anticipation.

3. The images along the highway from the airport to my hometown.

4. The home of my grandparents, a place familiar to me.

5. A place where I used to play with my friends and I spent most of my childhood.

6. My grandmother who I hadn't seen for a long time. She called me by my Chinese name.

Run-on Sentences

7. (I)was surprised to hear that name, *because* (my friends) all use my American name.

8. Some things in my grandmother's apartment were still the same some looked different.

9. I looked around, I saw my cousin looking at me, she had grown a lot.

10. At the time I left, she was just seven, I could see that now we were the same height.

11. We used to be really close to each other, but at that moment, she was quiet, she just looked at me.

12. Maybe she was shy, or there was a gap between us, I wasn't sure.

Activity 4 • Edit student writing for fragments and run-on sentences

In the paragraphs below:
- <u>Underline</u> verbs and ⟨circle⟩ subjects.
- Highlight the **fragments**. (There are two fragments.)
- Highlight in a different color the **run-on sentences**. (There are four more.)
- Rewrite or fix the punctuation of any fragments or run-on sentences.
- Work with a partner or small group to compare your revisions.

In this society, ⟨everyone⟩ <u>has</u> their expectations; ⟨people⟩ <u>expect</u> a lot of things.   1

For example, teachers have expectations of their students, they expect their students

to gain knowledge from them. Parents expect their children to earn lots of money

after they graduate from college, some people even expect they will have better lives.

In the article "Return to Vietnam," Elsa Arnett describes her expectations when she   5

sees the tofu custard. Arnett moved to the United States when she was four. The first

time she went back to her birthplace, she was 33 years old.

Since she spent most of her time in the United States. She couldn't remember a

lot of things about Vietnam, most of the things that she knows about Vietnam are

from her relatives. When she arrives in Vietnam. She sees children sitting on top of   10

the water buffalo and girls riding on their bicycles. She can smell the fragrance of the

anise from the noodle soup, and she also hears people speak Vietnamese in the street.

All these things make her feel this country is very familiar, her memories come back

little by little.

Activity 5 • Edit your writing for fragments and run-on sentences

Using your own or a partner's writing from After Reading, p. 25, or Topics for Writing, p. 26, follow steps 1–3 in Activity 4. Then do the following:
- Exchange papers with a partner to check each other's work.
- If time permits, put examples on the board of independent clauses, dependent clauses, fragments, and/or run-on sentences and discuss them.
- Make corrections where necessary.

2.2   Subject-Verb Agreement

Preview: Assess What You Know

In English, verbs must agree with their subjects. Errors in subject-verb agreement often come from spoken English because speakers don't always pay attention to subject-verb agreement rules. Other errors come from problems writers have in keeping track of the subject or in recognizing the correct subject-verb agreement form to use. To assess your understanding of subject-verb agreement, do the following:

Each of these sentences has a problem with subject-verb agreement. <u>Underline</u> the verb and (circle) the subject. Try to find and correct the problem.

NOTE: *All verbs should be in present tense.*

1. To Arnett,(Vietnam)<u>feel</u> like home, but(it)<u>isn't</u>.

2. There is several reasons why Arnett feels uncomfortable in Vietnam.

3. The trip along the bumpy roads impress Arnett.

4. One of her important experiences are tasting the tofu custard.

5. Each of her tangled memories set Arnett apart from Vietnam.

6. Traveling through the Hanoi streets awaken memories for Arnett.

7. The background information about Arnett's childhood help us understand her experience of going to Vietnam for the first time.

Grammar Tips: Check Your Work

With a partner or a small group, check your answers in the Preview by using the information in Chart 2.2 that follows. Be prepared to explain your answers by referring to specific sections of the chart. Figure out what you still need to learn.

CHART 2.2	**Problem Areas for Subject-Verb Agreement**[3]	
Problem Area	**Rule / Tip**	**Example**
1. Present tense (a) Present perfect tense (b)	Third person singular subjects (*he, she, it, Arnett, the writer, the story, …*) require a verb that ends in *-s*.	a. (Vietnam)<u>feels</u> like home. b. (She)<u>has</u> not <u>forgotten</u> her childhood.
2. Verbs with *be* [4]	First person singular (*I*) requires *am* or *was*. Third person singular (*he, she, it*) requires *is* or *was*. All other subjects take *are* or *were*.	(I)<u>am</u> interested in her experiences. (I)<u>was</u> in Vietnam last year. (Arnett)<u>is</u> writing an article. (The schoolgirls)<u>are</u> riding bicycles.
3. Sentences with *there*	The verb must agree with the noun (subject) that follows the verb.[5]	**There** <u>are</u>(several reasons)why Arnett feels uncomfortable. On the street **there** <u>was</u>(a man)selling tofu custard.

Problem Area	Rule / Tip	Example
4. Information comes between the subject and verb	Keep track of the subject: circle it and underline the verb.	(The trip) along the bumpy roads <u>impresses</u> Arnett. (The way) that the tofu custard tastes <u>isn't</u> familiar to Arnett.
5. Special pronouns	Remember that certain words and expressions are always third person singular: *each, every, one of,* …	(One) of her important experiences <u>is</u> tasting the tofu custard. (Each) of her tangled memories <u>sets</u> Arnett apart from Vietnam.
6. Complex phrases and clauses as subjects, for example: a. *-ing* words or phrases b. *to* + verb (infinitives) c. *wh-* clauses d. *that* clauses	These are always third person singular.	a. (Traveling through the Hanoi streets) <u>awakens</u> memories for Arnett. b. (To return to Vietnam) <u>has been</u> exciting for her. c. (What she liked best) <u>was</u> finding out about her roots. d. (That she went) <u>isn't</u> surprising.
7. Noncount nouns[6] as subjects	Noncount nouns are always third person singular: *news, research, information*	(The background information) <u>helps</u> us understand her experience.

[3]See Reference Chart 2.3, p. 175, for more information.

[4]When *be* follows a modal *(can, should, must, may,* etc.*),* there is no change in the verb for different subjects. Examples: *Going to the place of your birth **can be** exciting. However, these return trips **may be** upsetting.*

[5]In informal speech and writing, you may find *there* + *is* + plural noun, for example, *There**'s several reasons** why I think so.* In academic writing, it is safest to follow the subject-verb agreement rules.

[6]See Reference Chart 1.4, p. 163, for more information about noncount nouns.

Practice

Activity 6 • Identify subject-verb combinations in student writing

Using the student writing below, do the following:

- <u>Underline</u> the verbs and (circle) the subjects.
- Highlight any subject-verb combinations that are third person singular in the *present* tense or the *present perfect* tense.
- Highlight in a different color any subject-verb combinations that have a form of *be* as the main verb or as part of the verb.

Refer to Chart 2.2 on p. 33 to review subject-verb agreement with present and present perfect tenses and with forms of *be*. Also see Reference Chart 2.3, p. 175.

As soon as (Arnett) <u>arrives</u> in Vietnam, (she) <u>can feel</u> the heat. (It) <u>is</u> so hot that   1

(she) almost <u>chokes</u>, and (her sweat) <u>drenches</u> her shirt in a few minutes. She remembers that when she was a child, on hot days such as this one, her mother usually turned on the electric fan, sat on an armchair, and played with her.

As Arnett travels from the airport to downtown Hanoi, the taxi is shaking all the   5
time because of the bumpy highway. She has never seen such a bumpy and sandy highway in the United States. She has to hold on to the seats in order to stabilize herself. As she looks through the window, she sees some villagers wearing conical hats working in the field. She feels sorry for them because they have to work so hard under the bright sun. At the same time, she feels lucky that she does not have to do such   10
hard work. In her memories, her mother also has a conical hat. She used to hang her hat on the hook in the living room when she came home from work. In the distance, children are laughing and playing on top of a water buffalo. Suddenly, Arnett hears some noise from the other side. As she turns around she sees a group of schoolgirls riding on bicycles on their way home from school. She thinks it is so beautiful to see   15
the tails of their *ao dai* dresses flying in the wind because the clothes are of attractive colors. She has seen *ao dai* dresses on TV but has never worn this dress before, so she decides to buy one for herself as soon as she gets to Hanoi.

Activity 7 • Edit student writing with subject-verb agreement problems

Using the student writing below, do the following:

- <u>Underline</u> the verbs and (circle) the subjects.
- Write *sva* above the verb where there is a subject-verb agreement error. (See Chart 2.2 to help you find problems.)
- Make corrections. (Note: There are six additional subject-verb agreement errors.)

                                                  sva s

(Everything) that (Arnett) <u>see</u> in Vietnam <u>is related</u> to her limited memory and her   1
imagination about Vietnam. She compares what she thought before and what she see   2
in reality; for example, she see exactly the same exotic fruits, hear the same language   3
in her home country. She feel very happy and comfortable about that; however, later   4
she feels disappointed about the fact that the tofu custard in Vietnam is not as good   5
as before and even worse than the tofu custard in the U.S. At the end of the article,   6
she realize that Vietnam is not her home anymore. It is not a place for her to live be-   7
cause she has already been Americanized for a long time and the U.S. have replaced   8
Vietnam to become her home.   9

Activity 8 • Partner dictation: Edit your partner's writing for subject-verb agreement

Using writing you did for Topics for Writing on p. 26, follow these steps:

- Select a paragraph from the paper that contains examples of subject-verb agreement, for example, one with present tense verbs or present or past tense of be.
- Give your partner a brief oral summary of your paper, but don't show your partner your writing.
- Dictate the paragraph to your partner.

   First, read the paragraph all the way through once.

   Then read the paragraph again, one clause at a time.

   While you read, your partner will write down what you say.

   When you are finished, read the paragraph aloud all the way through again.

- Using the three steps in Activity 7, check the dictated paragraph with your partner.
- Switch roles with your partner and repeat steps 1–4.

2.3 Verb Tenses for Writing about a Reading

Preview: Assess What You Know

Sometimes writers are confused about verb tenses in their writing. They may be unsure about using different tenses within a paragraph. This section reviews some verb tenses used in academic writing to discuss events or information from a reading.

The paragraph below is part of a student composition on a topic related to "Return to Vietnam." The student describes key events from the reading in order to support the point he is making.

Analyze the use of the different verb tenses in the paragraph by following these steps.

NOTE: *All the verbs in the paragraph are correct.*

- Read the paragraph all the way through once.

   Notice the first two verbs: *find, are.* Why are these verbs in the present tense?

- Notice that the writer uses the present tense to describe the events that Arnett tells about in the reading (i.e., the events during her trip to Vietnam).
- Read the paragraph again. As you read, <u>underline</u> verbs; put a wiggly line under time expressions. (Be sure to include the complete time expression, not just the signal word.)
- Notice the changes in verb tense. As you read the paragraph again, put an X above any verb that shows a tense shift from the last verb—for example, a shift from present to past tense or a shift from past to present tense.

NOTE: *You will find 10 shifts in tense.*

After reading the article "Return to Vietnam," I <u>find</u> there <u>are</u> several ways to look   1

at the significance of the tofu that Elsa Arnett <u>purchases</u> in the streets of Hanoi.   2

Arnett, *San Jose Mercury News* journalist, and her family <u>left</u> Vietnam when she   3

<u>was</u> four years old. After thirty-some years, she finally has the chance to go back to   4

her native country. When she sees the tofu custard seller in the market, she is over-   5

joyed with excitement because the tofu custard was her favorite dessert when she was   6

a child. She has thought about eating it hundreds of times in the United States, but   7

the tofu custard she has eaten in the United States has never tasted as good as the   8

ones that she had in Vietnam in her childhood. Seeing the Hanoi tofu seller gives her   9

the first chance of eating the "real" tofu custard since she left Vietnam. From the   10

above description of the tofu custard, I can see that Arnett has clear and vivid memo-   11

ries of the custard. It is something that she remembers very well and misses very   12

much. So her expectation of the tofu is very high. She thinks the taste of the tofu will   13

be the same as she remembers from childhood. But when she tastes the tofu custard,   14

she is greatly disappointed. The tofu custard does not taste the same to her anymore.   15

She thinks of it as tasteless and without flavor. Her experience shows how different   16

memory and reality can be.   17

■ On a separate piece of paper, copy the chart below and continue filling out the columns. Focus on the verbs that show a change or shift in tense. (You should have eight additional shifts.) If you can, name the tense and give a reason for the writer's choice of tense.

Verbs showing tense shifts	(line #)	Tense/Reason for the tense
1. Arnett and her family <u>left</u>	(line 3)	Past: Event that occurred before her trip to Vietnam
2. she finally <u>has</u> the chance	(line 4)	Present: To write about events and information during the trip

Grammar Tips: Check Your Work

With a partner or a small group, check your answers in the Preview by using the information in Charts 2.3A and 2.3B that follow. Be prepared to explain your answers by referring to specific sections of Charts 2.3A and 2.3B. Figure out what you still need to learn.

CHART 2.3A	Verb Tenses for Writing about a Reading	
Verb Tense	**Use**	**Example**
Simple present[7]	a. To give opinions, beliefs, ideas	a. Arnett **learns** an important lesson about memory and reality.
	b. To state facts or general truths	b. Our memories of an event **change** over time.
	c. To write about events and information in a reading (using a present time frame) Writers use present tense and a present time frame to make their writing more interesting and vivid to the reader.[8]	c. Arnett **sees** many wonderful things on the way into town from the airport.
Present perfect	d. To describe an activity or state that happened in the past but is related or relevant to the present.	d. As Arnett travels the streets in Hanoi, she realizes she **has not forgotten** the bits of Vietnamese culture she learned as a child.
Simple past	e. In a present time frame, to describe past events or activities clearly linked to a past point or period of time (*as a child* describes a past period of time)	e. As Arnett travels the streets in Hanoi, she realizes she has not forgotten the bits of Vietnamese culture she **learned** as a child.
	f. To write about events and information in a reading (a past time frame) Writers can use the past tense and a past time frame because the events happened in the past.	f. When Arnett first **arrived** in Vietnam, she **saw** many wonderful things on the way into town from the airport.
Past perfect	g. To show a relationship between two past events and to make clear which happened first: the past perfect shows which event happened first	g1. When she saw the tofu custard seller in the market, she was overjoyed because she **had thought** about eating this favorite dish hundreds of times in the U.S.
		g2. She **had** just **begun** feeling comfortable when she tasted the tofu; she then realized the present reality didn't match her memories.
Future	h. In a present time frame, to describe a state or event that will occur at a future point (*will* or *is/am/are going to*)	h. Arnett is excited when she realizes she **will have** the tofu custard again.
	i. In a past time frame, to describe a state or event that will occur in the future in relation to a past point of time (*would* or *was/were going to*)	i. Arnett was excited when she realized she **would have** the tofu custard again.

[7]Note that progressive tenses can be used as well to describe action ongoing over a period of time in the present (e.g., While Arnett **is traveling** to Hanoi from the airport, she sees many girls on bicycles.) or in the past (e.g., While Arnett **was traveling** to Hanoi from the airport, she saw many girls on bicycles.) See Chart 3.1A, p. 52, for more information.

[8]Note that Arnett uses present tense to tell the story of her trip to Vietnam. (The story of the trip begins on line 10.)

CHART 2.3B	Verb Tense Consistency for Writing about a Reading	
Problem	**Tips**	**Examples**
Confusion for the reader caused by shifts from one verb tense to another without a reason	a. Choose a past or present time frame and use verbs appropriate to that framework. b. For a *present* time frame: Use present, present perfect, future, and present progressive c. For a *past* time frame: Use past, past perfect, past progressive, and future with *would/was going to*. d. You can *shift* to another frame if ■ You use a <u>time expression</u> (e.g., *as a child*), or ■ You are shifting to *present* tense to give an opinion or state a general truth. (*See a, b in Chart 2.3A.*)	a. *For a text with problems in consistency, see Activity 10 on p. 40.* b. *For a correct example of a present time frame, see the text in the Preview on p. 36.* c. *For a correct example of a past time frame, see the text in Activity 9 below.* d1. Arnett <u>recognizes</u> the bits of culture she <u>learned</u> as a child. d2. Such sudden recognitions <u>are</u> common to most of us.

Practice

Activity 9 • Analyze verb tenses and tense shifts

The paragraph in the Preview is presented again below. It has been altered to show the choice of verb tenses if the writer chooses the past time frame to tell the events from the story. Verbs that are changed are in **bold**.

■ Read the paragraph all the way through once. Notice that the writer uses the past tense to describe the events during her trip to Vietnam.
■ Read the paragraph again. As you read, notice the shifts in verb tense.

   Put an X above any verb that shows a tense shift from the last verb—for example, a shift from present to past tense or a shift from past to past perfect tense.

NOTE: *You will find 8 shifts in tense, including the example.*

■ For each line with an X, write the letter of the corresponding verb tense use from Chart 2.3A. You can write these letters in the left margin.

          After reading the article "Return to Vietnam," I find there are several ways to look   1

f   at the significance of the tofu that Elsa Arnett **purchased** in the streets of Hanoi.   2

Arnett, *San Jose Mercury News* journalist, and her family left Vietnam when she was   3

four years old. After thirty-some years, she finally **had** the chance to go back to her   4

native country. When she **saw** the tofu custard seller in the market, she **was** overjoyed   5

with excitement because the tofu custard **had been** her favorite dessert when she was   6

a child. She **had thought** about eating it hundreds of times in the United States, but   7

the tofu custard she **ate** in the United States never **tasted** as good as the ones that she   8 had in Vietnam in her childhood. Seeing the Hanoi tofu seller **gave** her the first 9

chance of eating the "real" tofu custard since she left Vietnam. From the above de- 10

scription of the tofu custard, I can see that Arnett **had** clear and vivid memories of the 11

custard. It **was** something that she **remembered** very well and **missed** very much. So 12

her expectation of the tofu **was** very high. She **thought** the taste of the tofu **would be** 13

the same as she **remembered** from childhood. But when she **tasted** the tofu custard, 14

she **was** greatly disappointed. The tofu custard **did** not **taste** the same to her any- 15

more. She **thought** of it as tasteless and without flavor. Her experience shows how dif- 16

ferent memory and reality can be. 17

Activity 10 • Analyze and edit verb tenses: Practice the past time frame

Analyze and edit the paragraph below by following these steps. Some of the verbs in the paragraph are incorrect.

- Read the paragraph all the way through once. Ask yourself: Why are the verb tenses confusing?
- Analyze the paragraph to help you figure out what corrections to make:
    Underline verbs; put a wiggly line under time expressions.
- Read the paragraph again. Put a check (✓) above any verb that you think is in the wrong tense. Then ask yourself:
    Do verbs and time expressions match?
    Does the writer have a reason for shifting tense?
- Make corrections. Work with a partner or small group to compare your work.

NOTE: *There are 13 errors, including the example.*

Refer to Charts 2.3A and 2.3B to help you make decisions about appropriate tenses.

✓ *d*
After my graduation from high school, my mother decide to take me back to 1

Cambodia to see my grandfather and my relatives. I became so excited and 2

anxious to go back when I heard the word "Cambodia." Three weeks later we were on 3

the plane back to Cambodia. On the airplane I was thinking about how excited I am 4

to see my grandfather and the people that I miss since I left. 5

When we got to our grandfather's house, I cannot believe that everything has 6

changed. The floor and the ground were dirty, and the place was filled with pieces of 7

wood that were stacked on the inside of the house. The people in the house look like 8

strangers to me, but as I go closer to take a good look at them, I saw they were my rel- 9

atives from far away coming to welcome us home. After a while my grandfather 10

cooked pho noodles, my favorite food ever since I was a kid. I was so eager to eat 11 them because I remember how good they tasted to me as a child. After taking the first   12

two bites, I realize that they don't taste the same as they did when I was a kid. I kept   13

on eating them because I don't want my grandfather to find out that I don't like his   14

pho noodles anymore. After a month in Cambodia, I can't wait to be back home.   15

Activity 11 • Edit verb tenses and subject-verb agreement: present or past time frame

Read the excerpt below all the way through once. Ask:

- What time frame is the writer using to write about the events—present or past or both?
- Where does the writer shift tense? Are the time shifts correct?

Follow the steps below to help you analyze the text and make suggestions for editing.

- <u>Underline</u> the complete verbs and draw a wiggly line under time expressions.
- Put a check (✓) above any verb that you think is in the wrong tense.
- Write *sva* above the verb where you think there is a subject-verb agreement error.
- Make corrections in verb tense and in subject-verb agreement.

NOTE: *There are nine errors including the examples.*

Refer to Charts 2.3A and 2.3B to help you make decisions about appropriate verb tenses, and refer to Chart 2.2 to help you make decisions about subject-verb agreement.

When I was sixteen, I returned to my home country to be with my grandmother   1

before she died. This experience ✓ taught teaches me three important things. First of all, I   2

learn_{ed} that bad luck happen_s *sva* to everybody. It is just a part of our lives. We don't   3

need to feel sad about it, and also we should use a more positive attitude to face it.   4

For example, we can see it as an encouragement for us to try our best for our fu-   5

ture …. Secondly, I realize that nothing will stay with us forever, especially our family,   6

relatives, and friends. Death and sickness are all around us. We don't know when acci-   7

dents will happen. Nobody know what will happen tomorrow and even in the next   8

moments. Therefore, we need to treasure the time we have with our families, rela-   9

tives, and friends. Even though we have just a short conversation, it can be meaning-   10

ful to us. After my grandmother died, I had a deep feeling about it and want to make   11

changes in my life. Therefore, I now spend most of my time with my family. Also every   12

Sunday, I spend the whole day with my family instead of hanging out with my friends.   13

Even though sometimes we just stay in the house and watch television, I still feel   14

happy and satisfied. Finally, I learn that some things that I don't want or expect to   15

happen still has the possibility of happening. As with my grandmother, I don't want   16

her to pass away, but death is one of the processes of our lives. When it comes, no one   17

can escape it.   18

Wrap-Up

Activity 12 • Edit your writing for fragments and run-on sentences, subject-verb agreement, verb tense, and articles and nouns

■ Using Editing Guides 1.1 (p. 151) and 2.1–2.3 (p. 152) and other information in this chapter, edit a piece of your own writing (from Topics for Writing, p. 26, or After Reading questions 7 or 8 (p. 25) for problems with:

fragments and run-on sentences

verb tense in academic writing

subject-verb agreement

articles and nouns

■ For the structures you edit, clearly show on your paper each step described in the Editing Guides. In addition, check your writing to see if you've used any of the word partnerships listed in "Using Vocabulary Accurately," p. 26. Correct any problems you find, and add examples to your word partnerships list. (See p. 150.)

Activity 13 • Class editing workshop: Edit for common structure problems

At home: Follow the directions for Activity 12. In addition, write questions in the margins of your paper next to places where you're not sure of your editing choices.

In class: Working with a partner or a small group, trade papers, and talk about each other's questions and writing. Refer to the grammar charts in the chapters and in Appendix B and the Editing Guides in Appendix A to help you. If time permits, put examples from your writing and editing on the board to discuss as a class.

3

Verb Tenses for Generalizations and Support, and Reporting Ideas

Overview of the Chapter

Read

Before Reading

Respond to these questions to help you think about and understand the reading that follows.

1. Discuss the following statement: "In negotiating with foreign business people, small things matter." What might the words "small things" refer to?
2. What problems in communication could arise when people from different cultures exchange e-mail messages?

"You Say Tomato" by Lalita Khosla

Lalita Khosla is a writer and filmmaker of Indian descent. Both her writing and her films contain elements of humor underlying potentially serious situations. In this article, she examines cross-cultural communication in business interactions and suggests what can be done to establish successful international business partnerships. The title, "You Say Tomato," comes from a popular American song of the 1930s. The song is about two people who can't agree on the pronunciation of certain words (e.g., "tomayto" vs "tomahto"), so they humorously talk about ending their relationship.

*In dealing with foreigners, Americans sometimes come across as **intrusive**, **manipulative**, and **garrulous**. This can get partnerships off to a bad start.*   1

In negotiating with foreign business people, small things matter. During seemingly endless negotiations with the Japanese Ministry of Trade and Industry (MITI), Minnesota Mining and Manufacturing's (3M) Harry Heltzer and a few of his   5
colleagues left the table and began preparing tea. Later, their **prospective** partners, executives of the Sumitomo Trading Co., asked why Heltzer and his crew had behaved so uncharacteristically. Heltzer, who later rose to be 3M's chief executive, smiled and explained: You guys know how to **haggle** with MITI; we just wanted to be out of your way.   10

That little gesture of trust made a deep and lasting impression on the Sumitomo people; 40 years later the Sumitomo 3M joint venture is one of the most successful in Japan and contributes more than 10% of 3M's total profits.

Americans aren't always so sensitive to foreign tastes and habits. More recently, for instance, at Hewlett-Packard a group of engineers in California began designing   15
software with HP's engineers in Grenoble, France. A **rift** nearly destroyed the project.

HP engineers in San Jose sent long, detailed e-mail to their **counterparts** in Grenoble. The engineers in Grenoble viewed the lengthy e-mail as **patronizing** and replied with quick, concise e-mail. That made the U.S. engineers believe that the

---

intrusive: violating the privacy of others
manipulative: controlling
garrulous: tiresomely talkative
prospective: likely to be

haggle: bargain
rift: break in friendly relations
counterparts: partners
patronizing: treating someone as inferior

French were withholding information. The process **spiraled** out of control. People   20
started blaming personalities. A cultural **logjam** rolled into place.

HP turned to Charis Intercultural Training, a consulting firm based in Pleasanton,
Calif., to help improve the relationship. "We went in as cultural **sleuths**," says Charis
President Marian Stetson-Rodriguez. Charis quizzed members of each team, asking
about their preferred communication styles. After six months of cultural training, the   25
relationship improved.

Helping business people avoid intercultural **faux pas** has become a $100-million
business for companies like Charis and San Francisco-based Meridian Resources.
Intel, for instance, uses Charis to provide 55 training classes to instruct Intel employees on cultural **nuances**.   30

Here are a few hints from the people at Charis and Meridian. By remembering
these **subtle** points, your partnerships may avoid running into trouble:

- Italians, Germans, and French don't soften up executives with praise before they
  criticize. Americans do, and to the Europeans that seems manipulative.
- Israelis, accustomed to fast-paced meetings, have no patience for American   35
  small talk.
- British executives often complain that their U.S. counterparts chatter too much.
  Our **penchant** for informality, **egalitarianism**, and **spontaneity** sometimes jars
  people.
- Europeans often feel they are being treated like children when Americans insist   40
  they wear name tags.
- Indian executives are used to interrupting one another. If Americans listen with-
  out asking for clarification or posing questions, the Indians may feel the
  Americans aren't paying attention.
- When negotiating with Malaysian or Japanese executives, periodically allow for 6   45
  seconds of silence. If you are negotiating with an Israeli, don't pause.
- Think twice before asking some foreigners questions like "How was your week-
  end?" That sounds intrusive to foreigners who tend to regard their business and
  private lives as totally **compartmentalized**.
- For more hints and suggestions, visit www.meridianglobal.com and click on Web   50
  Tools.

from *Forbes* magazine, May 21, 2001, p. 36

---

spiraled: quickly rose or fell
logjam: obstruction, deadlock, stoppage
sleuths: detectives
faux pas: social mistakes
nuances: slight differences

subtle: not obvious
penchant: definite liking
egalitarianism: equality
spontaneity: acting without planning
compartmentalized: separate

After Reading

Individually at home, or with a partner or a small group in class, write the answers to these questions to prepare for class discussion. Keep your answers in a notebook or binder to refer to later when you respond to the writing topics, develop your ideas for longer papers, or analyze your writing. Questions marked ¶ are especially suitable for paragraph length answers that can be used later when you analyze your own writing.

1. Lalita Khosla gives two examples to support her idea that "small things matter" in intercultural business relationships: one example shows a positive interaction; the other example illustrates a misunderstanding.

   In a brief paragraph, summarize the situation and outcome of the first example. Explain who the different people and groups are, what they did, and why they did it. In your paragraph, include the following:

the Japanese Ministry of Trade and Industry (MITI)	the hours of negotiations
the Minnesota Mining and Manufacturing Co. (3M)	the "little gesture of trust"
the Sumitomo Trading Company	the result for the joint venture
Harry Heltzer	

2. Why did the Sumitomo executives say that Heltzer and his crew behaved "uncharacteristically"? Why was this a *good* thing? How would Americans "normally" behave?

3. In a brief paragraph, summarize the situation and outcome of the second example explained in question 1 above. Explain who the different groups are, what they did, and why they did it. In your paragraph, include the following:

the HP engineers in California	the American view of e-mail
the HP engineers in France	the French view of e-mail
Charis Intercultural Training	how the problem "spiraled out of control"
the solution to the problem	

4. Khosla states that "Americans aren't always so sensitive to foreign tastes and habits." Explain what she means by using the two examples you described in questions 1 and 3.

5. In the last third of the article, Khosla describes some cultural differences that can cause misunderstandings in the business world. To help you understand her points, fill in the following chart.

Line #	"Foreign" culture	American culture	Possible misunderstanding for each culture
33–34	Italians, Germans, and French don't give praise before they criticize.	Americans give praise before they criticize.	Europeans think Americans are manipulating them by "softening them up" before criticizing. Americans may think the Europeans are too direct and critical.
35–36	Israeli meetings move at a rapid pace without "small talk."	American meetings include a lot of small talk.	Israelis are not patient with Americans in meetings. Americans think Israelis aren't friendly and are too businesslike.

Line #	"Foreign" culture	American culture	Possible misunderstanding for each culture
37–39			
40–41			
42–44			
45–46			
47–49			

6. Come up with one or two generalizations about Americans that are different from the ones in Khosla's article. Think of examples that support your generalizations.

7. What do you find humorous in the article? List examples and jot down your ideas about them.

¶ 8. First, freewrite your response to this question: What is the point or main idea of "You Say Tomato"? Then write one or two statements that express possible main ideas. Be prepared to discuss how you would support your statement(s) using the text.

¶ 9. What experiences have you had at work, at school, or in social situations that reflect Khosla's ideas in "You Say Tomato"? Make a list of some of these experiences. Write about how your experiences connect to Khosla's examples of how people from different cultures think or behave in different situations.

Write

Topics for Writing

Respond in writing to one (or more) of the following topics.

1. Imagine that a friend or relative is coming to the United States for the first time to take a trip, go to school, or start a new job. You want to prepare him or her for the behavior of Americans. Make a generalization about Americans. Support your generalization with examples, including information about misunderstandings that could occur.

2. Imagine that you want to prepare a friend, a co-worker, or a relative for his or her first trip to your home country. Make a generalization about the people in your home culture. Support your generalization with examples, including information about misunderstandings that could occur.

3. Find an article from a magazine, newspaper, or on the Internet that illustrates problems with cross-cultural communication. Topics to consider: sports, politics, education, international negotiations between governments. Compare the example(s) and information in the article with the example(s) and information in "You Say Tomato."

4. Discuss the significance of the following statement from "You Say Tomato": "In negotiating with foreign business people, small things matter." Use examples and information from the text to support your ideas.

5. What is Khosla's point in "You Say Tomato"? Do you agree with the ideas presented in the article? Why or why not?

> ### Strategies for Writing: Generating and Developing Ideas
> For a description of ways to generate ideas, such as freewriting, listing, and brainstorming, as well as ways to develop and support your ideas, refer to Strategies for Writing, pp. 185–190.

Using Vocabulary Accurately

As you write about a reading, pay attention to key words and word partnerships, words that occur frequently with each other or that form fixed expressions. For more examples, see Reference Charts 2.1 and 2.2, pp. 172–174. Create your own word partnerships list (see p. 150).

Some key word partnerships for this reading follow. Locate key words in the reading or in Topics for Writing and notice how they are used. For practice, write sentences using some of these expressions.

to be sensitive to (*something*)	to run into trouble
to view (*something*) as patronizing	to be used to (*doing something*)
a deep [and lasting] impression	a preferred communication style

Edit: Grammar Previews, Tips, and Practice

Listening/Writing Activity: Dictation/Dictocomp

The following dictation /dictocomp gives information related to the reading "You Say Tomato" on p. 44.

Close your book. As your teacher reads the sentences below (one time all the way through, then by clauses, then all the way through again), do the following:

- For a dictation, try to write exactly what you hear.
- For a dictocomp, take notes on key words and phrases.
- Then, individually or in groups, reconstruct the text, revising and correcting your work and paying attention to problem areas.

1. In intercultural business negotiations, small things matter.

2. An example of this occurred when an American company and a Japanese company were negotiating an agreement with the Japanese Ministry of Trade.

3. The representatives of the American company left the room so that the Japanese executives could handle the negotiation.

4. This demonstration of trust led to a forty-year relationship between the two companies.

5. But Americans aren't always so sensitive to foreign tastes and habits.

6. More recently, for instance, California software engineers created huge misunderstandings when they wrote lengthy e-mails to French software developers working for the same company.

7. It took six months of training by an intercultural consulting firm to repair the relationship.

8. Helping business people avoid intercultural misunderstandings has become a $100-million business.

3.1   Verb Tenses[1] for Making and Supporting Generalizations

Preview: Assess What You Know

When authors write to inform their readers, they use different verb tenses to make the information clear. They regularly use the simple present tense (e.g., *think, thinks*) to make general statements of fact—statements that are currently true—or to give opinions. The present perfect tense (e.g., *has become, have become*) is also used for this purpose. Writers support general statements with information using other tenses as well, such as the past (e.g., *occurred*) and the past progressive (e.g., *were negotiating*).

A. Examine the dictation for this chapter in the previous section and do the following:

- Identify sentences that are general statements of fact or opinion and label them "G" (e.g., #1).
- Identify sentences that support the generalizations and label them "S" (e.g., #2).
- <u>Double underline</u> any expressions that help you identify a sentence as a supporting sentence (e.g., #2: <u>an example of this</u>).
- Draw a wiggly line under time expressions in supporting sentences.
- <u>Underline</u> the verbs and identify their tenses (e.g., #1, <u>matter</u>: simple present).

B. Examine the pairs of sentences below, which are from the reading "You Say Tomato," and follow the instructions above.

Pair 1

_G_   1. Helping business people avoid intercultural faux pas *present perfect* <u>has become</u> a $100 million business for companies like Charis and San-Francisco based Meridian Resources.

_S_   2. Intel, <u>for instance</u>, *present* <u>uses</u> Charis to provide 55 training classes to instruct Intel employees on cultural nuances.

Pair 2

_____   3. British executives often complain that their U.S. counterparts chatter too much.

_____   4. Our penchant for informality, egalitarianism and spontaneity sometimes jars people.

---

[1]Information about the names and forms of verb tenses appears in Reference Charts 1.6, 1.7, and 1.8, pp. 167–168. Additional information about verb tense use appears in Chart 2.3A, p. 36, Chart 4.3, p. 86, Chart 4.4, p. 90, and Chart 5.4B, p. 118.

Pair 3

_____ 5. Think twice before asking some foreigners questions like "How was your weekend?"

_____ 6. That sounds intrusive to foreigners who tend to regard their business and private lives as totally compartmentalized.

C. Summarize what you know: Work with a partner or a small group to compare your answers for the exercises above. Then complete the following statements by circling the letters of the correct answers:

1. In general statements of fact or opinion, two verb tenses commonly used are:
   a. simple present.
   b. present progressive.
   c. simple past.
   d. present perfect.

2. When you are writing sentences that give information to support general statements of fact or opinion, you can use the past tense when you are talking about:
   a. a present event.
   b. a past event.
   c. an event that occurred before a past event.
   d. an action that started in the past and continues up to the present.

3. You can use the present tense when you are talking about something:
   a. true from the past up to now.
   b. true in the present.
   c. true in the future.
   d. true in the past.

Grammar Tips: Check Your Work

With a partner or a small group, compare your answers in the Preview by using the information in Charts 3.1A and 3.1B that follow. Be prepared to explain your answers by referring to specific sections of the charts. Figure out what you still need to learn.

CHART 3.1A   Verb Tenses for Stating Generalizations

In informative or persuasive writing, writers use the present tense or the present perfect tense to state facts, general truths, or opinions.

Time Reference/ Verb Tense	Verb Tense Use	Examples
Present time Simple Present tense	Gives writer's opinions, beliefs, or ideas, or states general truths. Describes activities, habits, or states related to a present time period that extends backward into the past and forward into the future.	In Khosla's view, small things **matter**. Americans **aren't** so sensitive. If Americans **listen** without asking for clarification, speakers **may feel** ignored.

Past   Now   Future

matter
aren't
listen
may feel

Time Reference/ Verb Tense	Verb Tense Use	Examples
Past up to present time Present Perfect tense	Describes activities or states related to a present time period. Describes an action that happened in the past and whose effect has extended to the present and may continue in the future.	Helping business people avoid intercultural misunderstandings **has become** a $100-million business. *(Here, the actual event—"become a $100-million business"—happened sometime in the past, but we don't know when. The fact that it happened is important to the point the writer is making.)*

Past   Now   Future

has
become

CHART 3.1B   Verb Tenses for Supporting Information

In informative and persuasive writing, writers use different types of information to support their ideas: Examples of things that happened in the past, examples of things that are true or happen in the present, examples of things that may happen in the future, or factual information such as statistics or quotations from other sources. The writer chooses the verb tense to correspond to the time that is relevant to this information.

Time Reference/ Verb Tense	Verb Tense Use	Example
Past time Simple Past tense	Describes a past action or state.	An example of this **occurred** when …. California software engineers **created** huge misunderstandings ….

Past   Now   Future

occurred
created

Time Reference/ Verb Tense	Verb Tense Use	Example
Past time Past Progressive tense	Describes an action ongoing over a period of time in the past. **were withholding**	That made the U.S. engineers believe that the French **were withholding** information. *(Here, the Americans believed that the French **were withholding** information at the time they wrote the e-mail, and that this action— withholding— would probably continue.)*
Past time Past Perfect tense	Shows a relationship between two past events.	Their prospective partners asked why Heltzer and his crew **had behaved** so uncharacteristically. *(Here, **behaved** happened first; **asked** happened second.)*
Present time Simple Present tense	Shows a present perception, opinion, or state. **sounds**	That **sounds** intrusive to foreigners …. *(This use of the simple present refers to the general present, not necessarily to the precise moment **now**.)*
Present time Present Progressive tense	Shows action over a present period of time. **are negotiating**	If you **are negotiating** with an Israeli, don't pause. *(If = whenever = at any time in the present time period.)*

CHART 3.1C　Expressions that Introduce Support

When academic writers want to give their readers a cue that they are presenting examples or other information to support their ideas, they use certain expressions to introduce the supporting information.

Grammatical Structure of the Expression	Examples
As a phrase *For example,* *For instance,*	American meetings often move slowly. **For example,** participants generally wait to speak until they are called on by a moderator and sometimes they have trouble staying on topic.
As a subject *One instance of this* *One example of this*	Americans give praise before they criticize. **One instance of this is** that a boss may begin a critique of an employee's work by saying something positive such as, "Overall you are doing a fine job." *(The pronoun* this *refers to the generalization in the previous sentence.)*

Grammatical Structure of the Expression	Examples
As a subject + verb	
a. *The author illustrates this by/with …*	a. **Khosla illustrates this** by describing how French and U.S. software engineers mistrusted each other. *(The pronoun* this *= a prior generalization about Americans' lack of sensitivity.)*
b. *The following example/quotation/information shows clearly that …*	b. **The following example shows clearly** that small things are important. *(Here, the sentence states the generalization, and the example follows in the next sentence(s) in the text.)*
c. *The following figures/statistics prove/support the point that …*	c. **The following figures prove** the success of companies which specialize in intercultural training programs: Both Meridian Resources and Charis, which provides 55 classes for Intel employees, have become $100-million businesses.

CHART 3.1D Grammar Problems and Tips: Generalizations and Support

Problem	Example of Problem Text	Solution
1. Inconsistent verb tense *several years ago* = past time In these sentences, all main verbs should be past tense to match the past time expression.	Khosla gives us an example of a successful relationship between two companies. Several years ago, they ⊘ **show** understanding of each others' cultures while they **were** in an important business meeting. During negotiations, the Americans just ⊘ **prepare** tea and ⊘ **give** some time to the Japanese executives to think and make the right decisions. These **were** little actions, but they ⊘ **make** them trust each other.	Check time expressions; think about the time of the events. <u>Underline</u> verbs and check time reference. Ask yourself: *Do tense and time expression match?* The correct verbs for the example are: **showed** **prepared** **gave** **made**
2. The relationship between generalization and support isn't clear enough. *An example (of this)* tells the reader that the general statement is in the preceding sentence. In this problem text, the example refers to the first sentence (a positive relationship), not the second (a negative relationship).	People who understand each other's cultural values and customs can keep a good relationship. *(positive)* On the other hand, people who misunderstand another culture can cause problems even though it might be a small difference. *(negative)* ⊘ **An example of this is** the relationship between an American company, 3M, and a Japanese company, Sumitomo. *(Is this example positive or negative?)*	Check the logic and order of sentences to make sure that the meaning of the example is clear and logically relates to the generalization. If not, rewrite to make it clear and logical in relationship to the generalization. *Correction:* **An example of a positive relationship is the one** between an American company, 3M, and a Japanese company, Sumitomo.

Practice

Activity 1 • Write generalizations and support, and then analyze tenses

Work individually or with a partner and do the following:

- Using your own words, write several generalizations that state a point that Khosla makes in the article, "You Say Tomato." (Write on a separate piece of paper.)
- For each of your generalizations, write supporting statements.
- <u>Underline</u> the verbs and identify the tenses.
- Explain your tense choices. Refer to Charts 3.1A and 3.1B.

Example:

Generalization: Companies operating globally <u>need to invest</u> money in cross-cultural training for their employees.
(present)

Support: For example, companies <u>can hire</u> experts to give workshops. This training <u>can prevent</u> misunderstandings such as the one that <u>occurred</u> between the French and American employees of Hewlett Packard.
(present, present, past)

Explanation: <u>need, can hire, can prevent</u>: present tense because they give the writer's opinion; <u>occurred</u>: past tense because the misunderstanding occurred in the past.

Activity 2 • Choose verb tenses in student writing

Read the paragraph of student writing below all the way through once and do the following:

- Draw a wiggly line under any time expressions.
- Choose the correct tense of the verb, and write it in the blank.
- Be prepared to explain your answers. Refer to Charts 3.1A, 3.1B, and 3.1C.

My friend is coming to America, and I want to prepare her for some of the cultural differences between Hong Kong and the United States based on my experience. The first problem she may face is "hugging." In Hong Kong, people usually __*don't hug*__ each other in public. Hugging _____ an action that you
1. hug, negative
2. be

_____ with a loved one in private. If you _____ female, you never
3. do
4. be

_____ males, except for the one you _____ in love with. If you
5. hug
6. be

_____, people _____ that you _____ too open-minded
7. do
8. think
9. be

and not a "good" girl. On the other hand, if you _____ male, you never
10. be

_____ females, except your girlfriend or your wife. If you _____,
11. hug
12. do

people _____ you _____ females. However, in America, it
13. think
14. respect, negative

_____ totally different. You _____ people hugging each other on
    15. be   16. see

the street, in cars, in shopping malls, and other places. For Americans, hugging each other

_____ just like shaking hands; it _____ just a normal thing. I
    17. be   18. be

_____ the first day I _____ to school in America. When I
    19. remember   20. go

_____ into my first class, which _____ a math class, the teacher
    21. go   22. be

_____ hands with me, _____ me, and then _____ me. I
    22. shake   23. hug   24. welcome

_____ shocked. In Hong Kong, teachers _____ that. If the teacher
    25. be   26. do, negative

_____, he or she _____ fired!
    27. do   28. modal + be

Activity 3 • Analyze and edit student writing for generalizations, support, and tense

For the student writing below, do the following:

- Identify the generalizations the writer is making. Mark the sentences "G."
- Identify the support the writer gives and mark these sentences "S."
- To analyze verb tenses,

    Draw a wiggly line under any time expressions and underline the verbs.

- Correct any problems with verb tense. (You will find seven total errors.)

G

Khosla tells us that misunderstanding foreign cultures can cause   1

big problems, and I agreed with her because of my experience of dealing with   2

S

someone from another country. I met a boy from Belgium when I went to a high   3

school in the United States as an exchange student. He is also an exchange student. 4

We did not go to same high school, but we sometimes met each other at parties and   5

events, and on trips. When I first met him, I thought that he was a very nice and gen- 6

tle person. But the second time we met, he tried to kiss my cheek. My culture doesn't 7

approve of this type of behavior. I was so surprised, and I don't understand why he   8

did that. And also, I am very confused. So I kept away from him, and I stopped talking 9

to him. It was a big problem for me at that time because I really want to be friends   10

with everyone, and I have always thought that it is important to try to be open while   11

living in a foreign culture. A solution to the problem was given by one of our friends. 12

He talked to me and the boy from Belgium and explain our cultures. He told me that   13

in Belgium young men kiss the cheeks of girls to greet them. Of course, this never   14

happened in my culture. He also talked to the boy from Belgium about my culture,   15

and we began to understand each other. Later, the three of us became great friends.   16

From my experience, I think that understanding other customs is very important   17

when dealing with foreign people.   18

3.2   Making Generalizations Less Certain

Preview: Assess What You Know

Writers often want to make their generalizations less certain or less assertive by using words that make the meaning less strong. They do this not only to make a point but also to avoid being too direct or to avoid overgeneralizing. Some examples are:

Certain: Americans come across as intrusive.

Less Certain: Americans **sometimes** come across as intrusive.

Certain: That is manipulative.

Less Certain: That **seems** manipulative.

Examine the generalizations that follow. Highlight the special expressions that make the statements less certain.

1. Americans sometimes come across as intrusive, manipulative, and garrulous.
2. This can get partnerships off to a bad start.
3. Americans aren't always so sensitive to foreign tastes and habits.
4. By remembering these subtle points, your partnerships may avoid running into trouble.
5. American small talk in meetings seems to annoy people from some other cultures.
6. Europeans often feel they are being treated like children.
7. Indians may feel that the Americans aren't paying attention.
8. Generally, Israeli business meetings move at a more rapid pace than American meetings do.

Grammar Tips: Check Your Work

With a partner or a small group, check your answers to the items in the Preview by using the information in Chart 3.2 that follows. Be prepared to explain your answers by referring to specific sections of the chart. Figure out what you still need to learn.

CHART 3.2 Strategies to Make Generalizations Less Certain[2]		
Strategy	**Expression**	**Example**
Use a modal auxiliary.	*may, might, can, could* (Use the simple form of the verb after a modal.)	This **can** get partnerships off to a bad start.
Use an adverb or noun showing probability.	**Adverbs:** *possibly, probably, generally*	**Generally**, Israeli meetings move at a more rapid pace. Americans **probably** come across as intrusive.
	Nouns: *a possibility, a probability*	There is **a possibility** that Americans will come across as too talkative.

Strategy	Expression	Example
Use a frequency adverb.[3]	*sometimes, always, often, usually, rarely, hardly ever*	Americans **sometimes** ask too many questions.
Use a verb that shows uncertainty.	*seem, appear, tend, suggest*	That **seems** manipulative.
Use a structure that shows uncertainty.	*It seems that …* *It is likely that …* *It is possible that …* *If …, (then) … may …*	**It seems that** Americans are more direct in asking questions.
Use a quantity modifier before a noun to limit the noun to a smaller group.	*most, many, some*	**Many** Americans are direct in asking questions.

[2]Writers can also use special expressions to make generalizations *more* certain. For example: Americans *definitely (always/without a doubt)* come across as intrusive. *All* Americans like to ask questions. Americans *never* feel uncomfortable asking questions.

[3]Single word adverbs of frequency—*usually, always, never, sometimes*—normally occur with the verb in a sentence: They come before the verb (They *sometimes ask* …) or after *be* (They *are often* aggressive …) or after the first auxiliary verb (They *can never* tell …). Most of these adverbs, with the exception of *always*, can also occur at the beginning of a sentence.

 Practice

Activity 4 • Analyze generalizations for degree of certainty

Examine the following generalizations from student essays and do the following:

- Indicate whether they are certain (+C) or less certain (–C).
- <u>Underline</u> any expressions that give you clues.

1. Americans <u>sometimes</u> form a line at the bus stop while waiting for the bus.   –C
2. Chinese people do not wait their turn and will squeeze their way onto the bus.
3. Americans are aggressive and assertive in business situations.
4. Japanese often dislike saying "no" directly.
5. People from Latin America do not think it is polite to make direct eye contact in certain situations.
6. All Americans like to show off their talents and material wealth.
7. Bargaining is acceptable and even expected in Mexican markets.
8. In some Arab countries, it is important to wear traditional clothing.
9. Americans will think you are rude if you don't call before stopping by to visit at someone's home.
10. Japanese are used to living in relatively small spaces, and they know they sometimes can't avoid bumping someone accidentally. Therefore, Japanese probably won't apologize if they bump into you in an elevator.

Activity 5 • Rewrite generalizations to make them less or more certain

- On a separate piece of paper rewrite the generalizations in Activity 4 above to make them less certain or more certain.
- Practice using different strategies in Chart 3.2.
- Be prepared to explain your choices of words or phrases.

  Examples:

  #1. Americans <u>always</u> form a line at the bus stop. (Change sometimes *to* always *to make the statement more certain.)*

  #3. Americans <u>can</u> be aggressive and assertive in business situations. (Use a modal to make the statement less certain.)

Activity 6 • Write generalizations and supporting statements

In the last part of the article "You Say Tomato," the author offers her American readers a few general statements about business people from several different cultures. For each generalization, she tells how cultural differences might result in misunderstandings. For example, in lines 33–34 she says, "Italians, Germans and French don't soften up executives with praise before they criticize. Americans do, so to Europeans that seems manipulative."

- Write two or three general statements about Americans or your "home culture." These statements may be about cultural or general habits or preferences. Topics to consider for your generalizations: The workplace, accepted behavior in public, communication styles, students and teachers, employers and employees.
- As you write your statements, use strategies for making your generalizations less certain. Highlight expressions you use for this purpose.

  Examples of Generalizations:

  Many Americans are openly social with people, even people they don't know. Americans are usually not comfortable with silence.

- Choose one of your statements and support it in a brief paragraph. Give information about possible problems or misunderstandings that might occur.
- <u>Underline</u> the verbs in your short paragraph and <u>double underline</u> expressions that introduce examples.
- Check your verb tenses and expressions and make corrections if necessary.
- If time permits, put paragraphs on the board to discuss as a class.

  Example of Generalization and Support:

  Most Americans <u>are</u> openly social with people, even people they <u>don't know</u>. <u>For example</u>, they sometimes <u>start</u> conversations with complete strangers at bus stops, in the supermarket line, and occasionally even on public transportation, as well as saying hello and smiling when they <u>meet</u> a hiker going in the opposite direction on a hiking trail. This sort of sociability <u>might lead</u> to misunderstandings with people from other cultures. Some Asians, <u>for instance</u>, rarely <u>talk</u> to strangers in this way and they <u>might think</u> these Americans <u>want</u> to take advantage of them in some way.

3.3 Reporting Ideas, Statements, and Thoughts

Preview: Assess What You Know

In academic writing, it is common to report what someone else has written or said. In reporting, writers provide two pieces of information: 1) the reporting signal—the identification of who wrote (or said) something, and 2) the idea, statement, or thought—what the person wrote, said, or thinks. Some common verbs for reporting are *say, point out, tell, write, mention, state, discuss,* and *advise.* Study these examples:

Reporting signal	**Idea/Statement**
Khosla points out	that cultural misunderstandings can easily occur in the business world.
According to the author,	interruptions are common among Indian executives.
Khosla advises us,	"If you are negotiating with an Israeli, don't pause."

We can use the same reporting structures to talk about thoughts and beliefs—someone else's or our own—using verbs such as *think, wonder, believe, feel,* and *understand.* For example:

Reporting signal	**Thought/Belief**
The French engineers thought	that the American engineers were patronizing them.
I believe	that this misunderstanding would not have happened if the French and Americans had received intercultural training.
Americans may not understand	why they are perceived as rude.

Examine the following sentences. For each,

- Double underline the reporting signal and put [brackets] around the idea, statement, or thought.

- Match the information in brackets to one of the grammatical patterns listed below. Write the letter at the end of the sentence.

A. quotation	E. *wh-* + *to* + verb
B. independent clause	F. *whether/if* clause
C. *that* clause	G. noun phrase
D. *wh-* clause (*where, when, how, …*)	

1. In the article, <u>Khosla discusses</u> [why misunderstandings between international business partners may occur.] *D*

2. The author describes two examples of intercultural misunderstanding.

3. Khosla says, "Americans aren't always so sensitive to foreign tastes and habits."

4. According to Khosla, cultural training can improve business relationships.

5. Khosla makes the suggestion that we go to the Meridian website to get more ideas about intercultural understanding.

6. She tells us what to do when negotiating with Malaysian or Japanese executives.

7. When international students arrive in the U.S., they may wonder why American students behave so informally in class—eating, drinking, putting their feet up, etc.

8. When my cousin first came here, she asked me whether this informal student behavior was typical in all classes.

Grammar Tips: Check Your Work

With a partner or a small group, check your answers in the Preview by using the information in Charts 3.3A and 3.3B that follow. Be prepared to explain your answers by referring to specific sections of the charts. Figure out what you still need to learn.

CHART 3.3A   Reporting Ideas, Statements, and Thoughts[4]

This chart shows patterns and offers tips for reporting in academic writing. For additional information about reporting, including quoting and paraphrasing, see Appendix C, Strategies for Writing, p. 188.

Examples		Pattern	Tips
Reporting Signal	*Message or Idea*		
1. Khosla tells us, … Khosla says, … To quote Khosla, … According to Khosla, …	"In negotiating with foreign business people, small things matter."	**A.** Direct quotation[5] *(here, a full clause)*	Use the exact words of the writer or speaker. Use a comma after the reporting signal, and use quotation marks around the exact words.
2. According to the author, …	interruptions are common and accepted among Indian executives.	**B.** Full clause	Use a complete clause (without *that*) after signals such as: *According to Khosla, …* *In Khosla's opinion, …* *As Khosla points out, …*
3. Khosla points out … The author thinks … It seems to her …	**that** cultural misunderstandings can easily occur in the business world and can be avoided.	**C.** *That* clause	In academic writing, don't omit *that* with these reporting signals. Be sure that you have a complete clause with a subject and a verb. You *must* paraphrase the author's words: Do not use the exact words of the author.
4. Americans may not understand …	**why** they are perceived as rude.	**D.** *Wh-* clause *(why, when, where, what, how)*	After the *wh-* word, do not use question word order: Use the statement order—subject + verb. Do not use *that*.
5. Khosla tells us …	**what to do** when negotiating with Malaysian or Japanese executives.	**E.** *Wh- + to +* verb	This structure is frequent when reporting advice, asking for advice, or reporting "or" questions.
6. My friends asked …	**where to go** to get information about cultural differences.		
7. They wondered …	**whether to search** the web or ask their advisor.		*Whether* can be used but *"if"* cannot.

Examples		Pattern	Tips
Reporting Signal	*Message or Idea*		
8. The French engineers probably wondered ...	**whether** the Americans were withholding information.	**F.** *Whether/if* clause	This structure reports a "yes/no" question. *Whether* is more common in academic writing than *if*.
9. They may have asked their boss ...	**if** the Americans were being impolite.		
10. The engineers in both countries did not understand ...	the communication **patterns** of the other culture.	**G.** Noun phrase	Although noun phrases do not report *complete* ideas or statements, they frequently follow verbs of mental activity (e.g., *understand, believe*) and speech (e.g., *describe, explain, talk about*).

[4]For more information on the grammar and meaning of various reporting verbs, see Reference Charts 3.1 and 3.2, pp. 177–179. See Chapter 4 for further work on verb tenses in reporting.

[5]See Reference Chart 3.1, p. 177, for information about punctuation of direct quotations.

CHART 3.3B Common Problems with Reporting

Problem	Incorrect Examples	Solution
1. Double reporting signal	⊘ According to the author, she says that small things can make a big difference.	Use only one signal. *Correction:* **According to the author, small things** can make a big difference. (or, **The author says that small things** ...)
2. Using exact words or nearly exact words when you should paraphrase	⊘ According to Khosla, if you are negotiating with an Israeli, don't pause.	Use quotation marks or rewrite the message using different words. *Correction:* **According to Khosla, you shouldn't pause when you are negotiating with Israelis.**
3. Using the wrong structure after *describe, discuss,* or *talk about*[6]	⊘ Khosla describes that cultural differences can cause problems. ⊘ Khosla discusses that small things can make a big difference.	*Describe, discuss,* and *talk about* are not followed by *that* clauses. They can be followed by a *wh-* clause, or *discuss* and *talk about* can be followed by *the fact that.* a. Change the *that* clause or b. Use a reporting verb that can be followed by a *that* clause. *Corrections:* a. Khosla **describes how** cultural differences can cause problems. b. Khosla **points out that** cultural differences can cause problems.

Problem	Incorrect Examples	Solution
4. Word order in *wh*-clauses	⊘ Khosla advises us where can we go to get more information about intercultural communication.	Use statement word order (subject + verb) rather than question word order. *Correction:* Khosla advises us where **we can go** …

[6]Like most verbs, these verbs can also be followed by nouns. For example: In the article, Khosla *discusses cross-cultural misunderstandings.*

Practice

Activity 7 • Analyze sentences for reporting signals and patterns

Examine the following sentences from the reading or related to the reading, "You Say Tomato."

- Double underline the reporting signal.
- Put [brackets] around the idea, statement, or thought.
- Identify the pattern of the reported idea, statement, or thought, and write the letter of the pattern from Chart 3.3A at the end of the sentence.

1. Khosla describes [how Harry Heltzer, from the American 3M Company, helped to build a good relationship with the Japanese Sumitomo Trading Company.] *D*

2. The prospective partners of 3M, executives of the Sumitomo Trading Co., asked why Heltzer and his crew had behaved so uncharacteristically.

3. Heltzer, who later rose to be 3M's chief executive, smiled and explained: You guys know how to haggle with MITI; we just wanted to be out of your way.[7]

4. In her article, Khosla states, "Americans aren't always so sensitive to foreign tastes and habits."

5. She explained how Hewlett-Packard engineers sent a long and detailed e-mail to their counterparts in Grenoble.

6. Unfortunately, the French thought that this e-mail was too long, and they sent a short and quick message in reply.

7. That made the U.S. engineers believe that the French were withholding information.

8. In the article, Khosla suggests what to do to prevent problems of miscommunication.

[7]Notice that quotation marks are not used after the reporting verb "explained." A colon introduces the direct quotation and may be a stylistic feature of the magazine in which the article appeared. This lack of quotation marks is unusual in academic writing.

Activity 8 • Identify and edit student writing for reporting signals and statements

The following problem sentences are from papers written by students on the article, "You Say Tomato." Follow the steps below to help you find and identify the problem.

- Double underline the reporting signal and put [brackets] around the idea, statement, or thought reported.
- Highlight the error. Refer to Charts 3.3A and 3.3B to help you identify the problem.
- Correct the error. (In most cases, there is more than one way to correct the error.)
- Be prepared to explain why the original statement is incorrect.

1. In "You Say Tomato," the author, Lalita Khosla, discusses *says* [that differences in culture may cause a lot of problems for international businessmen.]

2. Khosla describes different cultures can cause business people to misunderstand each other.

3. According to Khosla, she thinks some small things can affect our relationships with people from another culture.

4. In the article "You Say Tomato," the author Lalita Khosla says that the understanding and misunderstanding of cultural differences in negotiating with foreign business people.

5. If we don't know what are the cultures of the people that we are doing business with, misunderstanding in communication will occur.

6. In the article "You Say Tomato," Khosla talks about that some misunderstandings may occur when people from different cultures communicate with each other in business relationships.

7. In American culture, when someone sneezes, the other person says, "Bless you." But my friend from Taiwan didn't understand this, and when someone said that after she sneezed, she thought do Americans feel uncomfortable with sneezing?

8. My cousin is coming to the U.S. from China, and I told my cousin that how much she will like the life here.

Activity 9 • Write reported statements about a reading

The following is a brief excerpt about cultural differences from a university textbook on management by R.W. Griffin.[8] After you have read the excerpt, follow the instructions that appear below it.

> Some cultural differences between countries can be even more subtle and yet have a major impact on business activities. For example, in the United States most managers clearly agree about the value of time. Most U.S. managers schedule their activities very tightly and then adhere to their schedules. Other cultures don't put such a premium on time. In the Middle East, for example, managers do not like to set appointments and they rarely keep appointments set too far in the future. U.S. managers interacting with managers from the Middle East might misinterpret the late arrival of a potential business partner as a negotiation ploy or as an insult, when it is simply a reflection of diverse views of time and its value.

Report information from this excerpt and your own ideas using the following reporting signals. Wherever possible, use different information from the Griffin reading to complete the sentences.

1. Griffin points out _that even subtle cultural differences can have a major effect on business negotiations._

2. Griffin makes the point _____.

3. According to Griffin, _____.

4. In Griffin's words, _____.
   (Use a quotation.)

5. Griffin talks about _____.

6. Griffin says _____ but I wonder _____.

7. In his book, Griffin implies that American managers may not understand _____.

8. In reflecting on the information that Griffin provides, it seems to me _____.

---

[8]R.W. Griffin. *Management*, 4th edition. (Houghton Mifflin, 1999), p. 152.

Wrap-Up

Activity 10 • Edit your writing for verb tenses indicating generalizations and support, and for reporting ideas

- Using Editing Guides 3.1 and 3.2, pp. 177–179, and other information in this chapter, edit a piece of your own writing (from Topics for Writing, p. 48, or After Reading questions 8 or 9, p. 47) for problems with the following:

  Verb tenses for generalizations and support

  Reporting ideas

- For the structures you edit, clearly show on your paper each step described in the Editing Guides. In addition, check your writing to see if you've used any of the word partnerships listed in "Using Vocabulary Accurately," p. 48. Correct any problems you find, and add examples to your word partnerships list. (See p. 150.)

Activity 11 • Class editing workshop: Edit for verb tenses indicating generalizations and support, and for reporting ideas

At home: Follow the directions for Activity 10. In addition, write questions in the margins of your paper next to places where you're not sure of your editing choices.

In class: Working with a partner or a small group, trade papers, and talk about each other's questions and writing. Refer to the grammar charts in the chapters and in Appendix B and the Editing Guides in Appendix A to help you. If time permits, put examples from your writing and editing on the board to discuss as a class.

4

Passive Forms, Verb Tenses, and Generic Nouns

Grammar and Writing Goals

- To understand the use of active and passive forms
- To recognize generic nouns and choose appropriate articles
- To focus on verb tenses and accuracy when reporting ideas and information
- To review tense uses in academic writing
- To practice editing:
  Verb tenses
  Active and passive forms
  Generic nouns
  Reporting verbs
  Reported information

Overview of the Chapter

Read

Before Reading

Respond to these questions to help you think about and understand the reading that follows.

1. What are the advantages and disadvantages of e-mail communication? As you respond, think about these factors: time, accessibility, efficiency, privacy, convenience.

2. What kinds of nontechnical problems have you encountered when using e-mail? Have you ever been involved in an uncomfortable situation or conflict because of e-mail communication? Describe the problem and discuss how it could have been avoided.

"Communicating in the Online Workplace" by R. Kreitner

In a textbook designed for an introductory course in management, R. Kreitner discusses various forms of communication in today's workplace—e-mail, videoconferencing, and telecommuting. In a section on e-mail, he describes the growing popularity of e-mail and gives recommendations regarding an organizational e-mail policy as well as directions for writing clear e-mails.

Computers speak a simple digital language of 1s and 0s. Today, every imaginable   1
sort of information is being converted into a digital format, including text, numbers,
still and moving pictures, and sound. This process means nothing short of a **revolu-**
tion for the computer, telecommunications, consumer electronics, publishing, and
entertainment industries. Organizational communication, already significantly re-   5
shaped by computer technology, promises its own revolutionary change. This section
does not attempt the impossible task of describing all the **emerging** communication
technologies, which range from **voice recognition computers** to multimedia computers to virtual reality. Rather, it explores the impact of some established Internet-
age technologies on workplace communications. Our goal is to appreciate how new   10
and yet unknown technologies will change the way we communicate.

Getting a Handle on E-mail. E-mail via the Internet has **precipitated** a communication revolution **akin to** those brought about by the printing press, telephone, radio,
and television. The numbers are **astonishing**. If you are on the Internet, you are
ultimately linked to each of the 225 million people on earth capable of sending and   15
receiving e-mail. By 1998 "the volume of e-mail in the United States surpassed the
volume of hand-delivered mail." According to a recent survey of executives, "76 percent said they spend at least an hour each day reading and responding to e-mail, with
12 percent spending three hours a day." (This, on top of the one hour 42 percent reportedly spend each day on voice mail.) E-mail is a **two-headed beast**: easy and effi-   20
cient, while at the same time grossly abused and mismanaged. By properly managing

---

revolution: sudden and extreme change
emerging: newly developed
voice recognition computers: computers that respond to
    sound
precipitated: set off, started

akin to: similar to
astonishing: extremely surprising
ultimately: in the end
two-headed beast: something that has both extreme positives
    and negatives

e-mail, the organization can take a big step toward properly using the Internet. An organizational e-mail policy, **embracing** these recommendations from experts, can help:

- The e-mail system belongs to the company, which has the legal right to **monitor** its use. (*Never* assume privacy with company e-mail.) 25
- Workplace e-mail is for business purposes only.
- **Harassing** and offensive e-mail will not be tolerated.
- E-mail messages should be concise (see below). As in all correspondence, grammar and spelling count because they reflect on your **diligence** and credibility. 30 Typing in all capital letters makes the message hard to read and amounts to SHOUTING **in cyberspace**. (All capital letters can be appropriate, for contrast purposes, when adding comments to an existing document.)
- Lists of bullet items (similar to the format you are reading now) are acceptable because they tend to be more concise than paragraphs. 35
- Long attachments defeat the quick-and-easy nature of e-mail.
- Recipients should be told when a reply is *unnecessary*.
- An organization-specific priority system should be used for sending and receiving all e-mail. *Example:* "At Libit, a company in Palo Alto, Calif., that makes silicon products for the cable industry, e-mail is labeled as either informational or 40 action items to avoid time wasting."
- "Spam" (**unsolicited** and unwanted e-mail) that gets past filters should be deleted without being read.
- To avoid file **clutter**, messages unlikely to be referred to again should not be saved. 45

How to Compose a CLEAR E-Mail Message[1]

Concise	A brief message in simple conversational language is faster for you to write and more pleasant for your readers to read.
Logical	A message in logical steps, remembering to include any context your readers need, will be more easily understood. 50
Empathetic	When you identify with your readers, your message will be written in the right tone and words they will readily understand.
Action-oriented	When you remember to explain to your readers what you want them to do next, they are more likely to do it.
Right	A complete message, with no important facts missing, with all 55 the facts right, and with correct spelling, will save your readers having to return to you to clarify details.

from *Management*, (Houghton Mifflin, 1999), Chapter 12, pp. 378–9

---

embracing: including
monitor: regulate
harassing: verbally abusive
diligence: attentiveness

in cyberspace: through the network connections of the Internet
unsolicited: unasked for
clutter: messiness, overload of contents

---

[1]Joan Tunstall, *Better, Faster Email: Getting the Most Out of Email* (St. Leonards, Australia: Allen & Unwin, 1999), p. 37.

After Reading

Individually at home, or with a partner or a small group in class, write the answers to these questions to prepare for class discussion. Keep your answers in a notebook or binder to refer to later when you respond to the writing topics, develop your ideas for longer papers, or analyze your writing. Questions marked ¶ are especially suitable for paragraph length answers that can be used later when you analyze your own writing.

1. What does it mean to convert information into a digital format? What types of information are being converted? What kinds of industries are affected by this digital "revolution"?

2. Kreitner compares the "communication revolution" caused by the use of e-mail to the changes brought about by the printing press, telephone, radio, and television. Why does Kreitner say that the numbers are "astonishing"?

3. According to Kreitner, what are the advantages and disadvantages of e-mail?

4. Read through the recommendations for an organizational e-mail policy (lines 25–45). Focus on two or three recommendations that you think are useful and explain why. Are there any that you think are *not* useful? Why?

5. On a separate paper, complete the chart below to analyze the suggestions for composing CLEAR e-mails (lines 47–57). Refer to the example.

Suggestion	What to Do	Positive Results
Be concise.	Write brief messages. Use simple conversational style.	Faster to write More pleasant for readers to read

¶ 6. How has e-mail changed our lives in the following areas: How we communicate, how we use language, how we spend our time, how we interact with other people?

¶ 7. In the textbook excerpt, the writer says "Our goal is to appreciate how new and yet unknown technologies will change the way we communicate." How do you think communication in the future will differ from the way we now communicate?

¶ 8. Draw up an e-mail policy for your school. (See the bulleted information in the reading (lines 25–45) for an example of an e-mail policy for organizations.) Explain the reasons why the policy would be effective.

¶ 9. Write up your own set of directions for writing e-mail for one of these uses: a. teacher-student-student communication; b. friend-friend communication; c. family communication. For the use you choose, explain the reasons for the directions and information you give.

Write

Topics for Writing

Respond in writing to one (or more) of the following topics.

1. On the Internet or elsewhere, find information about the technologies mentioned in the reading: the printing press, the telephone, radio, television. For one of these, explain when it was first used, who invented it, and how it changed communication at that time.

2. Write about yourself and how your life has been affected by technology. Possible topics to consider: the way you communicate, how you use language, how you spend your time, how you interact with other people, the positive and negative impacts of technology on your life.

3. Imagine a world without computers. What would that world be like? Think about positive and negative outcomes. Consider how life would be different without computers at home, at school, and/or at work.

4. For all its benefits, technology can have a negative impact on people's lives. Describe the negative effects of computers, e-mail, cell phones, or the Internet on one person's life. How did this person become a victim of technology and what can we learn from his or her situation?

5. Choose one of the four situations below (A–D) and do the following:
   - Write an e-mail of 3–4 brief paragraphs to the person indicated (e.g., Frank Sung for situation A). Use your imagination and experience to provide appropriate background and details that fit the situation.
   - Use your chart from After Reading question #5 to follow the guidelines for composing CLEAR e-mails.
   - Start your e-mail message with a heading:
     Date:
     To:
     From:
     Subject:

Situations

A. *To: Frank Sung, Academic Advisor*
You need help deciding which course or courses to take next semester in order to prepare for your major classes. You are confused about the requirements and not sure if you can handle the workload.

B. *To: Mary Johnson, Dean, College of* _____
You want to complain about a grade your received in a class last semester. You have met with the instructor of the course and he is unwilling to change it. You have several reasons why you feel that you deserve a higher grade.

C. *To: Nancy Smith, Coordinator of the English Program*
You want to write either to give praise or complain about someone or some course. You have had a good (or bad) experience in one of your classes and want to report it to the coordinator.

D. *To: Elsa Ramirez, Director of the Tutoring Center*
You've never been to see a tutor before, but you find that you're struggling in a course that is very difficult for you. You write to find out what kind of help is available, how to get assistance, and to explain any special circumstances you have.

6. Interview someone who was not raised in the computer age. Ask that person to tell you what the world was like before the computer age: at home, at school, and/or at work.

7. Interview someone about how technology (computers, e-mail, fax, Internet, cell phones) has affected the way the person works. This person could be self-employed or work for a company or organization. Possible professions to choose from: business, education, medicine, health, journalism, science, social service. (See suggested questions for your interview below.)

Option A: Summary Write up a report of your interview.

Option B: Summary and Analysis Your paper should include the following:
- A summary of your interview.
- An analysis of your interview, including generalizations about the way technology has changed people's lives.
- Connections between the experience of the person you interviewed and, if appropriate, your own experience to support your generalizations.

Suggested Questions for Your Interview

1. Please describe your current job and how you use technology in your work:
   a. Whom do you communicate with and how do you communicate?
   b. How do you gather and store information?
   c. How does your business or profession depend on technology?

2. How long have you worked at your present job? How has your work changed as a result of technology? Describe some examples of changes that have occurred.

3. How much time each day do you spend on the computer, e-mail, or Internet-related activities?

4. Do you view technology in your workplace as a blessing or a curse?

5. What work-related problems have you encountered that are connected to technology (miscommunication, managing information, technical difficulties, personal or physical problems)?

6. How has technology affected you outside your work?

Before you interview someone outside your class, practice interviewing a partner and writing up the interview. Modify the suggested questions above so that partners can describe how they use technology in either their work or at school. If possible, put sample write-ups on the board to discuss. (See Activity 9 for a sample write-up of an interview.)

Strategies for Writing: Generating and Developing Ideas
For a description of ways to generate ideas, such as freewriting, listing, and brainstorming, as well as ways to develop and support your ideas, refer to Strategies for Writing, pp. 185–190.

Using Vocabulary Accurately

As you write about a reading, pay attention to key words and word partnerships, words that occur frequently with each other or that form fixed expressions. For more examples, see Reference Charts 2.1 and 2.2, p. 172–174. Create your own word partnerships list (see p. 150).

Some key word partnerships for this reading follow. Locate key words in the reading or in Topics for Writing and notice how they are used. For practice, write sentences using some of these expressions.

to attempt a task

to explore the impact of (*something*)

to have a positive/negative
    impact on (*someone/something*)

to be affected by (*someone/something*)

to encounter a problem

to change the way we communicate

to send/read/respond to e-mail

to e-mail (*someone/something to someone*)

to be in an uncomfortable situation

to depend on (*someone/something*)

a positive/negative outcome

a communications/digital revolution

Edit: Grammar Previews, Tips, and Practice

Listening/Writing Activity: Dictation/Dictocomp

The following dictation/dictocomp text gives information related to the reading "Communicating in the Online Workplace," on pp. 68–69.

Close your book. As your teacher reads the sentences below (one time all the way through, then by clauses, then all the way through again), do the following:

- For a dictation, try to write exactly what you hear.
- For a dictocomp, take notes on key words and phrases.
- Then, individually or in groups, reconstruct the text, revising and correcting your work and paying attention to problem areas.

1. In the last ten years, a revolution in personal and business communication has occurred.

2. This revolution has been brought about by new developments in computer software and equipment, the expansion of Internet services, and the widespread use of cell phones.

3. For most people, the availability of instant, easy communication is seen as a blessing.

4. For others, it is viewed as a curse.

5. How have your daily life and your communication with others been affected by these new technologies?

4.1 Active vs. Passive

Preview: Assess What You Know

Academic writing, such as the textbook excerpt that you read in this chapter, is generally formal and impersonal, and thus often contains passive verbs. A passive verb has two parts: a form of *be* and a past participle: "E-mail *is used* as a communication tool in most companies today."

Note: *Past participles of regular verbs end in* -ed. *For past participles of irregular verbs, see Reference Chart 1.9, p. 169.*

A. Examine the sentences in the dictation/dictocomp for this chapter and do the following:

- Underline the verbs and ⟨circle⟩ the subjects.
- Write "P" next to each sentence with a passive verb.

B. Examine the following sentences, underlining the verbs and ⟨circling⟩ the subjects. Write "C" if the passive verb in the sentence is correct. Write "⊘" if it is incorrect because of the form or use of the passive, and correct the error. You will find errors in three of the sentences.

1. In the modern workplace, ⟨a great deal of time⟩ is spent at a computer terminal. *C*

2. However, e-mail is often abuse and mismanage.

3. Some employees are used e-mail for personal purposes.

4. Yet this misuse of e-mail is often tolerated by the company.

5. Employers want their employees to stay with the company, so they are allow them to use e-mail however they want.

Grammar Tips: Check Your Work

With a partner or a small group, check your answers in the Preview by using the information in Chart 4.1 that follows. Be prepared to explain your answers by referring to specific sections of the chart. Figure out what you still need to learn.

CHART 4.1   Active vs. Passive: Problems with Forms and Use[2]

Problem Area	Rule / Tip	Examples
1. Forming the passive verb correctly	A passive verb must have a form of *be* and a past participle. <u>be</u> <u>past participle</u> a. *is* *labeled* b. *was* *converted* c. *should be* *deleted* d. *have been* *reprimanded*	a. ⃠ In some companies, e-mail **is label** as either an informational or an action item. *Correction:* **is labeled** b. ⃠ The information **converted** into a digital format. *Correction:* **was converted** c. ⃠ Spam **should delete** without being read. *Correction:* **should be deleted** d. ⃠ Some employees **have reprimanded** for excessive use of e-mail. *Correction:* **have been reprimanded**

2. Distinguishing the passive from the active	An active sentence has a Subject-Verb-Object (S-V-O) order. The subject is the agent (the person, animal, or thing that acts or causes the action of the verb). The object is the receiver of the action.
	
	A passive sentence puts the receiver in the subject position. If the agent is included, it comes after the verb and is preceded by the word *by.* (O-V-by S)
		<u>Active:</u>
		The company **will** not **tolerate** offensive e-mail.
		   (the company = *subject, agent*)
		   (offensive e-mail = *object, receiver*)
		
		<u>Passive:</u>
		Offensive e-mail **will** not **be tolerated** (by the company).
		   (Offensive e-mail = *subject, receiver*)
		   (the company = *agent*)
		a. ⃠ A problem with e-mail **was occurred** at my company. *Correction:* **occurred** (A problem = *agent, so the verb is active*)
		b. ⃠ The way we communicate **has changed** by e-mail. *Correction:* **has been changed** (e-mail = *agent*, the way we communicate ↑ *agent, so the verb is passive*)

3. Deciding when to use the passive	Use passive when: a. You want to avoid the informality of impersonal *you* or *they*. b. You want to put the receiver of the action rather than the agent in the subject position. c. The agent is unknown, obvious, or unimportant, or you don't want to mention the agent.	a. Recipients **should be told** when a reply is unnecessary. (**You** should tell recipients when....) b. When you identify with your readers, **your message** will be written in the right tone and in words they will readily understand. (*more effective than:* ... you will write your message in the right tone ....) c. See 4 c, d, e.

Problem Area	Rule/Tip	Examples
4. Knowing when to include the agent	Include the agent when: a. It provides important or necessary information. b. It is needed grammatically (some passive verbs require an agent or an adverbial). Do not include the agent when: c. It is obvious. d. It is unknown or unimportant. e. You don't want to mention the agent (to be polite).	a. The way friends communicate <u>has been affected</u> **by the availability of e-mail**. b. ⊘ Microsoft <u>was started</u>. **Possible corrections:** Microsoft <u>was started</u> **by Bill Gates**. Microsoft <u>was started</u> **in 1975**. c. Recipients <u>should be told</u> ~~**by the writer of the e-mail**~~ when a reply is unnecessary. d. This word processing program <u>was developed</u> in 1998 ~~**by someone**~~. e. The files on the disk <u>were</u> accidentally <u>erased</u> ~~**by my colleague**~~.
5. Forming the "*get* passive" correctly	The "*get* passive" is a more informal form of passive. It is made up of the verb *get* + past participle.	a. ⊘ Technology is convenient once you **get connect** to the Internet. *Correction:* **get connected** b. ⊘ Because my friend took classes on designing web pages, she **gets hired** to teach in an after school program for high school students. *Correction:* **got hired** c. ⊘ My friend is learning to design web pages so that she **will promote** at her office. *Correction:* **will get promoted** or **will be promoted**

[2] See Reference Charts 4.1 and 4.2, pp. 180–182, for further information on the passive, including other examples of usage and problems, and special cases.

 Practice

Activity 1 • Analyze the reading for additional passive forms

Review lines 25–57 of "Communicating in the Online Workplace" and look for additional passive forms.

■ Discuss with a partner why you think the passive is used. (Refer to Chart 4.1 to help you.)

Activity 2 • Analyze the meaning of active/passive and use of agents

With a partner or a small group, examine the following sets of sentences.

- <u>Underline</u> the verbs.
- Write "P" next to each sentence with a passive verb.
- In the passive sentences, <u>double underline</u> the agent if one is included.
- Explain how the meanings differ within each set of sentences depending on the information that is given in each sentence. (See the tips in Chart 4.1.)

Set 1

1. My friend <u>was told</u> to spend less time in his cubicle on personal e-mail. *P*

2. My friend's supervisor <u>told</u> him to spend less time in his cubicle on personal e-mail.

   Explanation: ___#2 makes it clear who told my friend.___

Set 2

1. The policy regarding e-mail was implemented two months ago.

2. The policy regarding e-mail was implemented by the new CEO two months ago.

3. Management implemented the policy regarding e-mail two months ago.

   Explanation: _____

Set 3

1. Organizational communication has been reshaped by computer technology.

2. Organizational communication has been reshaped.

3. Computer technology has reshaped organizational communication.

   Explanation: _____

Set 4

1. In this section, the impact of several Internet-age technologies on workplace communication is explained.

2. This section explains the impact of several Internet-age technologies on workplace communication.

3. In this section we explore the impact of several Internet-age technologies on workplace communication.

   Explanation: _____

Activity 3 • Edit sentences for active/passive errors

Each sentence contains a problem with active or passive constructions. Correct the sentences by following these steps.

- <u>Underline</u> the verb and (circle) the subject.
- Decide if the verb should be active or passive. Refer to Chart 4.1 and Reference Chart 4.2, p. 181.
- Check the form and correct any problems.

1. (The misunderstanding of those events) ~~are come~~ *comes* from small things.

2. I felt that I was not respect by any of the other students.

3. Israelis have no patience for Americans' small talk because they accustom to a fast pace during meetings.

4. Americans like to wear name tags because that is the custom they had taught when they were growing up.

5. Unlike Americans, Chinese people generally will not want to be hug or kiss in public.

6. Some people think that Chinese involve in arguments easily, but this is not the case.

7. It is just that in their culture they used to speaking loudly.

8. Chinese people are use to crowding on buses, so don't be shock when you see them crowd into a loaded bus.

Activity 4 • Edit student writing for active/passive errors

Using the student text and directions below, find and correct the errors with active and passive verbs. Be prepared to explain your answers by referring to Chart 4.1 and Reference Chart 4.2, p. 181.

- <u>Underline</u> the verbs.
- Write "C" above all the passive verbs that are written correctly. (You will find two.)
- Write "⊘" above all the incorrect passive verbs. Correct these verbs. (You will find five total errors.)

                    ⊘ *been*
Nonetheless, we <u>have</u> negatively <u>affected</u> by technology as well. Technology is not   1

always reliable. We have all probably been frustrated while using the Internet.   2

Often I get annoyed by having to wait a long time until I get connect to my server.   3

Worse than this, people so involved in their computers that they have lost their social   4

skills. However, the most frightening of all is how technology can be a harmful   5

weapon when it is mismanage. Certain websites have materials that are consider   6

hostile and threatening to people of different racial backgrounds.   7

Activity 5 • Choose the active or passive form of the verb

Read the following student text all the way through once. Think about the meaning and different options for verb tenses and forms as you read, and do the following:

■ Decide whether each verb should be active or passive and what the tense of the verb should be, then write the correct form of the verb in the space. Be sure to include any words in parentheses that are paired with the verbs.

■ Be prepared to tell why you chose the forms that you did. Refer to Chart 4.1 and Reference Chart 4.2, p. 181.

Everywhere in the world we ___*are surrounded*___ by new technologies. Our lives
                                    1. surround
_____ by new inventions that _____ the way we do
     2. (seriously) affect   3. change
business and communicate with one another. All companies now _____
                                                                    4. use
new technologies to help employees finish their projects. A wide range of technological

equipment and systems _____ in business. Our lifestyles
                              5. use
_____ by these new technologies. We now _____
     6. (also) change   7. use
the computer to type our papers instead of using typewriters. Also, letter writing

_____ by sending messages through e-mail. Scientists, software engi-
     8. (almost) replace
neers, and all the technical professionals from all over the world _____
                                                                        9. (still) work
on developing new technological advancements. In the future, our society

_____ than ever since there _____ more possibilities
     10. (more) advance   11. be
and unexpected events.

4.2 Nouns with Generic Meaning

Preview: Assess What You Know

In academic writing, nouns with generic, or general, reference are very frequent. In Chapter 3, you used nouns with generic reference in making generalizations. Compare generic and specific reference:

Generic Reference
Each of the <u>underlined</u> nouns refers to all members or representatives of a set, category, or group rather than to individual people or things.

<u>Europeans</u> often feel they are being treated like <u>children</u>.
(*Europeans* = all members of the set or group of people from Europe)

<u>Israeli business meetings</u> move at a more rapid pace than <u>American meetings</u>.

<u>Intercultural communication</u> can cause <u>serious problems</u> in <u>partnerships</u>.
(*Intercultural communication* = the idea of intercultural communication in general)

Specific Reference

These nouns refer to specific people or things. Whether the reference is specific or general has consequences for the choice of articles.

<u>The business meeting</u> that I attended last week seemed to move at a slow pace.

I have to attend <u>another business meeting</u> next week.
(The business meeting/another business meeting = individual, particular meetings)

A. In the sentences below, look at the <u>underlined</u> nouns.

■ Write "G" to the left of the nouns that have a generic reference. Write "S" to the left of those that have a specific reference.

■ Decide whether each noun is a count noun or a noncount noun and label each "C" or "N" on the right.

G 1. <u>Computers</u> are widely used in schools and in the workplace. *C*

S 2. <u>The computers</u> in my office are upgraded every other year. *C*

3. <u>The computer</u> I bought last year is already too slow.

4. <u>The computer</u> has revolutionized communication in the workplace.

5. <u>A personal computer</u> can save time in writing and revising papers for school.

6. My roommate uses <u>a computer</u> in the media center on campus to write all her papers.

7. <u>New technologies</u> make <u>communication</u> faster.

8. <u>The communication</u> from the Latin American office of my company contained good news about sales.

B. Based on your labels for nouns in the sentences in A above, complete the following table with the underlined articles and nouns.

Generic		Specific	
Count	*Noncount*	*Count*	*Noncount*
1. computers		*2. the computers*	

C. Based on your completed table, work with a partner or a small group to write some rules about patterns of articles and nouns for generic meaning.

Grammar Tips: Check Your Work

With a partner or a small group, check your answers in the Preview by using the information in Chart 4.2A that follows. Be prepared to explain your answers by referring to specific sections of the chart. Figure out what you still need to learn.

CHART 4.2A Article + Noun Patterns: Nouns with Generic Meaning[3]		
Article + Noun Pattern	**Tips**	**Examples**
Count Nouns		
1. No article + plural noun	*Meaning:* All members of the group or set (animals or things), the group in general	
	a. A plural noun is the most flexible and useful pattern. When in doubt, use this pattern.	a. **Computers** have changed communication in the workplace. **Most businesses**[5] today rely on **computers** for a range of different tasks.
	b. Be careful to avoid using the article *the* with a plural noun that has a generic reference.[4]	b. ⊘ **The computers** have changed communication in the workplace. *Correction:* **Computers**
2. *a/an* + singular noun	*Meaning:* Any member of a group This pattern is often used in	
	a. definitions	a. **A modem** is a device that connects a computer to a telephone line.
	b. generalizations	b. Access to **a computer** can change your life.
	c. descriptions	c. A person entering **a chat room** is expected to follow certain rules of behavior called "netiquette."
	Remember to use a *or* an *(d).*	d. ⊘ **Computer** can be a useful tool. *Correction:* **A computer**
3. *the* + singular noun[6]	*Meaning:* Any member of a group	
	a. This pattern is the most formal and is more restricted in use. It is especially used in technical and scientific writing to describe inventions, human groups, non-human groups, plants, parts of the body.	a. Spending hours in front of **the computer screen** can be especially hard on **the back** and **the neck**. *(invention, parts of body)*
	b. Remember to use *the.*	b. ⊘ **Computer** can be a useful tool. *Correction:* **The computer**

Article + Noun Pattern	Tips	Examples
Noncount Nouns		
4. No article + noncount noun	a. This pattern is used with all noncount nouns with general reference. b. Avoid using the article *the* with a noncount noun that has a generic reference. c. Also, do not use *a* or *an* with a noncount noun whether it is specific or generic.	a. Both **voice mail** and **e-mail** are commonly used in businesses and homes. b. ⊘ Many people prefer to receive **the voice mail** rather than **the e-mail**. *Correction:* **voice mail, e-mail**[7] c. ⊘ The company e-mailed **an information** to all employees. *Correction:* **information**

To help you decide if a noun has a generic reference, try putting *all* or *in general* with the noun:
1. **Computers** make **communication** faster.
   Computers (in general) make (all) communication faster. *(both generic)*
2. I bought **a computer** last week.
   I bought a computer (in general) last week. *(doesn't make sense, so not generic)*

[3]See Charts 1.1B and 1.1C and Reference Charts 1.3, 1.4, 1.5, pp. 162–166, for more information about article use.

[4]Another pattern, *the* + plural noun, is also possible, but it has a limited use in academic, scientific, and technical writing. See Reference Chart 1.5, p. 165.

[5]Nouns used generically can be limited to part of the group by quantifiers such as *most, many, much, few, little,* and *some.*

[6]Nouns in patterns 2 and 3 can usually be rewritten as pattern 1 (plural, with no *the*), for example, *Spending hours in front of* **computer screens** *can be hard on* **backs** *and* **necks**.

[7]*E-mail* and *voice mail* are commonly used as either count or noncount nouns (see Chart 4.2B). Another acceptable correction to this sentence would be: *Many people prefer to receive* **a voice mail** *rather than* **an e-mail**.

CHART 4.2B   Technology and General Nouns

This chart shows some count and noncount nouns that are commonly used either generically or specifically in writing about technology.

Category	Technology Terms[8]		General Terms	
Count	a computer a cell phone a pager a fax (machine) a format an attachment	a laptop a virus a server a website a drive a program	a process a revolution a survey an industry an organization a company	a workplace a policy a convenience a fact a detail
Noncount	cyberspace voice recognition virtual reality multimedia technical support	spam hardware software memory	information communication data privacy clutter	efficiency entertainment equipment stress

Category	Technology Terms[8]	General Terms
Commonly used as either count or noncount	e-mail/an e-mail technology/new technologies	change/major changes language/a digital language
Means of communication or delivery	send by phone/three phones — by fax/three faxes — by snail mail/three letters	

[8]Two important nouns are *the Internet* and *the World Wide Web*. Note that these are proper nouns that always use *the* and are usually capitalized. When used before other nouns as modifiers, they follow regular article rules; usage seems to vary concerning capitalization and spelling, for example, *Internet communication, an Internet service, an internet service, a Web site, a web site, a website.*

 Practice

Activity 6 • Write sentences using generic nouns

With a partner or a small group, brainstorm additional words related to technology to add to Chart 4.2B above.

- To decide if they are count or noncount or both, check with your classmates, your teacher, or your dictionary.
- Individually or with a partner or a small group, select three count nouns and three non-count nouns from the chart and write sentences using these nouns with generic reference. You might state your opinion, give a definition, make a generalization, or write a brief description. Underline these nouns and their articles.
- Exchange papers with a partner or another group and check each other's sentences for meaning and correct article use.

  Examples:
  I think <u>cell phones</u> and their users are very annoying in public places. *(opinion)*
  <u>A laptop</u> is a small portable computer that can be battery powered. *(definition)*
  <u>Voice recognition</u> is developing rapidly these days. *(generalization)*
  <u>Computer labs</u> are user-friendly when the chairs and tables are designed to reduce <u>physical stress</u>. *(description)*

Activity 7 • Recognize generic reference in sentences

Analyze the following sentences and check your answers with a partner or group:

- Label each <u>underlined</u> noun general reference, "G", or specific reference, "S".
- Label each <u>underlined</u> noun count, "C", or noncount, "N".
- (Circle) the article, determiner, or the plural.

1. Nowadays (most) businesses use <u>e-mail</u> rather than <u>printed memos</u> to
   communicate with <u>company employees.</u>
   (annotations above: G C over businesses, G N over e-mail, G C over printed memos, G C over company employees)

2. My friend received <u>an e-mail</u> from his boss yesterday telling him about <u>an upcoming</u>
   <u>meeting</u>.

3. <u>Many people</u> use <u>scanners</u> in their homes to copy <u>photographs</u> to send electronically
   to <u>family</u> and <u>friends</u>.

4. <u>The scanners</u> in <u>the campus media center</u> can be used by both <u>faculty</u> and <u>students</u>.

5. You can contact <u>most businesses</u> by <u>phone</u>, by <u>e-mail</u> or by <u>fax</u>.

Activity 8 • Edit student writing for noun and article errors

The following student text has a total of 11 errors in the nouns (and/or their related articles) with generic reference. Use Editing Guide 4.2, p. 155, to help you find and correct the errors.

Highlight all the nouns, <u>underline</u> any nouns that are incorrect, and write the correct form, including any needed articles, above them.

The most common technological devices being used today are <u>cellular phone</u>,   1
(handwritten above: cellular phones or the cellular phone; G over devices; G over cellular phone)

a portable computer, pager, and Game Boy. Computer can provide people with any   2

information they need from a source called Internet. Internet is similar to newspaper   3

and other sources where you can get information. One reason why computer is so   4

popular is because of e-mail. People everywhere write e-mail to each other rather   5

than sending letter through the post office.   6

4.3   Verb Tenses for Reporting Information

Preview: Assess What You Know

In academic writing, writers often report the ideas of others. The choice of verb tenses is important to make meanings clear. This section provides information about how to choose verb tenses for reporting verbs and for reported information. As you work with the activities and information that follow, refer to Chapter 3, which introduced ways to report ideas. (See Charts 3.3A and 3.3B, pp. 61–63, and Reference Charts 3.1 and 3.2, pp. 177–179, for information about direct quotations and about reporting verbs, their meanings, and their patterns.)

Look at the four short texts that follow, all of which contain reported information.

- <u>Underline</u> the reporting verbs (<u>say</u>, <u>tell</u>, ...). Write the tense in the left margin.
- <u>Double underline</u> the main verbs in the clauses that follow these reporting verbs. Write the tense above.
- After marking the text, try to come up with rules for verb tenses:

Reporting verbs:

   a. Use past tense when _____

   b. Use present tense when _____

Other verbs following reporting verbs:

   a. Use past tense when _____

   b. Use present tense when _____

   c. Use future tense when _____

Text 1 (from the reading):

present

past   According to a recent survey of executives, 76% <u>said</u> they <u>spend</u> at least an hour   1

each day reading and responding to e-mail. (This on top of the one hour 42%   2
present
reportedly <u>spend</u> each day on voice mail.)   3

Text 2 (from a student paper):

Last Friday in class I interviewed my classmate Allan Choi about his use of new   1

technologies for schoolwork. Allan told me that his computer is essential for his   2

homework for his classes. He also told me his teachers want short homework papers   3

typed as well, so he uses the computer for those too.   4

Text 3 (from a report on an interview):

In my interview with my friend Jeff, he talked specifically about his use of e-mail   1

and the Internet. Jeff told me that he is generally very positive about the way these   2

new technologies help in the workplace. He said that when he first started in his posi-   3

tion, he sometimes used e-mail, but now, he relies on e-mail extensively to communi-   4

cate with his boss, his team members, and other employees throughout the company.   5

Text 4 (from a newspaper article about eBay, a website for buying items by auction):

Chris Grubb says eBay users are mad as hell and they aren't going to take it any   1

more. Grubb is the brains behind a new Web site that lets customers of the San Jose   2

online auctioneer vent about recent fee increases. The name of Grubb's site is "Fire   3

eBay" (www.fireebay.com) The Web site urges, "Join auction users from all over the   4

world in making a stand." Grubb says the names of those signing will be sent to eBay   5

with a letter demanding the company reconsider the January fee increases, which   6

made it more expensive to sell goods on eBay.   7

(P. Delevett, *San Jose Mercury News*, 3/1/02, p. 1C)

Grammar Tips: Check Your Work

With a partner or a small group, check your answers in the Preview by using the information in Chart 4.3 that follows. Be prepared to explain your answers by referring to specific sections of the chart. Figure out what you still need to learn.

CHART 4.3 Verb Tenses for Reporting Information		
Problem Area	**Tips / Information**	**Examples**
1. Choosing the tense for the reporting verb[9] (e.g., *say, tell, report, mention, admit*, etc.)	a. *Past tense:* Commonly used because the act of speaking occurred in the past.	a. According to a recent survey of executives, 76% **said** …. *(See Text 1 in Preview.)* Allan **told** me that …. *(See Text 2 in Preview.)*
	b. *Present tense:* Often used in newspaper and other information reporting to create a sense of vividness, immediacy.[10]	b. Chris Grubb **says** eBay users are …. The Web site **urges** …. Grubb **says** the names of those signing on will be sent …. *(See Text 4 in Preview.)*
	c. *Present perfect tense:* Links a past event (e.g., *reported*) to the present, suggesting the past event is relevant to other information being presented.	c. Researchers **have reported** that three-fourths of executives spend about an hour a day reading and responding to e-mail. This suggests that executives are more actively engaged in communication with others now than they were when their secretaries handled most of their correspondence.

Problem Area	Tips / Information	Examples
2. Choosing the verb tense for the reported information	Choose the tense that reflects the meaning you need to express, e.g.,	
	a. *Present tense* for statements that are generally true, current habits, current states, etc.	a. … 76% said they **spend** … … he told me his computer **is** essential …
	b. *Past tense* for completed events or habits in the past	b. … he told me that when he first **started** in his position, he sometimes **used** e-mail …
	c. *Future tense* for future events or states	c. Grubb says the names … **will be sent** …

⁹It's a good idea to use the same time frame (past or present) for the reporting verbs throughout your paper.

¹⁰Note also that the verb "say" sometimes means the same as "believe" or "think" or "have the opinion" rather than referring to the actual act of speaking, for example, "Riverstone Networks, a communications industry up-and-comer, lost half its stock market value yesterday…. Now, analysts <u>say</u>, phone companies are postponing spending on development …."

Practice

Activity 9 • Analyze student writing for reporting verbs and verb tense

Below is a text that reports on an interview about the use of new technologies.

■ Read the entire text through once. Note the variety of tenses the writer uses.

■ Read the text again and do the following:

<u>Underline</u> the reporting verbs (<u>say</u>, <u>tell</u>, etc.). Write the tense in the left margin.

<u>Double underline</u> the other verbs. Write the tense above the verb.

Put [brackets] around sentences that contain reported information but no specified reporting verb.

■ Discuss with a partner: How does the reader know that the information in brackets is what Allan said?

Last Friday in class I interviewed my classmate Allan Choi about his use of new   1

past technologies for schoolwork. Allan <u>told</u> me that his computer *present* <u>is</u> essential for his   2

homework for his classes. [He has to write papers for several classes and he does all   3

his writing and rewriting on his computer at home.] He also told me his teachers   4

want short homework papers typed as well, so he uses the computer for those too.   5

One of Allan's classes has a course website, and he has to log on to it every week to   6

participate in a discussion board. Allan admitted to me that he is sometimes shy   7

about speaking up in class, so this is a good way for him to give his ideas and opin-   8

ions. This is the first semester he has used a course website. Last semester none of his   9

teachers required a class discussion board. He likes writing for the discussion board   10 because he doesn't have to worry so much about his grammar. His instructor some-   11

times posts required readings on this website; Allan said that reading such material   12

on the computer screen is very difficult for him, so he copies the articles and prints   13

them out in a format that is easier to read. Allan told me that he is very fortunate   14

because he has DSL at home, so he can access the Internet easily. As a result, he   15

spends a couple of hours every day at the computer doing non-school-related activi-   16

ties such as surfing the Internet and sending e-mail to friends here and to his family   17

in Hong Kong. Allan clearly depends on one of the new technologies—the personal   18

computer—in his life as a student.   19

Activity 10 • Edit student writing for errors with reporting verbs and verb tense

The following student text is a portion of a report of an interview that the writer conducted with a friend about uses of new technologies.

- Read the text through once. Notice that the writer uses forms of past tenses: past, past perfect, or past modal + simple form.
- Read the text again and use Editing Guide 4.3, p. 155, to mark the text.
- Consider where the writer could use the present or the present perfect tense to make the meaning more clear. Change the <u>double-underlined</u> verbs to show these tenses.
- Discuss your findings with a partner or a small group.

past   I <u>asked</u> Michael whether he <u>had</u> any problems with technology. He <u>said</u> [that   1
     past (could be "has had" or "had")
occasionally his company <u>had</u> trouble with networks.] [Last month, the employees   2
     past (could be "has had" or "has")

couldn't get online to gather information. As a result, they personally went to the   3

Document Control Department to get information.] In addition, he said that some-   4

times they had trouble with supporting documentation because they didn't know all   5

about technology. Their company had provided them with more knowledge by send-   6

ing them to training workshops to learn more to support documentation. He also told   7

me that he thought technology was wonderful. No matter how much he knew about   8

it, he still felt like he was learning computer skills for the very first time. As a result, he   9

continued attending school to expand his knowledge.   10

Activity 11 • Interview and write; edit for nouns and articles, and verb tense

A. Interview and Write

■ With a partner, choose one of the following topics to use for an interview:

   After Reading: #7, p. 70.

   Topics for Writing: # 3, 4, 6, or 7, pp. 71–72.

■ Develop a set of 5–6 questions to use for the interview. (See suggested questions for Topic #7 on p. 72.)

■ After interviewing each other, write a brief report (1–2 paragraphs) of your interview. (See sample report in Activity 9.)

■ If time permits, some students can put their paragraphs on the board for class discussion of content and ways of reporting.

B. Edit your own paper

Use Editing Guides 4.2 and 4.3, p. 155, to analyze and edit your writing.

C. Check a partner's paper

Exchange papers with a partner (not the person you interviewed) and read your partner's paper.

■ If you have questions about your partner's editing process, put a "?" in the margin.

■ Discuss the paper with your partner.

4.4 Variety of Tenses in Academic Writing

Preview: Assess What You Know

In Chapter 3 you reviewed how verb tenses are used to make and support generalizations. In this chapter, you have reviewed passive verbs and verb tenses for reporting information and ideas. In this section, you will continue your review of verb tenses used in academic writing—in particular, in articles and in textbook writing.

To check your knowledge of verb tenses used in "Communicating in the Online Workplace," pp. 68–69, answer the following questions.

A. What is the general time reference framework of the reading? Circle the number.

   1. present   2. past   3. future

B. Reread the first paragraph.

■ <u>Underline</u> the complete verbs and put a wiggly line under any time expressions.

■ Write the name of the tense in the margin beside the verb.

■ Which of the following verb tenses are used? Check those you found.

   1. _____ simple present   4. _____ simple past

   2. _____ present progressive   5. _____ present perfect

   3. _____ future

■ Circle the number of the tense most frequently used. Why is it most frequently used?

C. Reread the second paragraph (lines 12–24).

- <u>Underline</u> the complete verbs, put a wiggly line under any time expressions, and write the name of the verb tense in the margin.

- Which of the following verb tenses are used? Check those you found. See Reference Charts 1.7 and 1.8, p. 168, if you need help.

1. _____ simple present		4. _____ simple past	
2. _____ present progressive		5. _____ present perfect	
3. _____ future		6. _____ modal + verb	

Grammar Tips: Check Your Work

With a partner or a small group, check your answers in the Preview by using the information in Chart 4.4 that follows. Be prepared to explain your answers by referring to specific sections of the chart. Figure out what you still need to learn.

CHART 4.4	Verb Tense Use: Variety of Tenses in Academic Writing	
Verb Tense	**Description**	**Examples**

Present perfect	In general: Links a past activity, event, or state to the present.
	a. Indicates a situation that began in the past and continues into the present.
	
	b. Indicates an activity, event, or state that occurred at some unspecified (and unimportant) time in the past but is relevant to the present.
		a. The company **has used** e-mail for interoffice communication since 1997.
		He **has served** as the CEO of our company for three years.
		
		b. The company **has begun** using its website to attract customers and sell products.
		  (activity occurred once)
		The company **has updated** its website several times in the past few months.
		  (activity occurred more than once)
		She **has served** as the CEO for several different companies. *(condition/state that occurred in the past, i.e., she **has been** the CEO in the past.)*

Past	c. Describes events, activities, or states in the past. **Note:** *The past progressive* (was working) *describes a state that continued over a period of time in the past.*	c. By 1998, the volume of e-mail in the United States **surpassed** the volume of hand-delivered mail. According to a recent survey of executives, 76 percent **said** they spend at least an hour each day reading and responding to e-mail .... When my friend was working at a start-up company, he **used** the Internet several hours a day.
Present	d. Describes current habits, opinions, and general statements of fact.	d. Seventy-six percent said they **spend** at least an hour each day reading and responding to e-mail ....

Practice

Activity 12 • Analyze and edit student writing for verb tense

Using the following piece of student writing about e-mail, do the following:

- Edit for verb tenses by using Editing Guide 2.3, p. 152. You will find a total of six errors.
- Discuss your changes and reasons with a partner. Refer to Chart 4.4.
- If time permits, put examples on the board for class discussion and further correction.

X (opinion)

E-mail <u>has changed</u> my life in many ways. Mainly, this new technology <u>makes</u> it   1

easier and cheaper for me to keep in touch with my loved ones on the other side of   2

the world. Before e-mail, I called my family in Jakarta every week and it is very expen-   3

sive. Despite the advantages of e-mail, I had a problem with it. My sister in Jakarta   4

and I became very addicted to being online. I spend at least an hour a day writing to   5

her and reading messages from her. Unfortunately, I ended up feeling miserable   6

about my school and work. I spent lots of time on the e-mail and forgot about things I   7

normally did in my life such as studying, working, and sleeping. As a consequence, I   8

am behind on everything. As a result of this experience, I've learned my lesson from   9

e-mail addiction. Luckily, I figured out how to manage my time and energy for my   10

school, work, and family. Now I've just used e-mail every weekend. Weekdays I've   11

spent my time on my school and work. We all have to manage our time when we use   12

the new technology and try not to get too addicted to it.   13

Activity 13 • Edit your writing for verb tense

Look at a piece of writing that you did for this chapter for After Reading or Topics for Writing.

- Edit your paper for verb tenses using Editing Guide 2.3, p. 152.
- Exchange papers with a partner.
- Check each other's analysis and corrections and discuss any questions you have about your paper or your partner's paper.

Wrap-Up

Activity 14 • Edit your writing for verbs, nouns, and articles

■ Using Editing Guide 2.3, p. 152, Editing Guides 4.1, 4.2, and 4.3, pp. 154–155, and other information in this chapter, edit a piece of your own writing (from Topics for Writing, p. 71, or After Reading questions 6–9, p. 70) for problems with:

Passive verbs and verb tenses

Count and noncount nouns and articles

■ For the structures you edit, clearly show on your paper each step described in the Editing Guides. In addition, check your writing to see if you've used any of the word partnerships listed in "Using Vocabulary Accurately," p. 73. Correct any problems you find, and add examples to your word partnerships list. (See p. 150.)

Activity 15 • Class editing workshop: Edit for verbs, nouns, and articles

At home: Follow the directions for Activity 14. In addition, write questions in the margins of your paper next to places where you're not sure of your editing and vocabulary choices.

In class: Working with a partner or a small group, trade papers, and talk about each other's questions and writing. Refer to the grammar charts in the chapters and in Appendix B and the Editing Guides in Appendix A to help you. If time permits, put examples from your writing and editing on the board to discuss as a class.

5

Connecting Ideas

Overview of the Chapter

Read

Before Reading

Respond to these questions to help you think about and understand the reading that follows.

1. How does the health of our minds affect the health of our bodies? What is the connection between emotional health and physical health?

2. What role do parents and family play in influencing the choices we make? What are the benefits and drawbacks of having family involved in our decisions?

"Sen-jo and Her Soul Are Separated" by Zenkei Shibayama

A story from ancient times in China, "Sen-jo and Her Soul Are Separated" still appeals to audiences of different cultures and belief systems. Modern readers are drawn to the story because of what they can learn from the characters and their responses to the inner conflicts they face—the decisions they make and the outcomes of their choices.

The story of "Sen-jo and Her Soul are Separated" is taken from a **T'ang Dynasty**   1
legend. In Koshu in China in that dynasty there lived a man named Chokan. He had
two daughters, but as the elder one died young he loved the younger daughter Sen-jo
all the more and made much of her. Since she was an unusually beautiful girl, many
young men wished to marry her. Sen's father selected a good youth named Hinryo   5
from her many suitors and decided to give Sen-jo to him. Sen-jo, however, had a
secret lover named Ochu, who was Chokan's nephew. When Ochu was a child, Sen's
father had told him in jest, "Ochu and Sen-jo will make a well-matched couple. You
two had better get married when you grow up." This remark made them believe that
they were engaged, and in the course of time they found that they were in love with   10
each other.

Sen-jo, who had suddenly been told by her father to marry Hinryo, **was greatly
cast down** and depressed. As for Ochu, when he heard of it he was so distressed that
he decided to leave the village, for he could not bear to live anywhere near her. One
evening he secretly left his homeland by boat without even telling Sen-jo. At midnight   15
he noticed a vague figure running along the bank as if to follow his boat. He stopped
to see who it was, and to his great surprise and joy he found it was his beloved. He
was overcome with joy at the truth of her heart, and they embraced each other in
tears. As they could not now dare to return to Sen-jo's father, they traveled to the **remote** country of Shoku, where they were married.   20

Five years passed after they had left home. Sen-jo, who was now the mother of
two children, could not forget her native country, and her longing for her parents and
home increased day by day. One day, in tears, she confessed her painful longing to

---

T'ang Dynasty: rulers of China from C.E. 618 through 907   **remote:** far away
was greatly cast down: felt extremely sad

her husband. "Loving you and following you, I left my home without permission, and I have stayed with you in this remote country. I wonder how my parents are getting on. Having left home as I did, against my parents' wishes, an ungrateful daughter like myself may never be able to return home." Ochu, who was in fact also longing for his homeland, calmed her saying, "Let us then go back to Koshu and beg your parents' pardon." Immediately they hired a boat and returned to Koshu, their dear old home.

Leaving Sen-jo at the port, Ochu first went to Chokan's house by himself, apologized for their ungrateful act, and told him the whole story. Chokan was **astonished** and asked Ochu, "Which girl are you talking about?" "Your daughter Sen-jo, Father," replied Ochu. Chokan said, "My daughter Sen? From the time you left Koshu she has been sick in bed and has been unable to speak." Ochu was equally taken aback and tried to explain, "Sen-jo certainly followed me and we have lived together in the country of Shoku. She has borne two children and is physically very well. If you do not believe what I say, please come with me to the port, for she is there in the boat waiting for me."

Chokan, **mystified**, sent an old servant to the boat to check, and he returned to report that it was unmistakably Sen-jo. Chokan then went to her room in his house, and sure enough, his daughter Sen was still there sick in bed. In **bewilderment** Chokan told the sick Sen-jo the whole story, whereupon, looking extremely delighted, she got out of bed still without saying a word. In the meantime the Sen-jo who had come ashore arrived at Chokan's house in a cart. The sick Sen-jo went out from her home to meet her, and just as the Sen-jo from the boat alighted from the cart, the two Sen-jos became one.

Chokan, the father, spoke to Sen-jo, "Ever since Ochu left this village, you have not **uttered** a word, and you have always been absent in mind as if you were drunk. Now I see that your soul left your body and has been with Ochu." To this Sen-jo replied, "I did not know at all that I was sick in bed at home. When I learned that Ochu had left this village in **distress**, I followed his boat that night, feeling as if it were a dream. I myself am not sure which was the real me—the one with you, sick in bed, or the one with Ochu as his wife."

from *Zen Comments on the Mumonkan* by Zenkei Shibayama. Translated by
Sumiko Kudo. (San Francisco: Harper & Row, 1974)

---

astonished: extremely surprised
mystified: confused by the mysterious information
bewilderment: confusion

uttered: spoken
distress: anxious mental suffering

After Reading

Individually at home, or with a partner or a small group in class, write the answers to these questions to prepare for class discussion. Keep your answers in a notebook or binder to refer to later when you respond to the writing topics, develop your ideas for longer papers, or analyze your writing. Questions marked ¶ are especially suitable for paragraph-length answers that can be used later when you analyze your own writing.

1. This reading has nine characters. Four characters' names are given and five are not. List or make a diagram of the nine characters and explain their relationships to one another.

2. Discuss how marriage customs differ between the time period and place of the story and now in the United States.

3. Why do Sen-jo and Ochu believe they are engaged? How does this influence their actions and the outcome of the story?

4. Discuss what happens after Sen-jo's father announces that she is to marry Hinryo. Why is Ochu "overcome with joy at the truth of her heart"? Why do they feel that they cannot "dare to return"?

5. What happens in the five years after Sen-jo and Ochu travel to Shoku? Why is it important to know that Sen-jo and Ochu have two children? What causes Sen-jo and Ochu to leave Shoku and return to Koshu?

6. Compare the names of the two villages: Koshu and Shoku. Notice that both contain the same letters but in an opposite pattern. How does this similarity (and difference) relate to the meaning of the story?

7. Discuss what happens when the old servant returns from the boat. Why does the "sick" Sen-jo appear "extremely delighted"?

8. Explain how the sick Sen-jo and the Sen-jo from the boat "become one." What is Chokan's idea about the separation of the two Sen-jos? What does Sen-jo feel about who the "real" Sen-jo is?

¶ 9. Although we know from lines 25 and 28 that Sen-jo's mother is living, we do not learn her name or what she thinks or feels about her daughter's situation or actions. Why is the mother not part of the story? How might the story be different if we knew more about Sen-jo's mother?

¶10. Which Sen-jo do you think is the "real" one—the "one with [her parents], sick in bed, or the one with Ochu as his wife"?

Write

Topics for Writing

Respond in writing to one (or more) of the following topics:

1. How would a modern doctor in an American clinic treat the sick Sen-jo (before the return of the Sen-jo from the boat)? Describe some different treatments and discuss how effective you think they would be.

2. Write about a personal experience or an experience of someone you know that illustrates how someone can become separated from him/herself. (Optional: Compare this experience with the experience of Sen-jo described in the reading.)

3. Discuss how the story of Sen-jo illustrates the conflict between the loyalty we have for our parents and the loyalty we have to ourselves—our desires to make our own decisions and to be independent. Discuss the result of this conflict for parents and children. If you want, you can focus only on the legend. However, you can also support your ideas by making a connection between the story and a personal experience or an experience of someone you know.

4. What is the message or lesson of the story "Sen-jo and Her Soul Are Separated"? In your essay, explain the relevance of the message or lesson to our lives today.

5. Discuss how the story of Sen-jo illustrates the importance of communication. Explain the problems and results.

6. Who or what is responsible for the separation of Sen-jo from her "soul"? Explain how the following play a role: Chokan, Ochu, and Sen-jo.

7. Using the story of Sen-jo, explain the connection between our minds and our bodies and/or our emotional health and our physical health.

> ### Strategies for Writing: Generating and Developing Ideas
> For a description of ways to generate ideas, such as freewriting, listing, and brainstorming, as well as ways to develop and support your ideas, refer to Strategies for Writing, pp. 185–190.

Using Vocabulary Accurately

As you write about a reading, pay attention to word partnerships, words that occur frequently with each other or that form fixed expressions. For more examples, see Reference Charts 2.1 and 2.2, pp. 172–174. Create your own word partnerships list (see p. 150).

Some key word partnerships for this reading follow. Locate the key words in the reading or in Topics for Writing and notice how they are used. For practice, write sentences using some of these expressions.

to be engaged/married (*to someone*)
to become separated (*from someone*)
to be overcome with joy
to make the wrong/right decision
to marry (*someone*)

to apologize (*to someone*) (*for something*)
to make a bad/good decision
a connection between
    (our minds and bodies)
a conflict between (loyalty and desire)

Edit: Grammar Previews, Tips, and Practice

Listening/Writing Activity: Dictation/Dictocomp

The following dictation/dictocomp text gives information related to the reading "Sen-jo and Her Soul Are Separated" on p. 94.

Close your book. As your teacher reads the sentences below (one time all the way through, then by clauses, then all the way through again), do the following:

- For a dictation, try to write exactly what you hear.
- For a dictocomp, take notes on key words and phrases.
- Then, individually or in groups, reconstruct the text, revising and correcting your work and paying attention to problem areas.

1. In Koshu during ancient times, a man named Chokan had two daughters, but the elder one died. He then gave all his attention to Sen-jo, the younger one.

2. When Sen-jo and Ochu, Chokan's nephew, were children, Chokan said they were a well-matched couple.

3. Therefore, Ochu and Sen-jo believed they were engaged and grew to love each other.

4. Since Sen-jo was an unusually beautiful girl, many young men wished to marry her.

5. Because he had forgotten his previous comment to Ochu and Sen-jo, Chokan selected Hinryo to be the husband of his daughter.

6. Hearing this news, Ochu became so distressed that he secretly prepared to leave his homeland by boat.

7. Sen-jo was equally distraught. She ran along the water at midnight until her beloved Ochu stopped and recognized her. They embraced each other in tears, realizing they could not be without each other.

8. As a result, Ochu and Sen-jo left together for the distant land of Shoku without asking for permission from Sen-jo's parents.

5.1   Function and Punctuation of Joining Words

Preview: Assess What You Know

Joining words connect ideas and show meaning through logical relationships. In this book, the term "joining words" refers to three types of connectors:

- Coordinators such as *and, but*
- Subordinators such as *because, after*
- Transition expressions such as *however, in contrast*

Examine the sentences in the dictation and do the following:

- Draw a $\boxed{\text{box}}$ around the joining word(s).
- For each joining word you mark, choose a word from the list below that explains the meaning of the joining word and write the letter to the left of the sentence. (You will not need to use all the letters, but you need to use some letters more than once.)

    A. addition   F. example

    B. cause/reason   G. result

    C. choice   H. time relationship

    D. comparison   I. summary

    E. contrast/concession

E
H
    1. In Koshu during ancient times, a man named Chokan had two daughters, $\boxed{\text{but}}$ the elder one died. He $\boxed{\text{then}}$ gave all his attention to Sen-jo, the younger one.

- Explain the rules for punctuation for the three different types of joining words:

Coordinators (e.g., see #1) Rule: _____

_____

Subordinators (e.g., see #2, 4) Rule 1: _____

_____

Subordinators (e.g., see #6, 7) Rule 2: _____

_____

Transition expressions (e.g., see #3, 8) Rule: _____

_____

Grammar Tips: Check Your Work

With a partner or a small group, check your answers in the Preview by using the information in Chart 5.1A that follows. (A complete chart of connectors, Chart 5.1C, appears later in this section on p. 102.) Be prepared to explain your answers by referring to specific sections of the chart. Figure out what you still need to learn.

CHART 5.1A **Information about Joining Words**		
Joining Word Type and Function	**Punctuation**	**Examples**
Coordinators *and, but, or, yet, for, so, nor*[1] A coordinator joins two independent clauses that are equally important; the coordinator comes before the second clause.[2]	A comma comes before the coordinator. Some writers do not use a comma if the clauses are very short.	a. He had two daughters, **but** he loved the younger daughter more. *(contrast)* b. Sen-jo could stay at home with her father, **or** she could run away with Ochu. *(choice)* c. Ochu decided to leave the village, **for** he could not bear to live anywhere near Sen-jo. *(reason)* d. Sen-jo loved Ochu, **so** she followed him. *(result)*
Subordinators *because, although, when, if,* etc. A subordinator joins two elements to form one sentence: one element (the dependent clause) requires another element (the independent clause) to complete its meaning.	If the dependent clause with a sub-ordinator comes before the independent clause, use a comma after it *(e).* If the dependent clause comes after the independent clause, do not use a comma *(f, g).*	e. [**Since** Sen-jo was an unusually beautiful girl,] [many young men wished to marry her.] *(reason)* f. [Five years passed] [**after** they had left home.] *(time)* g. [Ochu was **so** distressed] [**that** he decided to leave the village.] *(result)*
Transition Expressions *in addition, therefore, for example, on the other hand,* etc. A transition expression, like a coordinator, joins two equally im-portant elements. These elements are independent clauses that are set off by punctuation that marks them as two separate sentences. The transition expression is always placed with the second sentence.	Use a semicolon after the first sentence, or use a period after the first sentence and begin the second sentence with a capital letter. Always set off transition expressions by commas.[3]	h. Chokan thought he had made a good choice of a husband for his daughter; **instead**, his decision caused her to feel cast down. *(contrast)* i. Sen-jo was in love with Ochu and dis-tressed at the thought of not being with him. **Therefore**, she secretly left her home and followed him up the river. *(result)* j. Sen's father selected a good youth named Hinryo and decided to give Sen-jo to him. Sen-jo, **however**, had a secret lover named Ochu. *(contrast)* *(Or:* Sen-jo had a secret lover named Ochu, **however**.*)*

[1]See Section 5.2 in this chapter for further information on the use of coordinators to join words and phrases. (e.g., She was homesick **and** lonely.)

[2]Although professional writers occasionally use **and**, **but**, and **or** at the beginning of a sentence, overuse is usually considered poor style. Avoid using **so** to begin a sentence in academic writing.

[3]Three connectors—*thus, also, then*—do not require commas when they are not at the beginning of the sentence. (e.g., He **then** gave all his attention to his other daughter, Sen-jo.)

CHART 5.1B **Common Problems with Joining Words**	
Problem / Tip[4]	**Examples**
1. Using more than one joining word to express contrast/concession. *Use only one joining word.*	⊘ **Although** Sen-jo was engaged to Hinryo, **but** she left her home for Ochu. *Correction:* **Although** Sen-jo was engaged to Hinryo, she left her home for Ochu. *Or* Sen-jo was engaged to Hinryo, **but** she left her home for Ochu.
2. Using a comma (or no punctuation) rather than a semicolon or period before a transition expression, resulting in a run-on sentence.[5] *Use a semicolon or period before the transition expression.*	⊘ Sen-jo was in love with Ochu, **as a result**, she left home and followed him up the river. *Correction:* Sen-jo was in love with Ochu. **As a result**, she left home and followed him up the river.
3. Creating a fragment by using a dependent clause without a main clause. *Join the dependent clause to the independent clause.*	Sen-jo left her home and ran away with Ochu. ⊘ **Because** she didn't want to marry Hinryo. *Correction:* Sen-jo left her home and ran away with Ochu **because** she didn't want to marry Hinryo.
4. Confusing joining words with expressions used as prepositions that have similar meanings. Compare: **Joining word** **vs.** **Expression used as preposition** instead instead of despite the fact that despite/in spite of because because of while during for example such as similarly like in addition in addition to/as well as *Use clauses after joining words; use nouns after expressions used as prepositions.*	a. ⊘ **Despite** <u>she was ill</u>, the sick Sen-jo got out of her bed and went to meet the other Sen-jo. *Correction:* **Despite** <u>her illness</u>, the sick Sen-jo … *Or* **Despite the fact that** <u>she was ill</u>, the sick Sen-jo … b. ⊘ **Because of** <u>Sen-jo loved Ochu</u>, she left Koshu. *Correction:* **Because** <u>Sen-jo loved Ochu</u>, she left Koshu. *Or* **Because of** <u>her love for Ochu</u>, Senjo left Koshu.
5. Using a transition expression to link sentences that are not next to each other. *Make the link clear by using a more complex phrase or by rewriting.*	Sen-jo and Ochu were very homesick. They had lived in Shoku for five years. ⊘ **Therefore**, they decided to go back to Koshu. (Therefore *links the last sentence to the first sentence in meaning, not to the second sentence.*) *Correction:* Sen-jo and Ochu were very homesick. They had lived in Shoku for five years. **Because of their homesickness**, they decided to go back to Koshu. *Or* Sen-jo and Ochu were very homesick though they had lived in Shoku for five years. **Therefore**, they decided to go back to Koshu.

[4]See Reference Chart 5.1, p. 183, for information on the connectors *so* and *so that*.
[5]See Chapter 2, section 2.1, p. 27, for additional information and practice on run-on sentences and fragments.

CHART 5.1C	**Common Joining Words and Their Meanings**

This chart lists commonly used coordinators, subordinators, and transition expressions that connect clauses and ideas. The joining words are listed according to their meaning; that is, the logical relationship of the sentences or ideas they connect.

Logical Relationship	Coordinators	Subordinators	Transition Expressions
Addition	and, not only[6] … but also, both … and …		in addition, furthermore moreover, also, besides
Contrast/Concession	but, yet	although, though, while, even though, whereas, in spite of the fact that, despite the fact that	however, nevertheless, on the other hand, still, in contrast, conversely, nonetheless, instead, on the contrary
Cause/Reason	for *(See c, Chart 5.1A)*	because, since, as, in that	therefore, consequently, thus, for that/this reason
Result[7]	so	so/such … that	as a result, therefore, thus, consequently, for this reason
Purpose		so that, in order that (in order to)[8]	
Choice/Option	or, nor *(negative)*, either … or, neither … nor		alternatively, on the other hand
Condition		if, even if, unless, provided that, as long as, in the event that, on condition that, whenever, wherever	otherwise
Time/Sequence		when, after, before, until, till, as, while, since, once, now that, whenever, as soon as, by the time that	then, first, second, third, …, finally, next, afterwards, after/before that, meanwhile, at first, eventually
Place		where, wherever	
Comparison/Similarity/ Contrast	but *(contrast)*	whereas/as if	similarly, likewise, in a similar way, also, in contrast
Explanation/Restatement			in other words, that is/i.e.
Example			for example/e.g., for instance
Summary/Generalization/Conclusion			in summary, in short, in general, overall, in conclusion

[6]*Not only* is followed by a clause with subject-verb inversion: *Not only **was she** depressed, **but** she was **also** upset.*

[7]See Reference Chart 5.1, p. 183.

[8]Non-finite clauses beginning with *in order to + verb* or simply *to + verb* are very frequently used to express purpose in academic writing. Example: The study was undertaken ***to show*** *the frequency of logical connectors in academic writing.*

Practice

Activity 1 • Analyze the reading for joining words

Working with a partner or a small group, use the story of Sen-jo to do the following:

- Find examples of sentences with the three types of joining words listed below. Draw boxes around the joining words. Some examples will require more than one sentence to clearly show the logical relationship that the joining word expresses. (See Chart 5.1A for examples.)

  Two sentences with coordinators

  Two sentences with subordinators

  Two sentences with transition expressions

- If time permits put your examples on the board. Be prepared to explain how the joining word shows a logical relationship between ideas (see Chart 5.1C) and why the punctuation is correct (see Chart 5.1A).

Activity 2 • Choose appropriate joining words

In pairs or small groups, read through the student writing below and then do the following:

- For each blank, choose the joining word that best expresses the logical relationship between the ideas in the sentence.

- Be prepared to explain the reasons for your choices by referring to specific sections of Charts 5.1A, 5.1B, or 5.1C.

Text A

My body follows the wish of my parents for me to major in computer science just as the sick Sen-jo's body accepts the wish of her parents to marry someone who is not the one she loves. Both of us are not really happy _____*because*_____ Hinryo is not her favorite, and
    1. because/besides
computer science is not my real interest. _____, my soul follows my interest to
    2. As a result/On the other hand
play music just as Sen-jo's soul follows her lover. Both of our souls are struggling to be
happy _____ we can realize what is in our hearts and can have our own lives.
    3. although/ so that

Text B

Yo-Yo Ma, who is a famous and successful musician, dreamed of becoming a cellist
_____ he was young. He realized that he could be content _____ he
    4. until/when   5. if/when
could be a cellist playing concertos. _____ his parents thought that being a
    6. Although/Because
cellist was not an ideal career for him, he still kept discussing his enthusiasm for the cello
with his parents and following his dream. _____, he achieved his dream
    7. Overall/Eventually
through persistence and hard work. His interest in playing the cello _____ let
    8. either/not only
him achieve his dream _____ helped him make a success of his life.
    9. or/but also

Activity 3 • Write sentences about the story of Sen-jo using joining words

With a partner or a small group, select one set of joining words from the eight sets listed below. Each group should work with a different set. Then follow the steps to practice using joining words and writing sentences with correct punctuation. Refer to Charts 5.1A, 5.1B, and 5.1C to help you.

A. however
   and
   because

B. since
   not only ... but also
   therefore

C. so
   nevertheless
   while

D. although
   or
   instead

E. nor
   then
   even though

F. when
   yet
   otherwise

G. for
   so that
   on the other hand

H. finally
   but
   so that

- For your three joining words, do the following:

  For the coordinator, write a two-clause sentence.

  For the subordinator, write a two-clause sentence.

  For the transition expression, write two sentences (or join them with a semicolon).

- The sentences should be "true" statements (not made-up information) about the situations or characters in the story of Sen-jo.

- Check each two-clause sentence or pair of sentences for meaning and punctuation.

  Examples for set A:

  and *(coordinator):* Sen-jo was not in love with Hinryo, and she didn't want to marry him.

  because *(subordinator):* Sen-jo did not want to marry Hinryo because she was in love with Ochu.

  however *(transition expression):* Sen-jo's father wanted her to marry Hinryo. However, she did not want to marry him.

Follow-up Class Discussion. Put several of the sentences on the board and discuss them.

- Are the sentences accurate according to the story?

- Do the joining words show the correct logical relationship?

- Are the sentences correctly formed and punctuated?

Optional: Joining Word Game. Each two-clause sentence or pair of sentences is worth 2 points: 1 for logic and 1 for form/punctuation. Partial points may be added or subtracted for other grammar or content features that the class decides to focus on. The pair or group with the most points is the winner. To break ties: each "tied" group gets an index card with another joining word on it to write an additional sentence or pair of sentences. The procedure is repeated until there is a winner.

Activity 4 • Practice using unfamiliar joining words and prepositions

To expand your use of joining words and prepositions, do the following:

- Select four joining words that you do not ordinarily use (or are not sure how to use) from Chart 5.1C. (Choose at least one coordinator, one subordinator, and one transition expression.)

- Select two expressions used as prepositions from the list in Section 4 of Chart 5.1B (or other prepositions you want to practice using).

- Using the six words you selected, write sentences on one of the following topics (or come up with your own topic). These sentences do not need to be directly about the story of Sen-jo.

    Loyalty to family, friends, ourselves

    Responsibility for our actions

    The importance of communication

- With a partner, discuss the meaning and form of your sentences. Help each other make corrections.

instead (transition expression); as well as (preposition):
When we don't agree with decisions our parents make for us, we often feel rebellious and angry; instead, we should react by asking them to explain their reasoning as well as telling them our point of view.

Activity 5 • Edit sentences with joining words

The following sentences with joining words have errors in punctuation and/or problems with logical relationships. To help you find the problems:

- Draw a box around the joining words in the sentences, even if they are incorrect.

- Refer to Charts 5.1A, 5.1B, 5.1C to figure out problems.

- Correct the errors and be prepared to explain your corrections.

1. Sen-jo doesn't talk to her parents ~~even~~ *even though* they want her to marry a man she doesn't love. *("Even" is not a subordinator.)*

2. In this story, the characters have a big communication problem. For example, no one tries to solve the problem.

3. People think that what parents say is right, because they have more experience in their lives.

4. Sen-jo and Ochu loved each other so much that they left their home without permission and lived somewhere else, nevertheless, they were longing for their homeland and went back to beg for their parents' pardon.

5. When Chokan tells Sen-jo that she should get married to Hinryo. Both Sen-jo and Ochu become distressed.

6. Without doubt, Asian men are viewed to be more important in society because that they have bigger responsibilities than women do.

7. Sen-jo was caught between her love for Ochu and her responsibility to her father so that her soul and body separated.

8. Sen-jo blamed herself for being an ungrateful daughter and leaving home against her parents' wishes. Because of daughters must obey their fathers and wives must obey their husbands in ancient China.

Activity 6 • Edit student writing for errors with joining words

The student text below contains errors in logic and punctuation related to joining words. With a partner or a small group, do the following:

- Draw boxes around the joining words.
- Find the errors and highlight them. Refer to Charts 5.1A, 5.1B, and 5.1C and Reference Chart 5.1 on p. 183 to help you. (There are three additional errors with joining words and two errors in punctuation.)
- Edit the text to correct the errors.
- If time permits, put problem sentences on the board and explain your corrections.

In the story, although Sen-jo is distraught when she hears that she has to marry   1

Hinryo, but she accepts the wishes of her parents without any complaint. Similarly, in   2

the traditional Taiwanese family, children have no right to talk back to their parents.   3

They easily lose their individualities because they have to submit themselves to their   4

parents. However, children often struggle to find ways to be themselves in spite of   5

their parents. They want their own relationships, interests, and goals, so that they   6

fulfill their desires to lead their own lives and make their own decisions. So for most   7

Taiwanese children, when the wishes of our parents are in conflict with our own   8

wishes our bodies and souls will be separated in order to resolve the conflict. The   9

body follows the wishes of the parents; instead, the soul tries to achieve the dream.   10

5.2 Parallel Structure in Joined Clauses, Phrases, or Words

Preview: Assess What You Know

In parallel structure, writers join two or more elements of equal importance with the coordinators *and, but, or,* and *yet.* The elements should be the same grammatical structure; for example, they could be all nouns, all infinitives, all adjectives, all verb phrases, or all clauses. If the elements are not the same, the sentence breaks the rules of parallel structure.

Some of the sentences that follow have problems with parallel structure. To help you analyze them, do the following for each sentence:

- Draw a box around the coordinator.
- <u>Underline</u> the element that comes after the coordinator.
- Identify the structure of the element; e.g., clause, verb, noun, adjective.

  Check the other element that comes before the coordinator to see if they are equal structures. <u>Underlining</u> that element will help you.

  Label sentences with equal elements "C" for correct. Label sentences with unequal elements "⊘" for incorrect, and make corrections. Be prepared to explain your decisions.

C 1. Chokan <u>loved his younger daughter</u> [and] <u>made much of her.</u> *equal verb phrases*

⊘ 2. Women have become more <u>self-reliant,</u> <u>educated,</u> [and] ~~competition.~~ *competitive* *adjectives before* [and]*; noun after*

3. Sen-jo could not forget her native country and missing her parents more every day.

4. Ochu went to Chokan's house by himself, apologized for their ungrateful act, and told him the whole story.

5. Because children have to do what their parents wish, they can't speak up for what they want and causing communication problems.

6. The mental harm of depression can lead a person to talk to herself all the time and not responding to anyone's attempt at communication.

7. In India, parents have greater expectations of their sons than of their daughters. Nonetheless, parents hope all their children will be respectful and obedient, regardless of whether they are boys or girls.

8. Is it an irreconcilable conflict when the wishes of our parents and what we want are different?

Grammar Tips: Check Your Work

With a partner or a small group, check your answers in the Preview by using the information in Chart 5.2 that follows. Be prepared to explain your answers by referring to specific sections of the chart. Figure out what you still need to learn.

CHART 5.2	Parallel Structure in Joined Clauses, Phrases, or Words
Types of Structures Joined	**Examples**
Independent clauses	<u>Chokan had two daughters</u>, but <u>one of them died</u>.
Verb phrases	Sen-jo <u>left her home</u>, <u>married her true love</u>, and <u>had two children</u>.[9]
Other verb forms a. Infinitives b. -ing forms	a. Sen-jo wanted <u>to obey her father</u> but also <u>to be with Ochu</u>. b. <u>Loving you</u> and <u>following you</u>, I left my home without permission.
Nouns a. Single nouns b. Noun phrases	a. Sen-jo was forced to choose between <u>Ochu</u> and <u>Hinryo</u>. b. Sen-jo was <u>an unusually beautiful girl</u> and <u>an obedient daughter</u>.
Adjectives	Chokan was <u>mystified</u> and <u>confused</u> by the information.
Adverbs	The sick Sen-jo ran <u>out of her house</u> and <u>down the street</u> to meet the other Sen-jo.
Dependent clauses a. *That* clauses b. Relative clauses c. *Wh-* clauses	a. Chokan thought <u>that Hinryo was a good man</u> and <u>that Sen-jo would be happy with him</u>. b. Ochu, <u>who loved Sen-jo madly</u> but <u>who could not live in the same town with her if she was married to someone else</u>, decided to leave Koshu. c. Ochu saw a woman running along the river and didn't know <u>who she was</u> or <u>where she was going</u>.

If you have trouble with parallel structure, follow these instructions:
1. Draw a box around the coordinator.
2. <u>Underline</u> structures after and before the coordinator.
3. Check to see if they are equal grammatical elements.
4. If the elements are not equal, make corrections.

[9]A comma is generally required after each element before the coordinator in a series of three or more elements. Although some writers do not use a comma after the element that appears immediately before the coordinator, if you use a comma, you will always be correct.

Practice

Activity 7 • Analyze student writing for parallel structure

Read the student text below and do the following:

- Underline at least six additional examples of different types of joined parallel elements.
- Above each example, write the type of structure joined.

My father had a mysterious experience that revealed to him the separation of   1

nouns
body and soul. Almost three years ago, my father suffered tissue damage in his brain   2

verb phrases
and was in critical condition in the hospital. While he was alone and unconscious, he   3

had a mysterious vision. In that vision, he was standing in front of a huge river by   4

himself. It was dark, nobody was around, and he could only see that stormy river   5

flowing by swiftly and dangerously. Suddenly, my father heard someone calling his   6

name. He looked up, and he saw his uncle who died in World War II on the other side   7

of the river. His uncle, still wearing a military uniform, was beckoning to my father   8

and telling him to come to his side. Since his uncle had been a war hero who died   9

right before my father was born, my father wanted to see him and to talk with him   10

face to face. Walking along the bank and shouting to his uncle across the river, my   11

father looked for a way to get across, but there was no bridge or boat around. He even   12

tried to swim across, but the river was just too wide and was flowing too fast. Finally,   13

my father gave up trying to cross and told his uncle that he couldn't find a way. Then   14

the river and his uncle disappeared, and my father found himself in his room in the   15

hospital.   16

Activity 8 • Edit sentences with parallel structure problems

The sentences below contain errors in parallel structure. For each sentence do the following:

- Put a box around coordinators.
- Underline the structures that appear before coordinators and the structures that follow coordinators.
- Check each pair or list of elements to be sure that they are parallel and punctuated correctly. (Refer to Chart 5.2.)
- Make corrections and be prepared to explain them.

1. The writer of the text above wants to show that when our bodies are close to dying
   illness (noun, adjective noun)
   because of aging or ill , we might encounter unusual experiences.

2. She demonstrates this idea by telling and discussed a story about her father.

3. Her father lay in a hospital bed and unconscious with damage to the tissue in his brain.

4. Lying alone in a room and sensed that he was by himself, her father had a mysterious vision.

5. Suddenly, he found himself near a huge river flowing swiftly and dangerous.

6. On the other side of the river, he witnessed his uncle, who had died in World War II, beckon and calling for him to come near.

7. Although the two men were able to talk and walking along the riverbank, they could not find a way to cross the high water.

8. Finally, the father's vision ended with the disappearance of his uncle and the lonely of his hospital room.

Activity 9 • Complete sentences by adding parallel elements

Use "Sen-jo and Her Soul Are Separated" on p. 94 to do the following:
- Complete each sentence with a parallel element that is true according to the story.
- Underline the parallel elements and identify the structures of these elements.

1. This story is about <u>Sen-jo</u> and *the separation of her body and soul.*

2. Sen-jo's father wanted her to marry Hinryo, but _____

3. Sen-jo was in love with Ochu, but not _____

4. Sen-jo and Ochu went to another country together and _____

5. In Shoku, both Sen-jo and Ochu were homesick and _____

6. They decided to leave Shoku and _____

7. When Ochu first talked to Chokan, he told him about their marriage and _____

   _____

8. The old servant went to the boat and _____

9. Chokan was astonished and _____

10. Which was the real Sen-jo, the Sen-jo who stayed home with her father or _____

    _____

Activity 10 • Analyze your writing and add detail and information

Using a piece of your writing from After Reading or Topics for Writing for this chapter, practice adding detail and information to your writing with parallel structure by doing the following:

- Find places in your writing where the description or ideas could be clarified or expanded with parallel structure. <u>Underline</u> these places.
- Trade papers with a partner and help each other find additional places where you could use parallel structure to develop ideas and description.
- Add detail and information to these places by expanding your writing with adjectives, adverbs, noun phrases, verb phrases, or other parallel structures.

Activity 11 • Edit your writing for joining words and parallel structure

Use Editing Guides 5.1 and 5.2, pp. 155–156, to help you do the following:

- Trade your expanded writing from Activity 10 with a partner and check each other's work for accuracy.
- Highlight structures that you think need correction.
- Discuss your suggestions for corrections with your partner.

5.3 Using Participial Phrases to Connect Ideas

Preview: Assess What You Know

In addition to using joining words, another way of joining ideas and streamlining your writing is to use a participial phrase instead of a full clause. A participle is a verb form with *-ing* (e.g., *taking*) or *-ed/-en* (e.g., *taken*). A participial phrase always contains one of these verb forms.

A. In the sentences below, the participial phrases are underlined. For each sentence, do the following:

- Restate each participial phrase as an independent clause.
- Circle the subject of the new clause.
- Circle the subject of the main clause of the original sentence.

1. <u>Believing they were engaged,</u> Ochu and Sen-jo grew to love each other.

   Ochu and Sen-jo believed they were engaged.

2. <u>Without realizing that Sen-jo and Ochu were in love,</u> Chokan selected Hinryo to marry Sen-jo.

   Chokan didn't realize that Sen-jo and Ochu were in love.

3. <u>Hearing this news,</u> Ochu became so distressed that he left Koshu.

   _____

4. <u>Loving Ochu and following him,</u> Sen-jo left her home <u>without asking permission from her parents.</u>

   _____

   _____

5. Sen-jo worried that she might never be able to return home, <u>having left home without her parents' permission</u>.

_____

6. <u>After living in Shoku for five years and becoming parents to two children</u>, Sen-jo and Ochu decided to go back to Koshu.

_____

7. <u>Taken from an ancient legend</u>, the story of Sen-jo is relevant today to help us reflect on conflicts between our desires and loyalties.

_____

B. Now work with a partner or a small group to answer these questions, which relate to rules for participial phrases.

1. Is the subject of each clause you have written in A, above, the same as the subject of the main clause of the sentence?

2. Where can a participial phrase occur in a sentence?

3. Can a participial phrase follow a preposition or joining word?

4. Where do you find commas in relationship to participial phrases?

C. Now write some rules related to participial phrases.

1. Rule for subjects: _____

2. Rule for placement in the sentence (at the beginning? at the end?): _____

3. Rule for punctuation: _____

Grammar Tips: Check Your Work

With a partner or a small group, check your answers in the Preview by using the information in Chart 5.3 that follows. Be prepared to explain your answers by referring to specific sections of the chart. Figure out what you still need to learn.

CHART 5.3	**Participial Phrases and Related Structures**	
Features	**Explanations**	**Examples**
1. Function	Participial phrases can streamline your writing by: ■ Not repeating a subject, and ■ Joining ideas without a joining word. The subject of the main clause and the participial phrase are the same.[10]	Ochu and Sen-jo believed they were engaged. Ochu and Sen-jo grew to love each other. _(Original sentences)_ **Believing** they were engaged, Ochu and Sen-jo grew to love each other. _(Sentence with participial phrase)_

Features	Explanations	Examples
2. Form	The participle can have several forms. The most common are: a. Verb + *ing* *(The negative form* not realizing *comes from the verb* didn't realize *in the full clause.)* b. *Having* + past participle *(The perfect form* having *shows that* left *occurred before* worried, *the main clause action.)* c. Past participle *(This form comes from a passive verb in the full clause: The story of Sen-jo was taken from an ancient legend.)* d. Sometimes the participial phrase follows a preposition or joining word to make the meaning clear: *after, before, until, upon,* and *when* show time relationships; e. *without* shows a negative meaning.	a. <u>Not **realizing** the consequences</u>, Chokan told Ochu and Sen-jo they were a good match. b. Sen-jo worried that she might never be able to return home, <u>**having left** [home] without her parents' permission.</u> c. <u>**Taken** from an ancient legend</u>, the story of Sen-jo helps us reflect on conflicts between our desires and loyalties. d. <u>After **living** in Shoku for five years</u>, Sen-jo and Ochu decided to go back to Koshu. e. Sen-jo left her home <u>without **asking** for permission</u>. *(She didn't ask ...)*
3. Related common structure	A related common structure is: a. An adjective, or b. *Being* + adjective.	a. <u>**Unhappy** to be so far from home</u>, Sen-jo wanted to return. b. <u>**Being worried** about her father</u>, Sen-jo decided to return home.
4. Order	Participial phrases can come before or after the main clause *(2a, 2b)*, or occasionally after a subject.	Ochu, <u>**thinking** Sen-jo would marry another man</u>, left the village in despair.
5. Punctuation	Use a comma *(1–3)* except when a preposition or joining word introduces the phrase after the main clause *(2e)*.	The couple decided to return to Koshu <u>**after** living in Shoku for five years.</u> *(no comma)*
6. Problem	The most common error is a "dangling modifier," when the subjects are not the same. This can often lead to very humorous sentences. *Rewrite the sentence to make the subjects the same (a) or use another structure in place of the participial phrase (b).*	⊘ <u>Being an unusually beautiful girl</u>, many young men wished to marry her. (subjects: *Sen-jo* vs. *many young men*) *Corrections:* a. Being an unusually beautiful girl, Sen-jo had many suitors. *Or* b. Because Sen-jo was an unusually beautiful girl, many young men wished to marry her.

---

[10]Although it is not as common, it is possible to have two different subjects. However, the subject of the participle must be included. (***Chokan being upset***, *Sen-jo was afraid to talk to him directly when she returned.*)

Practice

Activity 12 • Write sentences with participial phrases

Practice streamlining the sentences below by doing the following:

- Turn the first clause into a participial phrase and rewrite the entire sentence on a separate piece of paper.
- You may have to change pronouns in the second clause to nouns (See the example rewrite for item 2).
- <u>Underline</u> your participial phrases.
- Refer to Chart 5.3 to check your form and punctuation.

1. I wanted to have more independence from my parents. I decided to move out of my parents' home while I was in college.

   <u>Wanting more independence from my parents</u>, I decided to move out of their home while I was in college.

2. My older sister understood my desire for independence. She offered to help me.

   <u>Understanding my desire for independence</u>, my older sister offered to help me.

3. I realized I would have financial problems. I moved in with my older sister's family and offered to pay monthly rent.

4. I was working 20 hours a week and taking a full load of classes. I began to feel overwhelmed.

5. My sister saw that I was under pressure. She said she would lower my rent so that I could work fewer hours.

6. I knew that she needed the money. I refused to accept her offer.

7. I didn't want to move back home. I solved the problem by dropping two of my classes.

8. I look back on my experience. I can see that becoming independent isn't as easy as I thought it would be.

Activity 13 • Streamline your writing with participial phrases

Choose a piece of your writing from After Reading or Topics for Writing for this chapter and do the following:

- Use Editing Guide 5.3, p. 156, to identify participial phrases and find places where you could add them to your writing.
- Exchange papers with a partner and check each other's work for accuracy.

5.4 Conditional Sentences: Meaning and Verb Tenses

Preview: Assess What You Know

A conditional sentence consists of a dependent clause beginning with the subordinator **if** or **unless** and a main clause.[11] For example:

(if clause—conditional clause)   *(main clause—result)*
a. If parents and children communicate well, many problems can be avoided.

b. If children were as mature as adults, many problems could be avoided.

Factual conditionals (*a*) are used when the condition is possible and likely in the past, present, or future. (It is possible that parents and children can communicate well.)

Hypothetical conditionals (*b*) have a non-traditional use of verb tenses to show that the writer is referring to a condition that is impossible or unlikely to occur. (It is not likely that children are as mature as adults.)

The following Preview activity will help you assess what you know about these two types of conditionals and about the relationship between tense and time reference in conditional sentences.

Look at the sentences below and do the following for each:

- Underline the conditional sentence.
- Double-underline the complete verbs in the conditional sentence.
- Figure out the time reference of each conditional sentence and write "P" for past, "Pr" for present, or "Fut" for Future after each. *(Note that the tenses of the verbs in the conditional sentences are not always consistent with the time reference.)*
- On the line, label each conditional sentence according to one of these two types:
    F = Factual conditional: a general truth, fact, opinion, or a prediction
    H = Hypothetical conditional: a speculation (a guess) about the results of a condition that is unlikely or impossible

__*F*___ 1. My parents have definite ideas about the type of person I should marry. If they object to the person I want to marry, I will follow my own heart.   *Fut*

_____ 2. I feel very strongly that if a daughter doesn't want to marry the man her parents choose for her as her husband, she shouldn't do so.

_____ 3. The story of Sen-jo illustrates this point: if children don't have good communication with their parents, the opportunities for misunderstanding and grief are many.

---

[11]Either clause can come first in the sentence: for example, *Many problems can be avoided if parents and children communicate well.* Or: *If parents and children communicate well, many problems can be avoided.*

———— 4. Good communication between parents and their children is essential, but Sen-jo and her parents failed to communicate. <u>If Sen-jo had talked</u> with her parents about her love for Ochu, Chokan <u>might have allowed</u> their marriage; consequently, everyone <u>would have been spared</u> a great deal of grief.

———— 5. Ochu was in a miserable situation. If I had been in Ochu's position, I would have talked to Sen-jo's father instead of secretly leaving town.

———— 6. Fortunately, most of us are not in the same position as Sen-jo. If I were forced to choose between my own desires and the wishes of my parents, I would probably follow my heart.

Complete the following chart with the verbs that you have double-underlined in the conditional sentences. Write the name of the tense next to the verb in parentheses. Choose from the following:

P = Past   PM + Sf = Past Modal + Simple form

PP = Past Perfect   Pr = Present

PM + Pf = Past Modal + Perfect form   Fut = Future

Type of Conditional	Verb + tense in *if* clause	Verb + tense in main clause
Factual	1. object/want (Pr)	1. will follow (Fut)
Hypothetical	4. had talked (PP)	4. might have allowed, would have been spared (PM + Pf)

Using the chart, write rules for possible verb tenses:

1. Verbs tenses possible in **factual** conditionals:
   a. In the *if* clause _____
   b. In the main clause _____

2. Verb tenses possible in **hypothetical** conditionals:
   a. In the *if* clause _____
   b. In the main clause _____

Which type of conditional sentence (factual or hypothetical) never has present or future verb tenses?

Grammar Tips: Check Your Work

With a partner or a small group, check your answers in the Preview by using the information in Charts 5.4A and 5.4B that follow. Be prepared to explain your answers by referring to specific sections of the charts. Figure out what you still need to learn.

CHART 5.4A   Meaning of Conditional Sentences Common in Writing[12]

Writers sometimes have difficulty choosing the correct verbs in conditional sentences. In order to decide which verb tenses to use, they must first think about the meaning of the conditional sentence.

Basic Type	Meaning	Examples
Factual	a. These conditional sentences state general truths, facts, or opinions. *(If this, then this.)*	a. If I talk with my parents about my problems, they always help me. *(fact)* If a Chinese couple has a daughter and a son, they usually favor the son. *(opinion)*
	b. They also can express realistic predictions.	b. If my parents object to the person I want to marry, I will follow my own heart. *(prediction)*
Hypothetical	These conditional sentences speculate (or guess) about the results of a condition that is unlikely or impossible.	If I asked my parents to find a husband for me, they would be very surprised. *(Fact: It is unlikely that I will ask them.)*
	They are called "contrary to fact" sentences because they express possibilities that are the opposite of what is true or known.	If I were a parent, I would always try to support my children's wishes. *(Fact: I am not now a parent.)*
		If Sen-jo had talked to her father, then perhaps he would have allowed her to marry Ochu. *(Fact: Sen-jo did not talk to her father.)*

---

[12]While a conditional clause is usually introduced by **if**, **even if**, or **unless**, it can be introduced in other ways. For example, ***Had** Sen-jo **talked** to her parents about Ochu, they might have allowed her to marry him. **Should** you **marry** someone from another culture, you must be prepared to encounter differences.* (See Chart 5.4C.) The punctuation follows the same rule as for other clauses joined by subordinators. (See Chart 5.1A.)

CHART 5.4B   Verb Tenses in Conditional Sentences Common in Writing[13]

Type of Conditional and Time Reference	Example	
	Conditional Clause	*Main Clause*
Factual		
a. Present	a. If parents and children **communicate** well, ... *(present verb)*	... problems **are** often easily **solved**. *(present verb)*
b. Future	b. If my parents **object** to the person I want to marry, ... *(present verb)*	... I **will consider** their advice. *(future verb)*
c. Past	c. If I **talked** with my parents about my problems when I **was growing up**, ... *(past verb)*	... they always **helped** me. *(past verb)*
Hypothetical		
d. Present	d. If my parents **objected** to the person I wanted to marry, ... *(past verb)*	... I **might/would consider** their advice. *(past modal + simple form)*
	If I **were**[14] living in Mexico right now, ... *(past verb)*	... I **wouldn't be able to stay out** late with my friends. *(past modal + simple form)*
	If I **couldn't be** with my friends, ... *(past modal + simple form)*	... I **would be** unhappy. *(past modal + simple form)*
e. Past	e. If last year my father **had told** me to major in computer science, ... *(past perfect verb)*	... I **would have followed** his advice. *(past modal + perfect form)*
f. Past time in conditional clause/present time in main clause	f. Also, if I **had listened** to my friends, ... *(past perfect verb)*	... I **would now be** a computer science major. *(past modal + simple form)*

[13]This chart shows the basic patterns for these conditional sentences.

[14]*Were* is customary for all persons in careful speech and writing in <u>hypothetical</u> if-clauses. *Was* is often used for first and third person, especially in casual conversation.

CHART 5.4C   Problems/Tips for Using Conditional Sentences

Problem/Tip	Examples
1. Mixing hypothetical and real conditional verb patterns in the same sentence *Decide on your meaning and check your verbs carefully.* In this case, choose *a* if it is possible that the condition will be fulfilled (i.e., you might reject their advice). Choose *b* if it is unlikely that you will reject their advice.	⊘ If I **reject** my parents' advice, they **would be** upset. *Mixed patterns: reject = factual* *would be = hypothetical* *Corrections:* a. If I **reject** my parents' advice, they **will be** upset. b. If I **rejected** my parents' advice, they **would be** upset.

Problem/Tip	Examples
2. Not using the hypothetical verb patterns to talk about the results of a condition that is unlikely or impossible. *Think about what tense you are using for narration. Then think about what the facts are. (See Chart 5.4B.)* If you are talking about something that is very unlikely or something that is not true, use hypothetical patterns. a. Use past tense and a past modal + simple verb form for something untrue in the present (to match present narration). b. Use past perfect and a past modal + perfect verb for something untrue in the past (to match past narration).	Communication between parents and their children is essential. In the story, neither Ochu nor Sen-jo **communicates** well with her parents. The lack of communication **causes** a problem for them. ⊘ If Ochu **discusses** Sen-jo's marriage with her and **tells** her father that he **wants** to marry her, I believe the problem **won't come up**. *(Writer is using present narration. The conditional sentence is contrary to fact: Ochu did* not *discuss Sen-jo's marriage with her or her father. Therefore, use a hypothetical verb pattern, not the factual conditional pattern.)* *Corrections:* a. If Ochu **discussed** Sen-jo's marriage with her father and **told** him he **wanted** to marry her, I believe the problem **wouldn't come up**. b. In the story, neither Ochu nor Sen-jo **communicated** well with her parents. The lack of communication **created** a problem for them. If Ochu **had discussed** Sen-jo's marriage with her and **had told** her father he **wanted** to marry her, I believe the problem **wouldn't have come up**.
3. Not using *unless, even if, even though* correctly a. *unless* = if not b. use *if* or *though* after *even* *Use even if/even though when there is a reference to a previous statement or assumption (here, the possibility that they may communicate well).*	a. **Unless** parents and children communicate with one another, problems are sure to arise. **(If parents and children don't communicate …)** b. ⊘ **Even** they communicate well, there still can be problems. *Correction:* **Even if** (or **even though**) they communicate well, there still can be problems. *(They may communicate well, but there still may be problems.)*

Practice

Activity 14 • Write sentences using the past hypothetical

The following are some events that happened in the story, for which the writer uses past tense.

- For each event, write a sentence telling how it could/would/might have been different if the characters had done something else. Write on a separate piece of paper.
- Underline the verbs in both clauses.

1. When Sen-jo was a child, her older sister died.

   If Sen-jo's sister <u>hadn't died</u>, Chokan <u>might not have focused</u> so much attention on Sen-jo.

2. Chokan selected Hinryo to marry Sen-jo.

3. Sen-jo didn't tell her father that she loved Ochu.
4. Sen-jo followed Ochu to the river and ran away with him.
5. Sen-jo and Ochu had two children.
6. Sen-jo and Ochu were homesick for Koshu.

Activity 15 • Write about how things might have been different

When reading the story of Sen-jo, it is natural to reflect on what happened and how everything would have been different if someone had or hadn't done something. For example:

> If Sen-jo and Ochu had only talked to each other and to Sen-jo's parents, they could have lived happily in Koshu for those five years, and Sen-jo and her soul would not have been separated. Chokan would not have had to live with the Sen-jo who stayed in bed. Furthermore, Chokan and his wife could have experienced the joys of the birth and early childhood of their grandchildren. But of course, if the lovers had talked, then there would have been no story to help us think about our conflicting desires and loyalties.[15]

With a partner or a small group, do the following:

- Talk about what would be or would have been different in your life if you had done or hadn't done something.
- After your discussion, write your own story.
- Exchange papers with a partner and read each other's stories.
- Check your partner's paper for verb tenses in conditional sentences; highlight verbs you have questions about and discuss them with your partner.
- Correct any problems in your paper. Refer to Charts 5.4A through 5.4C.

Activity 16 • Edit student writing with problems in conditional sentences

The following student texts have some problems with conditional sentences.

- To help you figure out and correct the problems, use Editing Guide 5.4, p. 156.
- Discuss your corrections with a partner, a small group, or the whole class.

1. In the story, there is a communication problem among the family members.   1

The daughter and parents don't talk and a difficult situation results. I believe that   2

if they communicate~~d~~ with each other, the problem ~~can~~ could be solved.   3

---

[15]Note that in this example, the first sentence sets up the hypothetical situation, and in the next two sentences that follow, no *if* clauses are stated. We are able to infer these *if* clauses from the context. This pattern is common in both spoken and written English.

2.   Sen-jo was her parents' only child. They loved her so much. I think if she   1

tried to talk to them about the problem, they might listen to her and solve the prob-   2

lem. Ochu can also solve the problem if he asks Sen-jo to go to see her parents with   3

him. All of them can solve the problem if they have a talk. It's too bad that no one   4

tried to discuss the problem. *(7 errors)*   5

3.   I think if I don't try to do what I want to do and what I believe in, I might   1

regret it in the future. The thing that makes our life wonderful is to try to achieve what   2

we want to do. If we don't try to achieve our goals and follow our desires, our life   3

would be meaningless. *(1 error)*   4

4.   Lack of communication can be the cause of a separation of a person and   1

her/his soul. Sen-jo knows that if she follows Ochu and leaves her hometown, she will   2

disappoint her parents. If she stays at home with the parents, she will disappoint   3

Ochu. To cope with this difficult situation, Sen-jo separates into two people to satisfy   4

both her parents and Ochu. By making this unconscious decision, she probably   5

thinks that if there had been more than one Sen-jo, then everything would have been   6

resolved. *(2 errors)*   7

5.   When I was a child, my grandmother told me that in ancient China the way   1

people communicated was to write a letter and leave it in an envelope on the dining   2

table so people didn't have to talk with each other face to face. This statement relates   3

to the story of Sen-jo. Sen-jo had problems with communication with her parents. If   4

Sen-jo knows how to communicate with her parents she wouldn't have to face all the   5

problems like running away from home and feeling regret. She should have written a   6

letter to her parents and explained that she wants to marry Ochu instead of Hinryo.   7

Her parents might be able to understand her situation and not stop them from seeing   8

each other. This example shows how important communication is to the stability of a   9

family. *(5 errors)*   10

Activity 17 • Edit your writing for conditional sentences

Using a piece of your writing from After Reading, question 9 or 10, or from Topics for Writing, discuss your paper with a partner by following the steps below:

- Trade your writing with your partner and check each other's work for correct form and use of conditional sentences. Use Editing Guide 5.4, p. 156 to help you.
- Highlight any structures that you think need correction.
- Discuss your suggestions for corrections with your partner.

Wrap-Up

Activity 18 • Edit your writing for joining words and conditional sentences

■ Using Editing Guides 5.1 (p. 155) and 5.4 (p. 156), and other information in this chapter, edit a piece of your own writing (from Topics for Writing, p. 97, or questions 9 or 10 in After Reading, p. 96) for problems with:

Joining words

Conditional sentences

NOTE: *You may want to use the piece of writing that you already edited for conditional sentences for Activity 17.*

■ For the structures you edit, clearly show on your paper each step described in the Editing Guides. In addition, check your writing to see if you've used any of the word partnerships listed in "Using Vocabulary Accurately," p. 97. Correct any problems you find, and add examples to your word partnerships list. (See p. 150.)

Activity 19 • Class editing workshop: Edit for joining words and conditional sentences

At home: Follow the directions for Activity 18. In addition, write questions in the margins next to places where you're not sure of your editing choices.

In class: Working with a partner or a small group, trade papers, and talk about each other's questions and writing. Refer to the grammar charts in the chapter and in Appendix B and the Editing Guides in Appendix A to help you. If time permits, put examples from your writing and editing on the board to discuss as a class.

Looking at Patterns:

Relative Clauses and Complements

Overview of the Chapter

Read: "Four Skinny Trees" with Before Reading and After Reading Questions, p. 124

Write: Topics for Writing, p. 126

Edit: Grammar Previews, Tips, and Practice, p. 127
  Listening/Writing: Dictation/Dictocomp, p. 127
  6.1 The Structure of Relative Clauses, p. 127

Read: "Julia 'Butterfly' Hill" with Before Reading and After Reading Questions, p. 137

Write: Topics for Writing, p. 139

Edit: Grammar Previews, Tips, and Practice, p. 140
  Listening/Writing: Dictation/Dictocomp, p. 140
  6.2 Verb, Noun, and Adjective Complements, p. 141

Wrap-Up: p. 148

Grammar and Writing Goals

- To understand the structure and correct use of relative clauses
- To practice adding detail and information with relative clauses
- To understand the structure and correct use of patterns following verbs, nouns, and adjectives
- To practice editing:
  The structure and punctuation of relative clauses
  Patterns following verbs, nouns, and adjectives

Read

Before Reading

Respond to these questions to help you think about and understand the reading that follows.

1. Brainstorm: What types of trees do you know about? List them. Sketch a few different types of trees and compare how they look.

2. If you were a tree, what kind would you be? Why?

3. What do you think of when you hear the word "skinny"? How does "skinny" compare with other similar words such as "thin" or "slender"?

"Four Skinny Trees" by Sandra Cisneros

In this prose poem, Esperanza, the main character, describes four trees in the urban neighborhood where she lives, telling about her relationship with them and her feelings about them. Esperanza lives in the house on Mango Street with her sister Nenny, her parents, and other siblings. The author, Sandra Cisneros, uses short sentences and sentence fragments—common stylistic features of poems and stories.

They are the only ones who understand me. I am the only one who understands   1
them. Four skinny trees with skinny necks and pointy elbows like mine. Four who do
not belong here but are here. Four **raggedy excuses** planted by the city. From our
room we can hear them, but Nenny just sleeps and doesn't appreciate these things.

Their strength is secret. They send **ferocious** roots beneath the ground. They   5
grow up and they grow down and grab the earth between their hairy toes and bite the
sky with violent teeth and never quit their anger. This is how they **keep**.

Let one forget his reason for being, they'd all **droop** like **tulips** in a glass, each
with their arms around the other. Keep, keep, keep, trees say when I sleep. They teach.

When I am too sad and too skinny to keep keeping, when I am a tiny thing   10
against so many bricks, then it is I look at trees. When there is nothing left to look at
on this street. Four who grew despite concrete. Four who **reach** and do not forget to
reach. Four whose only reason is to be and be.

from *The House on Mango Street*, by Sandra Cisneros,
(New York: Vintage Contemporaries, 1989), pp 74–75

---

raggedy excuses: poor substitutes (for beautiful trees)   **droop:** drop or fall loosely from lack of water
ferocious: powerfully angry   **tulips:** type of flower with long, soft stems
keep: maintain or survive   **reach:** try to move forward

After Reading

Individually at home, or with a partner or a small group in class, write the answers to these questions to prepare for class discussion. Keep your answers in a notebook or binder to refer to later when you respond to the writing topics, develop your ideas for longer papers, or analyze your writing. Questions marked ¶ are especially suitable for paragraph-length answers that can be used later when you analyze your own writing.

1. Sketch the scene described in "Four Skinny Trees." Then compare your sketch with another person's version. Which sketches are the most accurate based on what the text tells us?

2. How does Esperanza describe the trees? What is unusual about her description? Why does she use "who" to talk about the trees?

3. Why does Esperanza call the trees "four raggedy excuses planted by the city"? Why does she call them "raggedy"? What does she mean by the word "excuses"?

4. What references to the city do you find in the reading? How do you think Esperanza feels about the city?

5. Throughout the piece, Esperanza compares the trees with humans. How do these comparisons help us understand Esperanza's personality and feelings? Using lines 5–9, respond to a and b below to help you answer this question:

   a. List words that describe the trees and make comparisons with humans.
   b. List words that tell us about Esperanza's personality and feelings.

6. Esperanza says an unusual thing: "keep keeping." Read and think about the meaning of the whole sentence. What word(s) could you use instead of "keeping"?

7. Esperanza says that the trees "teach" her, that they say "keep" when she sleeps. What do they teach her and do for her?

8. What feelings can we infer from the reading? What words give you these feelings? Underneath the headings below, describe the feelings you can infer and the words from the reading that give you these feelings.

Feelings	Words that give you these feelings
sadness, loneliness	"only ones who understand me"

9. *Situation:* Imagine that Esperanza has had a hard day at school and comes home feeling frustrated and sad. She has a conversation with Nenny, her sister, and tells her about the trees and how they help her.
   Topic: Write a dialogue between Esperanza and Nenny. In the dialogue, Esperanza describes the four trees and explains how they help her during difficult times. Include Esperanza's discussion about the trees and Nenny's responses to her sister's ideas and feelings.

¶10. What kind of person is Esperanza? Describe her and explain what she is like: her physical appearance, personality, and the way she responds to her environment.

¶11. What is Esperanza's relationship to the skinny trees? What do they mean to her? Why?

¶12. Discuss the line "Let one forget his reason for being, they'd all droop like tulips in a glass with their arms around the other." How does this image help you understand how the trees help Esperanza "keep keeping"?

Write

Topics for Writing

Respond in writing to one (or more) of the following topics.

1. Write about something or some place in the natural world (a tree, a beach, an animal, a sunset, the moon) that you find beautiful, interesting, relaxing, comforting, or inspiring.
   - Describe that thing or place in detail: color, shape, appearance, smell, actions, etc.
   - Discuss why you respond to this thing or place the way that you do.
   - Use the words *who, that, which, when, where,* etc. to introduce clauses in your description.

2. Write an essay about "Four Skinny Trees." Discuss why the trees are important to Esperanza, and explain what they mean to her. Use descriptive words and clauses to make your ideas clear.

3. Explain why the four trees are important to Esperanza. Then write about something or someone who is important to you (*your* "four skinny trees"). Discuss an example from the past that shows why the person or thing is meaningful. Be sure to make a connection between your ideas and Cisneros' ideas at the end of your paper.

4. Revise one of your written responses to After Reading questions 10–12. Expand your writing by adding descriptive words and clauses to make your writing clearer and more vivid, and to add details.

> ### Strategies for Writing: Generating and Developing Ideas
> For a description of ways to generate ideas, such as freewriting, listing, and brainstorming, as well as ways to develop and support your ideas, refer to Strategies for Writing, pp. 185–190.

Using Vocabulary Accurately

As you write about a reading, pay attention to key words and word partnerships, words that occur frequently with each other or that form fixed expressions. For more examples, see Reference Charts 2.1 and 2.2, pp. 172–174. Create your own word partnerships list (see p. 150).

Some key word partnerships for this reading follow. Locate key words in the reading or in Topics for Writing and notice how they are used. For practice, write sentences using some of these expressions.

to be a poor/bad excuse for (*something*)
to be important to (*someone*)
to be inspired by (*someone/something*)
to be an inspiration to (*someone*)

to pay attention to (*someone/something*)
an inspiring/comforting/relaxing place
a hostile environment

Edit: Grammar Previews, Tips, and Practice

Listening/Writing Activity: Dictation/Dictocomp

The following dictation/dictocomp text gives information related to the reading "Four Skinny Trees" on p. 124.

Close your book. As your teacher reads the sentences below (one time all the way through, then by clauses, then all the way through again), do the following:

- For a dictation, try to write exactly what you hear.
- For a dictocomp, take notes on key words and phrases.
- Then, individually or in groups, reconstruct the text, revising and correcting your own work and paying attention to problem areas.

> 1. Esperanza describes four skinny trees that she sees outside her bedroom window.
>
> 2. These four trees grow despite the concrete that surrounds them.
>
> 3. The trees, which are strong and have ferocious roots, speak to Esperanza.
>
> 4. But they seem to have no effect on her sister, who pays no attention to them.
>
> 5. These are trees whose strength inspires Esperanza.

6.1 The Structure of Relative Clauses

Preview: Assess What You Know

Compare A and B:

A. Esperanza writes about four trees. The trees grow outside her window.
B. Esperanza writes about four trees <u>that grow outside her window</u>.

Sentence B combines the two sentences in A into a single, more complex sentence. The underlined part of sentence B is called a relative clause (or an adjective clause). It describes the noun phrase "four trees."

Relative clauses are common in academic writing. Using them to describe nouns can make your writing clear and vivid as well as more sophisticated.

Use the text of the dictation above. For each statement do the following:

A. Identify relative clauses and the nouns they modify

- Draw [brackets] around each relative clause. (A relative clause is usually introduced by relative pronouns: *who, which, that, whose, whom, where, when.*)
- Draw an arrow from each relative clause to the noun it describes.
- Double underline the relative pronoun.

Example:

1. Esperanza describes four skinny trees [that she sees outside her bedroom window].

B. Identify the function of relative pronouns

For each relative clause in brackets, do the following:

- Circle the subject
- Underline the verb.
- Write "O" over the object if there is one.

Example:

1. Esperanza describes four skinny trees [that she sees outside her bedroom window].

In 2, 3, and 4, the relative pronoun is the subject. For those clauses:

- Name the noun that the relative pronoun refers to.
- Show the subject-verb agreement:

Sentence	Pronoun = Noun	Subject-Verb Agreement
2	*that = concrete*	*concrete . . . surrounds*
3		
4		

- What is the subject-verb agreement in the relative clause in sentence 5?

C. Punctuation and meaning of relative clauses

- Highlight relative clauses that are set off by commas. (The use of commas shows that the information in the clause is not essential to identify the noun.)
- Be prepared to explain how the clauses not set off by commas are needed to identify the noun being modified. Be prepared to explain how the clauses that are set off by commas do <u>not</u> seem necessary to identify the noun.

Grammar Tips: Check Your Work

With a partner or a small group, check your answers in the Preview by using the information in Charts 6.1A and 6.1B that follow. Be prepared to explain your answers by referring to specific sections of the charts. Figure out what you still need to learn.

CHART 6.1A   Relative Clause Structures

A relative clause is a modifier that describes a noun and is usually introduced by a relative pronoun *(who, whom, which, that, whose)* or a relative adverb *(when, where).* The chart is organized according to the function of the relative pronoun or adverbial.

Function of Relative Pronoun	Examples

1. Subject[1]
a. Person
 	
b. Thing
	a. The girl **who/that admires the trees** is encouraged by them.
	  The character **whose name is Esperanza** admires the trees.
	b. The trees **that/which inspire her** are skinny.
	  (The verb agrees with the noun that the relative pronoun represents: the <u>girl</u> **who** <u>admires</u> the trees; the <u>trees</u> **that** <u>inspire</u> her)
	  (When the relative pronoun is whose, *the verb agrees with the noun following* whose: a girl **whose** <u>name</u> <u>is</u> Esperanza; the trees **whose** <u>strength</u> <u>inspires</u> her)

2. Object[2] a. Person b. Thing	a. The girl **[that/whom] the trees inspire** is named Esperanza. b. The trees **[that/which] she sees from her window** are tall and skinny. *(Object relative pronouns can sometimes be omitted. Brackets show pronouns that can be omitted in examples 2a, 2b, 3a, and 3b; e.g.,* The trees ~~that~~ **she sees from her window** are tall and skinny.)

3. Object of Preposition
a. Person
 	
b. Thing
	a. The trees mean nothing to the sister **[that] Esperanza lives <u>with</u>.**
	   ... **[whom] Esperanza lives <u>with</u>.**
	  (most formal →) ... **<u>with</u> whom Esperanza lives.**
	b. The apartment **[that] Esperanza lives <u>in</u>** is on Mango Street.
	   ... **[which] Esperanza lives <u>in</u>** ...
	   ... **<u>in</u> which Esperanza lives** ...

4. Possessive a. Person b. Thing	a. The narrator is a young girl **whose name is Esperanza**. b. The story, **whose characters have difficult lives**, was written by Sandra Cisneros. *(Generally, in academic writing you should avoid* whose *when writing about inanimate things:* The story, **which features characters that have difficult lives**, was written by Sandra Cisneros.)
5. Adverbial a. Place b. Time	a. The street **where Esperanza lives** is a hostile, urban one. b. She thinks about a time **when she will be strong like the trees**.

[1]When the relative pronoun is the subject, the relative clause can sometimes be shortened to a reduced relative clause. See Reference Chart 6.1, p. 184, for information and examples.

[2]In informal speech and writing, *who* is sometimes used for an object relative pronoun. In careful writing, avoid *who* as a direct object or an object of a preposition.

CHART 6.1B   Punctuation and Meaning of Relative Clauses

The two kinds of relative clauses, restrictive and nonrestrictive, provide different kinds of information.

Type of Relative Clause	Examples

Restrictive
Defines or limits the meaning of the noun: It tells *which one* or *what kind*; it gives essential information so that we can identify the noun. No commas are used.
	a. The trees **that the young girl sees** are tall and skinny.
	   (The clause identifies the trees—it tells which ones.)
	b. Esperanza has a sister **who pays no attention to the trees**.
	   (The clause provides essential information about Esperanza's sister.)

Nonrestrictive
Gives extra, non-essential information about the noun. It is set off by commas. *(a, b)* It frequently follows a proper noun.
 	
c. You cannot use *that* as the relative pronoun in a nonrestrictive clause.
 	
d. You cannot delete the relative pronoun in a nonrestrictive clause. (See Reference Chart 6.1, p. 184, for ways to reduce some relative clauses.)
	a. The trees, **which are strong and have ferocious roots**, keep growing.
	   (These particular trees have already been identified in sentence a in the section above.)
	b. Esperanza's sister, **who shares a bedroom with Esperanza**, pays no attention to the trees.
	   (The writer tells more about the sister: she shares a room with Esperanza.)
	c. ⊘ The House on Mango Street, **that was written by Cisneros**, has won many awards.
	   Correction: …, **which was written by Cisneros**, …
	d. ⊘ This famous book, **Cisneros published in 1989**, has won many awards.
	   Correction: …, **which Cisneros published in 1989**, …

CHART 6.1C   Problems with Relative Clauses: Formation and Punctuation

Problem	Information / Tips	Examples
1. Missing subject	Identify the verb and make sure it has a subject. Add a relative pronoun if there is no subject.	a. ⊘ The trees are like people **always <u>comfort</u> and <u>teach</u> Esperanza**. *Correction:* … people **who always comfort and teach Esperanza**.

2. Double subjects	Identify verbs and subjects and eliminate extra subjects.
	   a. Two subjects in relative clause
	
	   b. Two subjects in the main clause
		
		a. ⊘ Esperanza <u>likes</u> the four trees **that they <u>grow</u> outside her window.** (*grow* has two subjects: *that, they*)
		   Correction: … trees **that ~~they~~ grow outside her window.**
		b. ⊘ **These four trees**, which <u>grow</u> outside her window, they <u>keep</u> her company as she grows up. (*keep* has two subjects: *trees, they*)
		   Correction: **These four trees**, which grow outside her window, **~~they~~ keep her company** …

Problem	Information/Tips	Examples
3. Double objects	When a relative pronoun is the object of the verb or of a preposition, do not repeat the pronoun object. Remove the second object.	a. ⊘ Nobody seems to recognize the feelings **that Esperanza has them about the trees**. (Objects: *that, them*) *Correction:* ... the feelings **that Esperanza has** ~~them~~ **about the trees**. b. ⊘ The trees struggle to survive despite the concrete **(that) they live in it**. (Objects: *that, it*) *Correction:* ... concrete **(that) they live in** ~~it~~.
4. Missing preposition	When a relative clause describes a noun that is the object of a preposition, you must include the preposition. Do not use *that* after a preposition; use *which*, *whom*, or *whose*.	a. ⊘ The trees struggle to survive despite the concrete **[that] they live**. *Correction:* ... the concrete **[that] they live in**. *Or* ... the concrete **in which they live**.
5. Incorrect punctuation	Use commas to set off a nonrestrictive clause. Proper nouns (*Esperanza, Mango Street*) and unique nouns (*her mother*) are always modified by *nonrestrictive* relative clauses.	a. ⊘ Esperanza **who is the main character in the story** lives in a house on Mango Street. *Correction:* Esperanza, **who is the main character in the story**, lives ... b. Esperanza's sister, **who shares a room with her**, pays no attention to the trees. (*Nonrestrictive is correct because Esperanza has only one sister.*)

CHART 6.1D   Problems with Relative Clauses: Unclear Modification

Other problems with relative clauses lead to sentences that make no sense because the modification is unclear. The reader has trouble figuring out which noun is being modified and, therefore, cannot understand what the sentence means.

Problem	Information/Tips	Examples
6. Misplaced relative clause	Place the relative clause as close as possible to the noun it modifies.	a. ⊘ The trees fight back to survive in the difficult urban environment, **which show their anger by reaching violently to the sky**. *Correction:* The trees, **which show their anger by reaching violently to the sky**, fight back to survive in the difficult urban environment.
7. Unclear reference to the noun	Identify the noun that the clause describes. Rewrite the sentence to make the noun and relative pronoun match (*who* does not match the noun *Esperanza's opinion*).	a. ⊘ I agree with Esperanza's opinion **who thinks that the city doesn't take care of its trees**. *Possible corrections:* I agree with Esperanza, **who thinks that the city doesn't take care of its trees**. (*who = Esperanza*) *Or* I agree with Esperanza's opinion, **which is that the city doesn't take care of its trees**. (*which = opinion*)

Problem	Information/Tips	Examples
8. A relative clause that modifies the entire sentence rather than a specific noun	Such structures are frequent in spoken English, but are generally not appropriate in writing. Rewrite the sentence to make the meaning clearer.	Esperanza describes the four skinny trees as "raggedy excuses," **which reveals her feelings about how poorly the city provides for them**. *(acceptable in speech)* *Correction for writing:* Esperanza reveals her feelings about how poorly the city provides for the trees by describing them as "raggedy excuses."
9. Misuse of the relative pronoun to connect ideas	Change the relative pronoun to one that matches the noun, or change the relative pronoun to a joining word.	⊘ Esperanza is different from her sister **that** the trees are not special. *Possible corrections:* Esperanza is different from her sister, **who** doesn't think the trees are special. *Or* Esperanza is different from her sister **because** she sees the trees as special while her sister doesn't.

Practice

Activity 1 • Analyze relative clauses in sentences from the reading

Using these sentences from "Four Skinny Trees," do the following:

- Put [brackets] around the relative clauses.
- Draw arrows to the nouns these clauses describe.
- Show the subject-verb agreement for each relative clause by (circling) the subject and underlining the verb.
- With a partner, discuss the author's choice of *who* when it doesn't refer to people:
   What other choices does she have?
   Why do you think she chose to use *who*?

1. They are the only ones [(who) <u>understand</u> me].

2. I am the only one who understands them.

3. Four who do not belong here but are here.

4. Four who grew despite concrete.

5. Four who reach and do not forget to reach.

6. Four whose only reason is to be and be.

Activity 2 • Write sentences with relative clauses

A. Using the sentences from the dictation, p. 127, follow the steps below:

- On separate paper, for each noun modified by a relative clause, write a different relative clause.
- Put [brackets] around your new clauses.
- Work with a partner to check the form and meaning of your clauses.

    Example: *Esperanza describes four skinny* **trees** *that she sees outside her bedroom window.*

    Possible new clauses:

    Esperanza describes four skinny trees [that inspire her].

    Esperanza describes four skinny trees [that her sister doesn't even notice].

B. Combine each of the following pairs of sentences into one more complex sentence by making the second sentence into a relative clause.

- On separate paper, write each new sentence and put [brackets] around the relative clause.
- Work with a partner to check the form and meaning of your sentences.

1. To Esperanza, the trees are like special people.

    These special people always comfort her when she is sad and teach her how to survive difficulties.

    To Esperanza, the trees are like special people [who always comfort her when she is sad and teach her how to survive difficulties].

2. Like the trees, Esperanza has to find a way to survive in harsh surroundings.

    The trees struggle to live in the concrete.

3. The trees grow in the hostile environment of the city.

    Esperanza lives in the city.

4. Four skinny trees become a symbol of strength for Esperanza.

    Esperanza is often lonely and discouraged.

5. The trees seem to have a persistence for living.

    Esperanza gains strength from this persistence.

6. Whenever Esperanza feels troubled, she relies on the trees for strength.

    The trees can give her strength.

Activity 3 • Edit sentences with relative clause problems

The following sentences from student writing contain some errors with relative clauses. With a partner or with the whole class, do the following:

- Put [brackets] around the relative clause.
- Figure out what the error is and identify it. (Refer to Charts 6.1A through 6.1D.)
- Correct the errors.

1. For many people, it is important to have a spiritual connection with something
   that
   [~~is~~ part of nature]. *(missing subject, Chart 6.1C, Problem 1)*

2. Nature, that can give people power, encouragement, and comfort, is accessible even in urban environments.

3. A person who she keeps her anger and loneliness to herself is likely to become bitter and frustrated.

4. We all need interaction with others who we can rely on them to support us during both difficult and easy times.

5. Like Esperanza, I find myself living in a place where I don't want to be in.

6. People are likely to be frustrated who are not living in agreeable situations.

7. Reading about Esperanza makes me realize how we can be supported by the natural world that we live.

Activity 4 • Write and analyze a chalkboard composition

Step 1: Write the paragraph

As a class or in groups, work together to develop a paragraph on the chalkboard to describe what you can see outside your classroom window. Also, describe your response (reaction) to the scene. In your paragraph:

- Try to include some natural features.
- Describe this view for someone who has never been in your classroom.
- Include some relative clauses in your description.

Example paragraph

Only the first relative clause has been identified. Can you find the others?[3]

> Our classroom is on the first floor in the Humanities Building. When you look   1
> out the large windows on the east wall, you can see a beautiful green lawn and five   2
> small trees with bright green leaves. Because our building is only eight years old, the   3
> trees [(that) grow outside our window] are relatively young. The tree on the left is the   4
> tallest and has the biggest trunk. The other four trees, which seem to be a different   5
> species, are fuller and have white blossoms. The trees remind us of a family that has   6
> one strong older brother and four younger sisters who wear flowers in their hair.   7
> When we look out the window during our class, the trees make me think of times   8
> that my family would spend together far from the city.   9

Step 2: Analyze the paragraph

For the paragraph(s) the class writes, do the following:

- Identify all the relative clauses by putting [brackets] around them.
- Draw arrows from the relative clauses to the nouns they describe.
- Circle the subjects of the relative clauses and underline the verbs in the clauses.
- Double underline the relative pronouns.

     In which clauses could you omit the relative pronoun? Put an "X" on any object pro-
     nouns you can omit. (Note: In the example paragraph, you can omit *that* in the last
     sentence.)

Activity 5 • Write and edit your own relative clauses

Individually at your desk or with a partner or a small group at the board, look at Topics for
Writing #1, p. 126, and follow the directions as given.

- Write at least one paragraph. Begin your paper in this way:

  An event ⎫
  A place ⎬ that I find ⎧ inspiring ⎫
  An animal⎮   ⎪ interesting ⎬ is _____.
  etc.   ⎭   ⎪ comforting ⎪
                      ⎩ etc.   ⎭

- When you have finished, follow the analysis procedures in Step 2 in Activity 4.
- Correct any problems (refer to Charts 6.1A through 6.1D).

---

[3]Note that this example paragraph has reduced relative clauses: *the large windows [on the east wall]*
(reduced from *the large windows which are on the east wall*), and *the tree [on the left]* (reduced from *the tree
which is on the left*). See Reference Chart 6.1, p. 184.

Activity 6 • Edit student writing for relative clauses and parallel structure

- Use Editing Guides 6.1, p. 157, and 5.2, p. 156, to help you analyze this piece of student writing and correct the errors.

- Find examples of errors to discuss with the class. (You will find five relative clauses with problems, including the example, and two errors in parallel structure.)

"Four Skinny Trees," written by Sandra Cisneros, is a prose poem about the four   1

skinny trees outside the window of the narrator, Esperanza. The four trees seem   2

important to the narrator because they both share the same similarities, *which are that they're* ~~who are~~   3

skinny and do not belong there. The narrator feels that only she can understand the   4

trees, and only the trees, that shares her feelings, can understand her. When she feels   5

sad, lonely, hopeless, and giving up, then it is these trees that she looks at, which gives   6

her the encouragement not to give up so easily. Even though the trees do not seem to   7

belong in this concrete where they are growing in, their will to live is strong. Cisneros   8

writes, "They send ferocious roots beneath the ground, grow up and down grabbing   9

the earth between their hairy toes and bite the sky with their violent teeth and never   10

seem to quit their anger." Because of this, the skinny trees give the narrator the   11

strength and supportive she needs to keep growing in a society which she feels like   12

she doesn't belong in it.   13

Activity 7 • Improve your writing by adding relative clauses

Using a piece of writing from After Reading, p. 125, or Topics for Writing, p. 126, practice adding detail and information with relative clauses by doing the following:

- Find places in your writing where the description or ideas could be clarified or expanded with relative clauses. Also look for short, choppy sentences that could be combined by using relative clauses (as in Activity 2B). Underline these places.

- Trade papers with a partner and help each other find additional places where you could use relative clauses to develop ideas and description or combine sentences.

- Use relative clauses to add detail and information to the places you identified in the steps above.

Activity 8 • Edit your writing for relative clauses

- Trade your expanded writing from Activity 7 with a partner and check each other's work for accuracy. Use Editing Guide 6.1, p. 157, to help you.

- Highlight structures that you think need correction.

- Discuss your suggestions for correction with your partner.

Read

Before Reading

Respond to these questions to help you think about and understand the reading that follows.

1. Imagine a giant tree, one that is a thousand years old and 180 feet high and in a forest of similar huge trees. Now imagine building a platform in that tree and living in it— for a week, a month, a year. What might that experience be like?

2. Look up the word "legacy" in your dictionary. How do our natural resources—water, forests, sources of energy— relate to the word "legacy."

"Julia 'Butterfly' Hill" by Stephen Browning

When Julia Hill was 22 years old, she was nearly killed in a car accident. This life-threatening experience inspired her to set out for the Far East on a spiritual journey. Her route led her through California, and the reading that follows describes the turn her life took at that point.

When Julia "Butterfly" Hill came to the West Coast in 1997, she didn't plan to spend the next two years sitting in a tree. But she discovered some other young people in California trying to prevent the logging of some of the last **remnants** of the great redwood forest that once stretched along 400 miles of coastline from Southern Oregon to Big Sur, just south of Monterey Bay, California. So it was that the 23-year-old Julia decided to climb into a 180-foot-tall, thousand-year-old California Coast Redwood tree, which she eventually named Luna, in an attempt to save it and the forest in which it grew.

After a month in the tree, she had broken the American record for the longest time tree-sitting. Then after 42 days, she broke the world record. After 100 days, it became clear that she was not just tree-sitting, but was "living" there, and plainly intended to continue living there until her tree and its forest were permanently protected.

She remained sitting in the tree until December 18, 1999—two years and eight days after she first climbed up into its branches. She had reached an agreement with the lumber company to spare the tree and to create a three-acre **buffer zone**. Like Esperanza in "Four Skinny Trees," who developed a close relationship with the trees outside her window, Hill formed a **spiritual bond** with Luna that helped to give her the **stamina** and **conviction** to save it. She says,

> I didn't go into the tree looking to become an activist. I didn't come to California looking to become an activist. I had a question in my heart that said, "I have to be more than what society tells me and … what my parents taught me, [more than] believing in certain laws so that I can go to a better hereafter."

1

5

10

15

20

---

remnants: remains
buffer zone: neutral area (between the tree and the loggers)
spiritual bond: deep connection

stamina: inner strength
conviction: determination

Hill wants the legacy she leaves not to be "how many houses and cars" she can   25
buy or the amount of "jewelry and clothes" she can accumulate. In her words, "A
steering wheel slamming into my skull in a car wreck in August of 1996 steered me in
a new direction and said, 'There's got to be something more.' And I went in search of
that."

Since her tree-sitting experience, Hill has continued working towards that "some-   30
thing more." For example, in July of 2002 she went to Ecuador to support the native
Mindo community, who were working to halt construction of a new oil pipeline
through the Amazon rainforests. After visiting the protected areas where trees were
being illegally cut down, she went to the capital, Quito, to participate in a meeting
with community representatives and oil company officials. But when the company   35
cancelled the meeting, Hill and 50 Ecuadorians staged a protest outside the oil company's offices. Hill and seven other protesters were arrested and jailed, and Hill was
subsequently deported from Ecuador to the United States. Hill questions this outcome and what she sees as a contradiction on the part of the government:

Why is it that transnational oil companies can come to Ecuador, invade people's   40
lands, **ravage** ecosystems, and be welcomed by the Ecuadorian government, and
those who come to lend their solidarity to those **impacted** by these projects are mis-
treated and deported?

For her actions, both during the time she lived in the giant redwood and her ef-
forts to protect trees in South America, Julia "Butterfly" Hill has become the youngest   45
person to be honored in the Ecology Hall of Fame. She has written about her tree-sitting experience in her book *The Legacy of Luna: The Story of a Tree, a Woman and the
Struggle to Save the Redwoods*. Her practical tips for environmentally sound living appear in her book *One Makes the Difference: Inspiring Actions that Change Our World*.

"Julia 'Butterfly' Hill" was based on the following various online sources:
http://www.ecotopia.org/ehof/hill/index.html,
http://www.ecotopia.org/ehof/hill/bio.html, http://www.circleoflifefoundation.org/news/ecuador.html,
http://www.circleoflifefoundation.org/inspiration/spiritactive.html, and http://www.amazonwatch.org.

---

ravage: devastate; heavily destroy   **impacted:** affected

After Reading

Individually at home, or with a partner or a small group in class, write the answers to these
questions to prepare for class discussion. Keep your answers in a notebook or binder to refer
to later when you respond to the writing topics, develop your ideas for longer papers, or analyze your writing. Questions marked ¶ are especially suitable for paragraph-length answers
that can be used later when you analyze your own writing.

1. Describe Julia "Butterfly" Hill: her age, her values, her life experience.

2. Why did Hill first travel to California? What caused her to remain there?

3. What was Hill attempting to accomplish by living in the giant redwood? Was she
   successful?

4. Explain the connection between Hill's serious car accident and her desire to save
   the ancient trees. What does she mean by "There's got to be something more" than
   to leave the legacy of "how many houses and cars" she can buy or the amount of
   "jewelry and clothes" she can accumulate?

5. Why did Hill go to Ecuador? Who are the Mindo people and why did she want to work with them? What happened during her stay in Ecuador?

¶ 6. Explain Hill's view of the Ecuadorian government: its support for the oil companies and its lack of support for the people who are affected by corporate policy.

¶ 7. For her actions, Hill was deported from Ecuador and returned to the United States. In your opinion, was she successful or unsuccessful in achieving her goals?

¶ 8. The reading compares Esperanza from "Four Skinny Trees" with Julia Hill and mentions that "Hill formed a spiritual bond with Luna that helped to give her the stamina and conviction to save it." How does this quote show a connection between the relationship that Esperanza has with her trees and the relationship that Hill has with Luna?

Write

Topics for Writing

Respond in writing to one (or more) of the following topics.

1. Was Julia "Butterfly" Hill successful in achieving her goals? As you answer this question, consider Hill's actions both in the redwood forest of California and the rainforest of Ecuador. In developing your response, think about the following: her commitment to preserving ancient trees and other natural resources; her actions and the response of government, business, and the media; her desire to find something "more."

2. How are Julia Hill and Esperanza similar? How are they different? Compare the two: their personalities, their beliefs, their actions, their interactions with the natural world.

3. Using your imagination and the limited information from the reading, write about what you think Hill's experience living in the redwood tree for two years was like: how she survived, how she kept contact with the outside world, how she coped with the weather, her loneliness, her fear.

4. As an activist, Julia Hill believes in the conservation of the forests so strongly that she is willing to take risks that could endanger her life or cause her to be arrested. Explain what causes her to take such unusual actions. (Optional: Give your opinion. Do you admire Hill or disapprove of her actions? Why?)

5. Compare your ideas and beliefs to those of Julia Hill. In an essay, first give a summary of the reading that focuses on Hill's purpose for her actions. Then discuss an example that is important to you: an environmental issue, a public protest, an experience with nature, or your ideas about "finding something more." In your paper, show the connection between your example and the story of Julia Hill.

6. Sitting in Luna or protesting on the steps of the oil companies are acts of civil disobedience, nonviolent resistance for the purpose of making change in policy or laws. Other famous people such as Mahatma Gandhi and Martin Luther King have encouraged similar actions to produce social change. Using the Internet or other sources, find information about people who have practiced civil disobedience. Compare the actions and successes of the person you researched with the actions and successes of Julia Hill.

> ### Strategies for Writing: Generating and Developing Ideas
>
> For a description of ways to generate ideas, such as freewriting, listing, and brainstorming, as well as ways to develop and support your ideas, refer to Strategies for Writing, pp. 185–190.

Using Vocabulary Accurately

As you write about a reading, pay attention to key words and word partnerships, words that occur frequently with each other or that form fixed expressions. For more examples, see Reference Charts 2.1 and 2.2, pp. 172–174. Create your own word partnerships list (see p. 150).

   Some key word partnerships for this reading follow. Locate key words in the reading or in Topics for Writing and notice how they are used. For practice, write sentences using some of these expressions.

to spend time (*doing something*)
to be/go/fight against (*something*)
to be/find something more
   (*than someone tells you*)
to do something meaningful for
   (*someone/society*)
to have a passion for (*something*)
to form a bond with (*someone/something*)

to have a connection to nature/
   to the natural world
to live in a tree
to protect the environment
to break/set a record
to give support to (*someone*)
an environmental activist
an act of civil disobedience

Edit: Grammar Previews, Tips, and Practice

Listening/Writing Activity: Dictation/Dictocomp

The following dictation/dictocomp text gives information related to the reading "Julia 'Butterfly' Hill," on p. 137.

Close your book. As your teacher reads the sentences below (one time all the way through, then by clauses, then all the way through again), do the following:

- For a dictation, try to write exactly what you hear.

- For a dictocomp, take notes on key words and phrases.

- Then, individually or in groups, reconstruct the text, revising and correcting your work and paying attention to problem areas.

1. When Julia "Butterfly" Hill arrived in California, she discovered that young people were trying to prevent the logging of ancient redwood trees.

2. Inspired by their actions, Hill decided to climb into a 180-foot-tall redwood tree.

3. People wondered how long she could sit in the tree, and she surprised them by living there for two years.

4. Hill developed a bond with the tree that helped to give her the stamina and conviction to save it.

5. She later continued working toward her goal of preserving forests in Ecuador, where she led protests against oil companies that wanted to construct pipelines in protected areas.

6. Julia Hill's work as an environmentalist shows that working to make change can involve taking risks.

6.2 Verb, Noun, and Adjective Complements

Preview: Assess What You Know

In Chapter 3, section 3.3 showed structures used after verbs to report ideas, statements, and thoughts. Some structures reviewed there were: *that* clauses, *wh-* clauses, *whether/if* clauses, and noun phrases. (See Chart 3.3A, p. 61, and Reference Chart 3.2, p. 178.) Verbs, nouns, and adjectives can also be followed by other structures, such as infinitives (*to go, to live*) and gerunds (*going, living*). All these structures are called *complements* because they complete the meaning of the verb, noun, or adjective.

To assess what you know about patterns following verbs, examine the dictation and do the following:

- Underline the verbs and double underline the verb forms or clauses following the verbs.
- Try to identify the structure that you have double underlined. Look for these patterns following verbs:

  + *to* + verb   + verb + *-ing*   + *wh-* clause   + *that* clause

> *that clause*
>
> 1. When Julia "Butterfly" Hill arrived in California, she <u>discovered</u> <u>that young</u>
>   *to + verb*
>   <u>people were trying to prevent the logging of ancient redwood trees</u>.[4]

- Look for other examples of infinitives (*to* + verb) or gerunds (verb + *-ing*) in the dictation sentences that follow nouns and adjectives and double underline them. Underline the nouns and adjectives and label the part of speech.

Example:
>   *nouns*
>
> 4. Hill developed a bond with the tree that helped to give her <u>the stamina and conviction</u> to save it.

---

[4]In this sentence there are complements after each of the two verbs (*discovered* and *were trying*). It is not uncommon in complex sentences to have complements within complements.

Grammar Tips: Check Your Work

With a partner or a small group, check your answers in the Preview by using the information in Charts 6.2A and 6.2B that follow. Be prepared to explain your answers by referring to specific sections of the chart. Figure out what you still need to learn.

CHART 6.2A   Verb Complements[5]

When a verb is followed by another verb structure, that second structure—called a verb complement—can be in several different patterns. The choice of pattern depends on the *first verb*. There are no simple rules about which verbs take which pattern, so you have to learn them by memorization. Some verbs can be followed by only one pattern; some can be followed by two, and some by three.

A list of reporting verbs and their patterns appears in Reference Chart 3.2, p. 178. The verbs listed in the chart below are the verbs that appear in the patterns used most frequently in academic writing.

Complement Pattern Following the First Verb	Example	Common Verbs that Take the Pattern
1a. + *to* + verb (infinitive)	a. Julia Hill <u>didn't intend</u> <u>to become</u> an activist.	a. appear, attempt, be found, begin, continue, decide, fail, intend, seem, tend, try, want, work
b. + noun/pronoun + *to* + verb	b. Her auto accident <u>inspired</u> <u>her</u> <u>to set out</u> for the Far East on a spiritual quest.	b. advise, allow, cause, enable, expect, find, force, get, inspire, require, want *The infinitive (to + verb) often expresses an action that comes after the action of the first verb.*
2. + verb + *-ing* (gerund)	She <u>continued</u> <u>sitting</u> in the tree for two years.	begin, be used for, continue, experience, go, go on, involve, keep, keep on, remain, remember, spend (time, etc.), start, stop
3. + noun/pronoun + simple form of verb	Hill <u>made</u> <u>the lumber company</u> <u>pay</u> attention to her actions.	have, help, let, make *(Help can also be followed by to + verb after the noun or pronoun; e.g., ... help them <u>see</u> ... or ... help them <u>to see</u> ...)*
4. + *wh-* clause or + *that* clause	Many people <u>didn't understand</u> <u>how she could live in the tree so long</u>.	explain, know, realize, see, show, understand
5. + *that* clause	Hill <u>believes</u> <u>that one person can make a difference</u>.	argue, believe, conclude, ensure, feel, find, indicate, know, mean, realize, say, see, show, suggest, suppose, think

Complement Pattern Following the First Verb	Example	Common Verbs that Take the Pattern
6. + *that* clause with simple form of verb *(subjunctive)*[6]	Julia's supporters <u>suggested</u> <u>that she continue her work in other rainforest areas</u>.	advise, agree, ask, demand, insist, order, prefer, propose, recommend, request, require, stipulate, suggest, urge *(See pattern 9 in Chart 6.2B for related nouns.)*

[5]See Chapter 3, Chart 3.3A and B, and Reference Chart 3.2, p. 178, for further information about *that* clauses, *wh-* clauses, and direct quotations after certain verbs.

[6]These verbs (and their related nouns, see Chart 6.2B, pattern 9) have a common meaning: The subject of the first verb is trying to control or bring about the action in the *that* clause. In the example, the supporters wanted to bring about the action in the *that* clause, i.e., they wanted Julia to continue her work. The control can be strong (e.g., *demand, insist, require*) or weak (e.g., *ask, request, suggest, recommend*).

CHART 6.2B Noun and Adjective Complements

Infinitives, gerunds, and *that* clauses can also appear after adjectives and abstract nouns. These patterns often occur in academic writing.

Complement Pattern Following a Noun or Adjective	Example	Common Abstract Nouns and Adjectives that Can Take the Pattern
7. + *to* + verb *(infinitive)*	a. She made an <u>attempt</u> <u>to save</u> the redwood tree. b. It must have been <u>difficult</u> <u>to live</u> for so long in that situation.	a. **Nouns:** ability, capacity, chance, decision, desire, effort, failure, inability, plan, opportunity, power, right, tendency, willingness b. **Adjectives:** determined, difficult, due, easy, free, hard, important, (im)possible, shocked, (un)able, (un)likely, (un)willing
8. + *that* clause	a. The <u>fact</u> <u>that she lived in a tree for two years</u> made Julia Hill something of a celebrity.[7] b. It became <u>clear</u> <u>that she was not just tree-sitting</u>.	a. **Nouns:** assumption, belief, conclusion, desire, determination, doubt, hope, idea, notion, possibility, reason, wish b. **Adjectives:** apparent, certain, clear, confident, (im)possible, sure, surprised, true, (un)likely
9. + *that* clause with the simple form of the verb *(subjunctive)*	a. Hill ignored the <u>demand</u> <u>that she come down</u> from the tree. b. It was <u>essential</u> <u>that she show</u> her commitment to saving the trees.	a. **Nouns:** advice, claim, demand, observation, point, recommendation, suggestion *(See pattern 6 in Chart 6.2A for the identical pattern with related verbs.)* b. **Adjectives:** essential, important, necessary, vital
10. + preposition + verb + *-ing*	a. Julia was <u>enthusiastic</u> <u>about</u> <u>living</u> in the tree. b. Julia had no <u>doubts</u> <u>about</u> <u>going</u> to Ecuador.	*(See Reference Chart 2.2, p. 174, sections C and D, for a list of common adjective and noun + preposition combinations.)*

Complement Pattern Following a Noun or Adjective	Example	Common Abstract Nouns and Adjectives that Can Take the Pattern
11. + *of* + verb + *-ing*[8] (nouns only)	She continues working towards her <u>goal</u> <u>of</u> <u>finding</u> meaning in her life.	chance, cost, effect, idea, means, method, possibility, problem, process, risk, way
12. + verb + *-ing* (special expressions)	She didn't plan to <u>spend the next two years</u> <u>sitting</u> in a tree.	*Verb* + *-ing* *occurs after these common expressions:* spend (waste) time/money, have difficulty/trouble, have a hard/difficult time, be accustomed to, be used to, look forward to, be opposed to

[7]These structures may look like relative clauses, but they are not. Compare: Relative clause: *Julia had a belief <u>that inspired many followers</u>. (She had a <u>belief</u>. The <u>belief</u> inspired many followers.)* When the sentences are combined, *belief* is replaced by the relative pronoun *that*. (*that* = belief) Abstract noun + *that* complement: *Julia had a belief <u>that the redwood trees could be saved</u>. (Julia had a belief. The redwood trees could be saved.)* Here, *that* is not a relative pronoun but acts like an equal sign: *belief = the redwood trees could be saved.*

[8]The gerund (verb + *-ing* form) always occurs after prepositions (except *to* when it is part of an infinitive as in patterns 1 and 7) when a verb form is needed. For example, *Julia didn't worry <u>about upsetting</u> the lumber companies by living in the tree. She had a good reason <u>for staying</u> there.* See Reference Chart 2.2, pp. 173–174, for examples of preposition combinations with verbs, nouns, and adjectives.

CHART 6.2C	**Common Problems with Complements**	
Problem	**Examples**	**Corrections**
1. Leaving out *to* in the infinitive	⊘ Hill <u>wants</u> the companies **stop** cutting down the trees.	Hill <u>wants</u> the companies **to stop** cutting down the trees.
2. Not using verb + *-ing* after a preposition	a. ⊘ Nothing could stop her <u>from</u> **protect** the trees. b. ⊘ She devoted herself <u>to</u> **protect** trees.	a. Nothing could stop her <u>from</u> **protecting** the trees. b. She devoted herself <u>to</u> **protecting** trees.
3. Using the wrong complement	⊘ Hill did not stop trying to reach her <u>goal</u> **that she prevented** them from destroying the rainforests.	Hill did not stop trying to reach her <u>goal</u> **of preventing** them from destroying the rainforests. (*That clause after* goal *is inappropriate. See Chart 6.2B, pattern 11.*)

4. Leaving out the verb in a *that* clause	⊘ The article <u>illustrates</u> **that Hill's remarkable stay of over two years in a redwood tree**.	The article <u>illustrates</u> **that Hill's remarkable stay of over two years in a redwood tree** <u>had a positive outcome</u>.
		    (*Add a verb to the* that *clause.*)
		Or
		The article **describes** Hill's remarkable stay of over two years in a redwood tree.
		    (*Change the main verb.*)

Problem	Examples	Corrections
5. Using two "markers" of a complement *(Both that and how mark complement clauses: Use only one marker.)*	⊘ This article <u>shows</u> **that how** effective one person's actions can be.	This article <u>shows</u> **how** effective one person's actions can be. *Or* This article <u>shows</u> **that** one person's actions can be highly effective.
6. Not following *demand, suggest, recommend, urge* with a *that* clause + simple verb form	⊘ The lumber company <u>demanded</u> Hill **to come down** from the tree.	The lumber company <u>demanded</u> **that Hill come down from the tree**. *(See Chart 6.2A, pattern 6.)* *Or* The lumber company <u>**told**</u> Hill **to come down** from the tree. *(Change the verb.)*
7. Using the wrong complement after verbs of perception *(see, hear, feel)*	a. ⊘ A large gathering of people <u>heard</u> Hill **to protest** against the oil companies on the street in Ecuador. b. ⊘ The reporters <u>saw</u> Julia **was sitting** in the redwood tree.	a. A large gathering of people <u>heard</u> Hill **protesting** (or **protest**) against the oil companies ... b. The reporters <u>saw</u> Julia **sitting** in the redwood tree. *(After verbs of perception, use verb + -ing or simple form, as appropriate.)*

Practice

Activity 9 • Analyze the reading to find examples of complements

Using the portion assigned to you of "Julia 'Butterfly' Hill," do the following:

- Find examples of at least five patterns from those listed in Charts 6.2A and 6.2B.
- <u>Underline</u> the verb/noun/adjective + complement and write the number of the pattern in the margin.
- Add new examples of verbs/adjectives/nouns that are followed by complements to the appropriate lists in the charts.
- Compare and discuss your findings with the class.

Activity 10 • Compose sentences using verb complements

Using the context of the reading or another topic, practice using verb complement patterns by following the steps below:

- On a small index card, write one of the verbs from the common verbs column in Chart 6.2A, and also write its associated pattern, for example:

> *enable*   verb + noun/pronoun + to + verb   (1b)

- Find a partner, and tell your partner your verb (but don't show your card). Your partner will make a sentence using the verb with the appropriate pattern.

  Example: *Living in a tree for two years enabled Julia Hill to save many redwoods.*

  If the sentence is incorrect, help your partner to correct the sentence.

- Then your partner will tell you his/her verb and you will make a sentence. When you have both made correct sentences, exchange cards, and move on to new partners.

- Continue to practice making sentences with new partners and exchanging cards as many times as possible.

Activity 11 • Write sentences with complements of nouns, adjectives, and special expressions

Using the context of the readings, "Four Skinny Trees" or "Julia 'Butterfly' Hill," complete the sentences below by doing the following:

- Add *to* + verb, verb + *-ing*, or a *that* clause to complement the underlined noun, adjective, or special expression.

- Refer to Chart 6.2B for examples of patterns and to check your work.

1. Esperanza is <u>sad</u> *to see the poor condition of her four friends, the trees outside her window.*

2. As a young, sensitive girl, Esperanza is <u>surprised</u> _____

   _____

3. She <u>has a difficult time</u> _____

4. From looking at the trees, Esperanza gets <u>inspiration and strength</u> _____

   _____

5. Julia Hill had the <u>desire and will</u> _____

6. After two years of living in harsh conditions, Hill <u>got used to</u> _____

   _____

7. Because she is <u>determined</u> _____

8. In spite of the obstacles she has faced, Hill <u>looks forward to</u> _____

   _____

Activity 12 • Identify and correct errors with complements of verbs, nouns, and adjectives

The sentences that follow have problems in complements of verbs, nouns, or adjectives. To help you locate the errors do the following:

- <u>Underline</u> the verbs, nouns, or adjectives that are followed by complements and <u>double underline</u> the complements.

- In the left margin, identify the appropriate pattern in Charts 6.2A and 6.2B.

- Make corrections and check your work with a partner or a small group.

/2 1. Hill <u>spent a long time</u> <u>to sit</u> in the tree.

    sitting (handwritten above "to sit")

  2. The protesters were very emotional and some started to shouted when the police came.

  3. Hill went to Ecuador because she wanted the people feel supported.

  4. The oil company didn't let the protesters to demonstrate outside their building.

  5. Many environmentalists suggested Julia to continue her protests.

  6. These activists are impressed with Julia's ability to getting results.

  7. Hill seems confident to get the support of people concerned with protection of our natural resources.

  8. There is a good possibility her starting new environmental organizations.

Activity 13 • Edit student writing for verb complements

- Use Editing Guide 6.2, p. 157, to help you analyze this piece of student writing and correct the errors.
- Highlight at least four correct forms of verbs + complements and label them in the left margin according to the patterns in Chart 6.2A.
- With a different color, highlight four examples of incorrect forms of verbs + complements. Correct the errors and label the patterns according to Chart 6.2A.

5   Julia Hill <u>believes</u> <u>that we must protect trees</u> to benefit people and the earth   1

and that it is important to continue working toward "something more." Hill keeps try-   2

ing her best to do what she can to protect the environment, no matter what kinds of   3

difficulties she meets. To save Luna, a 180-foot-tall, thousand-year-old California   4

Coast redwood, she decided to sit in the tree and ended up to live in the tree for more   5

than two years. Her goal was to make the lumber companies guaranteed protection   6

for Luna and other old-growth redwoods. Continuing to pursue her convictions, Hill   7

went to Ecuador to support the native protests to protect trees in the Amazon rain-   8

forests. Although Hill experienced be arrested and deported by the local government,   9

she still knew that how important her work was to the Mindo community. Her dili-   10

gent actions in California and South America caused many people to admire her ef-   11

forts on behalf of the people and forests. Around the world, people saw how Hill was   12

continuing to pursue danger and hardship to preserve the legacy of the earth's natu-   13

ral resources for future generations.   14

Wrap-Up

Activity 14 • Edit your writing for relative clauses and complements

- Using Editing Guides 6.1 and 6.2, p. 157, and other information in this chapter, edit a piece of your own writing (from Topics for Writing, p. 126 or p. 139, or from After Reading questions 10–12, p. 126, or questions 6–8, p. 139) for problems with:

  relative clauses

  complements

- For the structures you edit, clearly show on your paper each step described in the Editing Guides. In addition, check your writing to see if you've used any of the word partnerships listed in "Using Vocabulary Accurately," p. 127 or p. 140. Correct any problems you find, and add examples to your word partnerships list. (See p. 150.)

Activity 15 • Class editing workshop: Edit for relative clauses and complements

At home: Follow the directions for Activity 14. In addition, write questions in the margins next to places where you're not sure of your editing choices.

In class: Working with a partner or a small group, trade papers, and talk about each other's questions and writing. Refer to the grammar charts in the chapter and in Appendix B and the Editing Guides in Appendix A to help you. If time permits, put examples from your writing and editing on the board to discuss as a class.

Appendix A: References for Editing

For each chapter, see also the Reference Charts in Appendix B, beginning on p. 159.

Creating Your Own Reference Materials

Grammar Reference Cards

Grammar Reference Cards are index cards with examples and grammar tips that you can use as a reference tool when you write papers for English or other classes. You create the cards based on the grammar structures you need to be reminded about when writing and editing your essays. Punch a hole in the upper left hand corner of your cards and keep them together with a metal ring. Use your teacher's comments or what you learn from this book to help you figure out what to include on your cards.

For example, if you're having trouble with tense shifts and consistency, create a reference card like the one shown below. Use information from the charts in the chapters as well as examples from your paper to help you include important information and reminders.

Verb Tenses for Generalizations and Support

Grammar Tips

1. Use present tense for statements of fact, opinion, or general truth.
2. Use a past tense (past, past progressive, or past perfect) for examples from the past that support generalizations.

Example Sentences

1. Humorous situations <u>can arise</u> from cross-cultural communication. (general truth)
2. People traveling in foreign countries usually <u>experience</u> some type of misunderstanding due to problems in communication. (fact)
3. When my friend <u>traveled</u> in Mexico last summer, she <u>had</u> a humorous interaction with a hotel manager. (past example)
4. Two days after she <u>met</u> him, she <u>told</u> him that she <u>was embarazada</u> because she couldn't remember his name. (past example)
5. ⊘ Later she <u>is</u> very embarrassed to find out that embarazada means "pregnant" in Spanish. (past example)

To fix it

Ask yourself: Do the tenses and time expressions match?

Later = last summer in Mexico; is (present) should be <u>was</u> (past)

Vocabulary Reference Lists

Word Partnerships

Create your own word partnerships list with key words and fixed expressions from the readings or from your teacher's notations on your papers. You can learn these special expressions through memorization and practice. Categorize them in a way that makes sense to you and write examples and notes to help you remember how to use them correctly. Occasionally ask your teacher or a partner to check your list to be sure that your sentences with the key words are accurate. If you want, you can use index cards for your word partnerships and information.

Word Partnerships List
Nouns
a drastic departure
Her reaction to the situation was a drastic departure from her normal behavior.
Verbs
to be concerned about (needs a form of be)
He was concerned about making the right decision. NOT: He concerned about

Word Forms

Keeping lists and examples of troublesome word forms, including irregular verb forms and noncount nouns, will help you learn how to use them correctly. These lists will also give you a reference sheet to use when you write papers for your college classes. A good way to develop your list is to record the different forms of words according to their parts of speech.

Word Forms List

adjective	noun	verb	adverb
patient	patience	----	patiently
He is a patient person.	My mother has a lot of patience with my brother.		I waited patiently for my friend to arrive.

Editing Guides

The Editing Guides that follow cover the main grammar points in each chapter. They are designed to help you analyze your writing so that you can "see" problem areas and correct them on your own. The purpose of the guides is to help you

- review and learn the grammar information in the chapters;
- discover your own language patterns, including your patterns of error;
- develop a system for editing;
- become more confident and independent in your ability to find and correct problems.

Suggestions for Using the Editing Guides

- Pick the guides that cover the grammar you need to work on.
- Follow the steps carefully and show all the markings on your paper.
- Edit for one or possibly two items only, especially when first beginning to use the guides.
- If you have time, ask someone to review your markings and corrections.

Chapter 1

The steps below will help you edit your writing. Follow these steps sequentially, or work through only the sections that cover grammar you know you need to work on. Refer to the Chapter 1 charts and information noted to help you.

1.1 Articles and Nouns
(See Charts 1.1B and 1.1C, pp. 7–8, and Reference Charts 1.4 and 1.5, pp. 163–166.)

1. Identify and highlight common nouns.
2. Ask yourself: What kind of noun is it (count or noncount)? Then check:
   - Count nouns need one of the following:
     a. an indefinite article: *a, an, (some/any)*;
     b. another type of determiner: *this/that*; a possessive pronoun *(my, his, their)*;
     c. the plural form: Add -*s*;
     d. a definite article: *the*. (Use *the* only when the specific person, thing, or action you are referring to has been identified.)
   - Noncount nouns:
     a. do not take indefinite articles: *a, an* (~~an~~ indirectness).
     b. do not take plural forms: *information~~s~~*.
     c. take the definite article *the* for something that has already been introduced to the reader or that the reader can identify in some way.
3. Make corrections:
   - to count nouns by adding articles or forming plurals;
   - to noncount nouns by deleting articles and/or plurals;
   - to any previously identified noun which needs *the* in front of it.

Chapter 2

The steps below will help you edit your writing. First, review the Editing Guide from Chapter 1. Then follow these steps sequentially, or work through only the sections that cover grammar you know you need to work on. Refer to the Chapter 2 charts and information noted to help you.

2.1 Sentence Structure: Fragments and Run-on Sentences
(See Charts 2.1A and 2.1B, pp. 28–29.)

1. Identify structures.

   ■ Look for punctuation (periods or semicolons) that marks complete sentences.

   ■ Put [brackets] around all the word groups you've punctuated as sentences.

2. Analyze clauses.

   ■ Does each sentence have a main verb and subject?

   ■ If there are dependent clauses, are they attached to independent clauses?

   ■ Are the independent clauses punctuated with periods or semicolons?

3. Edit to make corrections in clause structure and punctuation.

2.2 Subject-Verb Agreement
(See Chart 2.2, p. 33, and Reference Chart 2.3, p. 175.)

1. Underline verbs.
2. Find verbs in present tense, in present perfect tense, and with forms of *be*, and circle their subjects.
3. Check for the following:

   ■ *There + be* at the beginning of a sentence: the subject follows *be*;

   ■ Subjects that have information between them and the verb;

   ■ "Special" subjects: *each, every, one, …*;

   ■ Complex subjects: *what she liked best, living in the U.S., to return to my roots*;

   ■ Uncountable nouns as subjects: *information, traveling, the realization*.

4. Check for subject–verb agreement: Use *-s* ending for verbs or *is/was* for third person singular.
5. Correct any errors.

2.3 Verb Tense: Consistency and Appropriate Shifts
(See Chart 2.3A, p. 38, and Chart 2.3B, p. 39.)

1. Read your writing all the way through once. As your read, put an "X" above any verb that shows a shift in tense. Ask yourself:

   ■ If writing about a reading, what time frame am I using to describe the events in the article? *(Use present or past tenses, but be consistent within the time frame.)*

   ■ Am I expressing an idea or opinion, or stating a fact or general truth? *(Use present tense.)*

   ■ For each verb marked with an "X," is the tense shift "correct"? That is, do I have a reason for shifting? *(Check time expressions and consistency.)*

2. Analyze sentences you have questions about to help you figure out corrections.

■ <u>Underline</u> complete verbs (these may include modals).

■ Draw a wiggly line under the *complete* time expression, not just the signal word.

3. If your writing shows a reason for the tense shift, write it above or in the margin. If it does not show a clear reason, go to step 4.

4. Correct errors.

■ Add or change time expressions to make your meaning clear.

■ Correct verb tenses and forms.

Chapter 3

The steps below will help you edit your writing. First, review the Editing Guides for Chapters 1 and 2. Then follow these steps sequentially, or work through only the sections that cover grammar you know you need to work on. Refer to the Chapter 3 charts and information noted to help you.

3.1 Verb Tenses for Generalizations and Support
(See Charts 3.1A and 3.1B, p. 52.)

1. As you read your paper, ask yourself the following questions:

■ What time reference am I using to describe the events in the article (present or past)?

■ Where am I making generalizations? Providing support?

■ When I shift tenses, do I have a reason for shifting?

2. Analyze sentences you have questions about to help you figure out corrections:

■ <u>Underline</u> verbs, identify tenses, and draw a wiggly line under time expressions.

■ Check that generalizations are in present tense or present perfect tense.

■ Analyze the support: present tense for present examples and past tense for past examples.

3. If your paragraph or essay shows a reason for tense shifts, write it in the margin. If your paragraph or essay does not show a clear reason, go to step 4.

4. Add or change time expressions to make your meaning clear, or make corrections to your verbs.

3.2 Reporting Ideas, Statements, and Thoughts
(See Charts 3.3A and 3.3B, pp. 61–62, and Reference Charts 3.1 and 3.2, pp. 177–179.)

1. <u>Double underline</u> the reporting signal and put [brackets] around the idea, statement, or thought reported.

2. Check your sentences for the following problems:

■ Not paraphrasing or quoting when you should:

⊘ The author says that Americans *have a penchant for informality, egalitarianism, and spontaneity* when they do business. *(The material in italics is directly from the article and needs to be quoted or paraphrased.)*

■ Double reporting signal words: ⊘ <u>In Khosla's opinion</u>, <u>she thinks</u> …

3. Write a check mark ✓ above the following verbs: *describe, discuss, talk about.*

   ■ Check to make sure these verbs are not followed by *that* clauses.

   ⊘ <u>Khosla describes</u> [that Europeans don't like wearing name tags].
           ✓

4. Highlight *wh-* and *how* clauses.

   ■ Check to be sure that *wh-* clauses use sentence word order (subject-verb).

   ⊘ The HP engineers wanted to know how <u>could they</u> work effectively.

5. Correct the errors.

Chapter 4

The steps below will help you edit your writing. First, review the Editing Guides for Chapters 1–3. Then follow these steps sequentially, or work through only the sections that cover grammar you know you need to work on. Refer to the Chapter 4 charts and information noted to help you.

4.1 Passive Verbs
(See Chart 4.1, p. 75, and Reference Charts 4.1 and 4.2, pp. 180–182.)

1. Follow the steps to identify tense shifts by using Editing Guide 2.3.

2. Check verbs with passive constructions for the following:

   ■ A form of *be* or *get* in the appropriate tense;

   ■ The correct subject-verb agreement;

   ■ A correctly formed past participle: *-ed* for regular past participles, irregular forms for other past participles. (See Reference Chart 1.9, p. 169.)

3. Since they often cause problems, pay special attention to the following verbs to be sure that you have used them correctly: (See Reference Chart 4.2, p. 181.)

   ■ *to be used to*

   ■ *to be accustomed to*

   ■ *to be involved with/in*

   ■ *to be addicted to*

   ■ *to happen, to occur* (not used in the passive)

4. Correct the errors.

4.2 Generic Nouns, Count and Noncount Nouns, and Articles
(See Charts 4.2A, 4.2B, pp. 81–82, and Reference Charts 1.4 and 1.5, pp. 163–166.)

1. Identify structures:
   - Highlight nouns in your writing.
   - Decide if the nouns are count or noncount.
   - Mark nouns with a generic (general) reference with a "G."
2. Analyze structures: (See Editing Guide for Chapter 1, p. 151.)
   - Check to make sure that count nouns have appropriate articles or determiners or are in the plural form.
   - Check to make sure that noncount nouns do not have inappropriate articles or determiners and are not in the plural form.
3. Correct the errors.

4.3 Reporting Information: Verb Tenses and Patterns
(See Chart 4.3, p. 86, Chart 6.2A, p. 142, and Editing Guides 3.1 and 3.2.)

1. Check reported ideas and information:
   - Underline the reporting verbs *(say, tell, …)*. Write the tense in the left margin.
   - Double underline the other verbs. Write the tense above the verb.
   - Put [brackets] around the idea, statement, or thought reported.
2. Decide if there is any confusion for the reader because of the tense of the reporting verbs or the tense of verbs used to report information.
3. Check the pattern of the material in brackets following a reporting verb. (Refer to Charts 3.3A and 3.3B, pp. 61–62, Reference Chart 3.2, p. 178, and Chart 6.2A, p. 142.)
4. Correct the errors.

Chapter 5

The steps below will help you edit your writing. First, review the Editing Guides for Chapters 1–4. Then follow these steps sequentially, or work through only the sections that cover grammar you know you need to work on. Refer to the Chapter 5 charts and information noted to help you.

5.1 Joining Words
(See Charts 5.1A–5.1C, pp. 100–102, as well as Charts 2.1A and 2.1B, pp. 28–29, and Reference Chart 5.1, p. 183.)

1. Read through your sentences. Put a box around each joining word that you find.
2. For each joining word that joins clauses, check for logic by asking yourself:
   - What is the logical relationship that the joining word shows: contrast, opposite idea, condition, etc.?
   - Does the joining word connect my ideas the way I want it to? Does it show the appropriate meaning? If not, what is a better choice?

3. For each joining word that joins clauses, check the punctuation by asking yourself:
   - What kind of joining word is it: subordinator, coordinator, transition expression?
   - What kind of punctuation, if any, do I need?
4. Correct the errors.

5.2 Parallel Structure
(See Chart 5.2, p. 108.)

1. Read through the sentences in your essay. Highlight or put a box around each coordinator that you find: *and, but, or, nor, yet*.
2. Underline the structures that appear before coordinators and structures that appear after coordinators.
3. Check each pair or list of elements to be sure that they are parallel.
4. Check punctuation.
5. Correct the errors.

5.3 Participial Phrases
(See Chart 5.3, p. 112.)

1. Underline all the participial phrases.
2. If you can't find any, look for places in your writing where you could use participial phrases, and highlight them. (*Hint:* Look for clauses with *because/since* that give reasons, or clauses with *after/before/when* that show time relationships.)
3. Rewrite the highlighted clauses as participial phrases. You may have to change pronouns in the second clauses to nouns.
4. Check participial phrases to make sure that the subject of the participial phrase is the same as the subject of the clause, i.e., that you don't have "dangling modifiers."
5. Correct the errors.

5.4 Conditional Sentences
(See Charts 5.4A–5.4C, pp. 117–119.)

1. Check for consistency in verb tense. (See Editing Guide 2.3, p. 152.) Ask yourself:
   - What time frame am I using to describe the events in the story (present or past)?
2. Underline the conditional sentences.
3. Double underline the verbs in the conditional sentences.
4. Think about the meaning of each conditional sentence: Is it a factual or a hypothetical conditional?
5. Check the verbs in the conditional sentences to determine if the tenses accurately show your meaning. (Compare your choices of verb tenses in the conditional sentences with the time frame you are using to tell the events from the story.)
6. Check for consistency.
7. Correct the errors.

Chapter 6

The steps below will help you edit your writing. First, review the Editing Guides for Chapters 1–5. Then follow these steps sequentially, or work through only the sections that cover grammar you know you need to work on. Refer to the Chapter 6 charts and information noted to help you.

6.1 Relative Clauses
(See Charts 6.1A–6.1D, pp. 129–131.)

1. Read through your sentences and put [brackets] around any relative clauses that you find.
2. For each relative clause, ask yourself the following questions:
   a. What are the subject and the verb of the relative clause?
      - Check for tense and subject-verb agreement.
   b. Is the relative pronoun a subject or an object in the relative clause?
      - Check for missing subjects, double subjects, double objects.
   c. Is the relative clause placed where it should be?
      - Check to make sure it is placed close to the noun it modifies.
   d. Is the relative clause punctuated correctly?
      - Check to make sure it has commas if it is nonrestrictive; that is, if it provides extra information that is not essential to identify the noun.
      - Check to make sure there are no commas if the clause is restrictive; that is, if it provides essential information to identify the noun you are referring to.
   e. Identify clauses which contain *that*.
      - Check to make sure *that* is used as a relative pronoun and not a joining word. (See Chart 6.1D, 9, p. 132, Chart 3.3A, p. 61, Charts 5.1A–5.1C, pp. 100–102, and Reference Chart 5.1, p. 183.)
3. Correct the errors.

6.2 Verb, Noun, and Adjective Complements
(See Charts 6.2A–6.2C, pp. 142–144.)

1. Look for these patterns of complements following verbs and <u>double underline</u> them: (See Chart 6.2A.)

   to + verb   verb + *-ing*   *wh-* clause   *that* clause   simple form of verb

   <u>Underline</u> the verbs that come before these complements.
2. Look for these patterns of complements following nouns, adjectives, or special expressions (e.g., *have difficulty*) and <u>double underline</u> them: (See Chart 6.2B.)

   to + verb (infinitives)   verb + *-ing* (gerunds)   *that* clauses
3. Check the accuracy of the forms of the complements by using Charts 6.2A–6.2C. If the verb, noun, or adjective that is followed by a complement is not listed in the charts, ask your teacher or a partner to help you check it. Then add it to the chart in the appropriate list.
4. Correct the errors.

Appendix B: Grammar Reference Charts

Chapter 1

| REFERENCE CHART 1.1 | Basic Parts of Speech |

The following definitions and examples will help you recognize basic parts of speech.

Part of Speech	Examples

Noun
Names a person, place, thing, or concept
Used as subjects, objects, objects of prepositions, modifiers of other nouns
	subject *direct object*
	Deborah Tannen has studied **indirectness**
	       object of preposition in
	in everyday **language**.
	       modifier
	Her **research** findings are published in books and articles.

Verb[1] Tells what a person, place, thing, or concept does or is	Tannen **is** a linguist. She **studies** conversational language. She **says** that indirectness **can lead** to misunderstandings.
Adjective Describes a noun or pronoun Comes before the noun or after the verb *be* or a verb of feeling or perception	According to Tannen, "Indirectness is a **universal** device for expressing ideas." Some people think indirectness is **dishonest**. *(after verb* be) To others, directness may seem **rude**. *(after verb of perception)*

Adverb
Describes a verb, an adjective, another adverb, or an entire clause
Tells how, where, when, why, etc.
	We **very often** become upset when someone is too indirect.
	      (very describes adverb often; often *describes verb)*
	However, we are **extremely** reluctant to ask people to explain what they mean.
	      (describes adjective reluctant)
	Unfortunately, this can lead to confusion. *(describes entire clause)*

Pronoun[2] Substitutes for a noun or a noun phrase	Tannen studies language as **it** is used in everyday life. *(it = language)* **She** is interested in sentences **that** are actually spoken, not **those** that are possible but never spoken. *(she = Tannen; that = sentences; those = those sentences)*
Determiner[3] Makes the reference of a noun more specific	Tannen published **her** book on indirectness in 1986. **The** book was very popular.

Part of Speech	Examples
Preposition Comes before a noun or noun phrase and links it to other parts of the sentence Usually a single word *(at, by, for, …)* but can be up to four words *(such as, rather than, as far as, in addition to, as a result of, …)*	The woman didn't ask her colleague **about** her refusal. The colleague said she was **in the middle of** work **on** a report.
Conjunction[4] Joins two clauses Can be coordinating *(and, but, or, nor)* or subordinating *(because, although, before, …)*	**When** her colleague refused her invitation a second time, the woman felt confused. Was her colleague really busy, **or** was she trying to say she didn't want to go to lunch?

Auxiliary verbs
Are used to build up complete verbs
  a. **Primary:** *be, have, do*
    Show the progressive, passive, perfect and negative
  b. **Modal:** *can, could, may, might, must, shall, should, will, would*
    Show a wide range of meanings, such as ability, permission, necessity, degree of certainty
  c. **Semi-modal:** *be going to, ought to, have to, have got to, had better, be supposed to, be about to, used to, be able to*
 	
Note: *Modals and semi-modals are always followed by the simple form of the verb.*
	a. My friend **is** <u>taking</u> a linguistics class this semester. She **has** always <u>been</u> interested in language, but until now she **didn't realize** just how interested she was.
	b. If she **can** <u>do</u> well in this class, she **may** <u>decide</u> to major in linguistics.
	
	c. If she decides that she **is going to** <u>change</u> her major, she **ought to** <u>see</u> an advisor.

[1]See Reference Charts 1.6–1.9, pp. 167–169, for more information about verb forms.
[2]See Reference Chart 1.2, p. 161, for more information on pronouns.
[3]See Reference Chart 1.3, p. 162, for more information about determiners.
[4]See Charts 5.1A–5.1C, pp. 100–102, on various types of conjunctions (joining words).

REFERENCE CHART 1.2 Pronouns

Pronouns refer to previously mentioned nouns or noun phrases. They also refer to the writer or person the writer is addressing. They can have a general or an unknown reference.

The author's first book was published in 1989. I read **it** right after **it** was published.

They say that **it** is **his** best book. (*They* = general reference, people in general who read the book)

Pronoun Type	Personal		Reflexive	Possessive	
	Subject	*Object*[5]		*Determiner*[6]	*Pronoun*
1. Pronouns that show person					
First person					
Singular	I	me	myself	my	mine
Plural	we	us	ourselves	our	ours
Second person					
Singular	you	you	yourself	your	yours
Plural	you	you	yourselves	your	yours
Third person					
Singular–masculine	he	him	himself	his	his
Singular–feminine	she	her	herself	her	hers
Singular–nonpersonal	it	it	itself	its	—
Singular–formal	one	one	oneself	one's	—
Plural	they	them	themselves	their	theirs
They found the information **themselves**.					
2. Relative pronouns	who,	whom,	—	whose	—
The woman **who** wrote the book is a linguist.	that	that			
3. Question forms	who,	whom,	**Adverbial**	whose	whose
When was the book published?	what, which	what, which	when, why, where, how		
4. Indefinite pronouns	anyone	anybody	anything		
I read **something** about the book on the Internet.	someone	somebody	something		
	everyone	everybody	everything		
	no one	nobody	nothing		

[5]Object forms can be used as direct objects, indirect objects, or objects of prepositions.
[6]Determiners are used before nouns. See Reference Chart 1.3.

REFERENCE CHART 1.3   Determiners[7]

Determiners are words used to specify the reference of nouns. The determiners marked in **bold** can also be used as pronouns.

She wrote **these** papers on conversational language last year. (*these* as determiner)

Of all the many papers she has written, I find **these** the most interesting. (*these* as pronoun)

Determiner type	Count noun		Noncount noun
	Singular	*Plural*	
Article	a report the report	the reports	the information
Possessive	my, your, his, her, its our, their Tannen's } report	my, your, his, her, its our, their Tannen's } reports	my, your, his, her, its our, their Tannen's } information
Demonstrative	**this** report **that** report	**these** reports **those** reports	**this** information **that** information
Quantifier	**each** report every report — — — — — — — — **either** report **neither** report **any** report no report —	— — **all** (of) the reports **many** (of the) reports **a great many** (of the) reports **a lot** of (the) reports **some** (of the) reports **(a) few** (of the) reports **several** (of the) reports **a couple** of (the) reports **enough** (of the) reports **both** (of the) reports — **any** (of the) reports no reports **none** of the reports	— — **all** (of the) information **much** (of the) information **a great deal of** (the) information **a lot** of (the) information **some** (of the) information **(a) little** (of the) information — — **enough** (of the) information — — **any** (of the) information no information **none** of the information
Numeral	**one** report	**two/three** (of the) reports	—

Related structures			
same/other/rest	**the same** report **another** report **the other** report	**the same** reports — **the other** reports **the others** (pronoun)	**the same** information **the rest** of the information
former/latter	**the former** report **the latter** report	**the former** reports **the latter** reports	**the former** information **the latter** information
certain/such (a)	a certain report such a report	certain reports such reports	certain information such information
wh- words	which/what report **whose** report	which/what reports **whose** reports	which/what information **whose** information

---

[7]Information on determiners is based on Biber, et al., 1999, *The Longman Grammar of Spoken and Written English,* p. 259.

REFERENCE CHART 1.4   Noncount Nouns

Noncount nouns have only one form (no plural). They can refer to concrete or abstract entities.[8]

Having no **paper** to print out his composition, he saved his **work** on the hard disk. (*paper* is concrete; *work* is abstract)

See Reference Chart 1.3 for determiners that occur with noncount nouns:

If he had had **a little** paper, he could have printed out **a great deal of** work.

1. Some common noncount nouns are:

academic terms	general abstract nouns (continued)	emotional states	fields of study
evidence	health	anger	economics
feedback	help	confidence	education
focus	justice	depression	finance
information	labor	fear	history
knowledge	language	happiness	linguistics
methodology	life	joy	mathematics
publication	luck	loneliness	music
research	nature	love	philosophy
selection	peace	pleasure	physics
variability	policy	pride	religion
	pollution	relief	science
qualities	power		technology
beauty	progress	**other states/conditions**	
courage	protection	childhood	**substances**
consistency	reality	adolescence	air
importance	regulation	youth	coffee
intelligence	safety	old age	food
mercy	security	marriage	gas
patience	sex	dependence	oil
purity	sound	freedom	paper
respect	speech	independence	rain
strength	time	poverty	water
	tradition	noise	
general abstract nouns	transfer	silence	**-ing nouns**
advice	travel		eating
authority	trust	**collections of concrete items**	hearing
context	truth	equipment	speaking
culture	truth	furniture	traveling
death	violence	machinery	(sports activities)
energy	waste		bowling
environment	wealth	**sports**	hiking
existence	work	baseball	jogging
experience	worth	soccer	
growth			

2. Many noncount nouns can also be used as count nouns.

Noncount (substance, material, abstraction)	Count (an individual instance or unit)
Education can help us learn about good communication.	One can get **a good education** in school or on the job.
Experience teaches us about language use.	I have had **several bad experiences** concerning misunderstandings.
Life can seem very difficult when we don't communicate well with others.	No one leads **a life** that is free of all problems in communication.
Doing **business** with strangers can lead to misunderstandings.	Those who run **a business** should consider training their employees regarding communication skills.

3. Some noncount nouns _cannot_ be used as count nouns; however, they can be used with other nouns that indicate a part of the whole.[9]

Noncount	Noun + of + noncount
The **advice** the writer gives us is very helpful.	In fact, she gives us **several pieces of good advice** about indirectness and directness.
If you need **information** about conversational style, you can find references on Tannen's web page.	**One useful item of information** that I found was the title of her book on gender and conversational style.

4. Many abstract nouns have verb counterparts (e.g., _success—to succeed; rejection—to reject_). When these nouns have a general meaning, you can use them either as noncount or count nouns. The meaning is the same.

Many people measure **success** (a success) in dollars.
Rejection (a rejection) of traditional customs is often undesirable.

Note: _When you have made an error with a noncount noun, put that word on your word forms list. (See Appendix A, p. 150.)_

---

[8]Concrete, substance-like noncount nouns _(paper, water, coffee, cheese)_ are often called _mass nouns._
[9]Count nouns also are used this way: _a bunch of grapes, a grove of redwood trees, two kinds of computers._

| REFERENCE CHART 1.5 | **Using the Definite Article *the*** |

To apply rules about *the*, you must first consider:
1. Is the noun a common noun, e.g., *invitation*, (A), or is it a proper noun, e.g., *Dr. Tannen*, (B)?
2. For a common noun (either count or noncount), does the noun have a *specific* reference to a person, group, or thing?

> I received an invitation. (A1)

Or does it have a *general* reference to a person, group, or thing as a whole class?

> Receiving *a lunch invitation* is common in the workplace. (A2)

A. With Common Nouns

Tips	*Examples*
1. Nouns with specific reference (See also Chart 1.1C, p. 8.)	
General rule: Use *the* only when you and the reader can both identify the person, thing, or action you are referring to. The reader can identify the referent in several ways:	
a. From information **in the text** mentioned directly or indirectly	Dr. Tannen did several *studies* of language use in the workplace. **The studies** showed differences in conversational style. *(direct)* In one of Tannen's *research projects*, **the participants** were recorded during a conversation at work. *(indirect: the participants of the research project)*
b. From information **in the sentence** — after the noun	**The misunderstanding** *that Tannen described in her article* seems quite common. **The article** *written by Tannen* appeared in 1987. **The invitation** *to go out to lunch* was turned down. **The point** *of the article* seems to be that we can improve our communication by awareness of different conversational styles.
— or before the noun superlatives: *the best, the longest, ...* sequential words: *the first, the next, ...* unique nouns: *the only, the same, the main, ...*	**The** *most interesting* **part** was learning about **the** *latest* **development** in linguistics. **The** *first* **section** described a misunderstanding. I have experienced **the** *same* **problem** as a result of indirectness.
c. From **knowledge shared** — by everyone or a large group — by smaller groups (e.g., a class, a family, a group of friends)	**The government** has reduced federal spending for research in **the sciences**. Teacher to students: "I hope you studied **the reading**."

Tips	Examples

2. Nouns with general reference (See also Chart 4.2A, p. 81.)

The is used in these special cases:

a. *The* + **singular noun**:
   In technical and scientific writing to describe classes of humans, non-humans, plants, parts of the body, inventions, etc.

The computer has brought about many changes in communication.
The snake is one of the most feared animals.

b. *The* + **plural noun**
   In academic, scientific, and technical writing to state facts about a human group, plants, animals, etc.
      *Warning: **Do not** use the with noncount nouns or with plural nouns used with a general meaning.*

Various organizations are dedicated to saving **the redwoods**, **the whales**, and **the wolves**.
⊘ **The directness** can often be misinterpreted as rudeness.
   Correction: **Directness** …
⊘ **The linguists** study both written and spoken language.
   Correction: **Linguists** …

B. With Proper Nouns

Proper nouns refer to specific people, places, geographical features, etc., so the choice is between using the or no article. The rules are not the same as for common nouns. Some basic guidelines follow, but there are many exceptions, so you will need to pay attention to how proper nouns appear in readings and check your dictionary.

Tips	Examples
a. Use *the* with **plurals**	the United States, the Rocky Mountains, the Great Lakes, the Hawaiian Islands
b. Use *the* with **of phrases**	the King of Thailand, the University of Ohio, the Cape of Good Hope, the Bay of Bengal
c. Use *the* with **some singular nouns** (e.g., rivers, canals, oceans, deserts, peninsulas, museums, hotels, ships, government bodies, publications)	the Suez Canal, the Nile, the Mediterranean Sea, the Izu Peninsula, the Sahara Desert, the Prado, the Ritz Carleton, the Titanic, the Senate
d. However, in general, ***do not*** use ***the*** with ***singular nouns***	Deborah, English, April, Mars, Georgetown University, Asia, Mexico, Lake Titicaca, Narita Airport
e. Some categories of **singular** proper nouns have both patterns (without *the* and with *the*)	London Bridge — the Golden Gate Bridge Jack's Restaurant — the Hard Rock Café Sports Illustrated — the New Yorker Oracle — the Nature Conservancy

REFERENCE CHART 1.6   Verb Forms

Verb tense forms and modal + verb combinations appear in Reference Charts 1.7 and 1.8, p. 168; forms of irregular verbs are in Reference Chart 1.9, p. 169; passive voice forms are in Reference Chart 4.1, p. 180.

Name	Regular Verb	Irregular Verb	Example
Simple form (dictionary form)	ask study	write	Linguists **study** both spoken and written language. In the past, they didn't **write** about spoken language as extensively as they do today.
-*s* form (for third person singular, present tense)	asks studies	writes does	In the reading, linguist Deborah Tannen **writes** about a misunderstanding between two American women. One woman **doesn't** ask the other to explain her response.
Past form	asked studied	wrote did	Tannen first **wrote** as a graduate student about everyday spoken language. **Did** she study written language?
Infinitive	to ask to study	to write	In the 90's, she decided **to study** spoken language in the workplace.
Perfect infinitive	to have asked to have studied	to have written	She was pleased **to have written** a book about her research, called *Talking from 9 to 5.*
Present participle (verb + -*ing*)	asking studying	writing	I'm not sure what Tannen is **studying** now. (*used as part of a progressive verb tense*) As a **visiting** scholar at Stanford, she had considerable time for **writing**. (**visiting**: *used as adjective;* **writing**: *used as noun*)
Past participle (verb + -*ed*/-*en*)	asked studied	written	She has **written** at least 19 books. (*used as part of a perfect verb tense*) Her carefully-**written** articles contain informative examples. (*used in a compound adjective*)
Perfect participle (*having* + verb + -*ed*/-*en*)	having asked having studied	having written	**Having studied** communication patterns between men and women, she presented her findings in the book *That's Not What I Meant.* (*used in a participial phrase describing* she)

REFERENCE CHART 1.7   Forms of Verb Tenses (Active)

The chart shows the verb tense forms for a regular verb (*create*) and an irregular verb (*take*).

Tense	Past	Present	Future[10]
Simple	created	create/creates	will create am/is/are going to create
	took	take/takes	will take am/is/are going to take
Progressive	was/were creating	am/is/are creating	will be creating am/is/are going to be creating
	was/were taking	am/is/are taking	will be taking am/is/are going to be taking
Perfect	had created had taken	have/has created have/has taken	will have created will have taken
Perfect progressive	had been creating had been taking	have/has been creating have/has been taking	will have been creating will have been taking

[10] We use the label *future tense* to refer to combinations with *will* or with *be going to*.

REFERENCE CHART 1.8   Forms of Modal[11] + Verb Combinations (Active)

Tense	Form	Examples
Simple	modal (or semi-modal) + simple form	should create might take have to take
Progressive	modal + *be* + present participle	should be creating might be taking ought to be creating
Perfect[12]	modal + *have* + past participle	could have created must have taken can't have taken
Perfect progressive	modal + *have* + *been* + present participle	could have been creating must have been taking should have been taking

[11]The modals are: *can, could, may, might, must, shall, should, will, would*. The semi-modals are: *ought to, have to, have got to, had better, be supposed to, be about to, be going to, used to, be able to*.

[12]*Can* occurs only in the negative (as *can't*) in modal perfects.

REFERENCE CHART 1.9	**Some Common Irregular Verbs**	
Form	**Irregular Verb**	**Regular Verb**
Simple form	The class should **begin** on time.	The class should **start** on time.
Past form	The class **began** at 9 yesterday.	The class **started** at 9 yesterday.
Past Participle form	The class has never **begun** late.	The class has never **started** late.

Irregular verbs with only one form for simple, past, and past participle:

bet	cut	let	read
broadcast	hit	put	set (also upset)
cost	hurt	quit	shut

Alphabetical list of other irregular verbs:

Simple form	Past form	Past Participle	Simple form	Past form	Past Participle
be	was/were	been	lead	led	led
become	became	become	leave	left	left
begin	began	begun	lend	lent	lent
break	broke	broken	lie (recline)	lay	lain
bring	brought	brought	lose	lost	lost
build	built	built	make	made	made
buy	bought	bought	mean	meant	meant
choose	chose	chosen	meet	met	met
come	came	come	pay	paid	paid
do	did	done	ride	rode	ridden
draw	drew	drawn	rise	rose	risen
eat	ate	eaten	run	ran	run
fall	fell	fallen	say	said	said
feel	felt	felt	see	saw	seen
fight	fought	fought	sell	sold	sold
find	found	found	send	sent	sent
forget	forgot	forgotten/forgot	show	showed	shown/showed
get	got	got/gotten	sit	sat	sat
give	gave	given	sleep	slept	slept
go	went	gone	speak	spoke	spoken
grow	grew	grown	spend	spent	spent
hang	hung	hung	steal	stole	stolen
have	had	had	take	took	taken
hear	heard	heard	teach	taught	taught
hide	hid	hidden/hid	tell	told	told
hold	held	held	think	thought	thought
keep	kept	kept	understand	understood	understood
know	knew	known	win	won	won
lay (put)	laid	laid	write	wrote	written

Note: *Circle verb forms that you have had difficulty remembering. Then add them to your personal word forms list. (See p. 150.)*

REFERENCE CHART 1.10 **Types of Phrases**		
Type of phrase	**Description**	**Example**
Noun phrase	A noun + the words that describe it	a frustrating **experience** two **women** working for the same company

Verb phrase	A phrase containing a verb
	  a. complete verb phrase = a central clause element (subject + complete verb)
	  b. incomplete verb phrase: not a central clause element (no tense or modal)
		a. (she) **had been feeling**
		   (she) **could understand**
		b. **to dispel** (infinitive)
		   having seen (participial)

Adjective phrase	An adjective + any modifiers	very **sorry** **unsure** of herself **eager** to make friends more **confusing** than the first response
Adverb phrase	An adverb + any modifiers	**instinctively** hardly **ever** very **quickly** more **quickly** than before
Prepositional phrase	A preposition + the noun that follows it and any modifiers of the noun	**in** her office **about** a very interesting case **by** doing more of the same

Participial phrase	A phrase beginning with a participle
	A participle is made from a verb:
	  Verb + *-ing*: expecting, writing
	  Verb + *-ed/-en*: confused, frustrated, told, asked
	Can serve as an adjective or adverb phrase
		Expecting directness, the woman was **confused by her colleague's indirectness**. *(adjective phrases—describe the woman)*
		Rejected twice, the first woman felt frustrated. *(adverb phrase—tells why)*

Infinitive phrase	A phrase beginning with an infinitive: *to* + verb	**to convey** information

REFERENCE CHART 1.11	Common Word Endings for Basic Parts of Speech[13]

Verbs, nouns, adjectives, and adverbs often have special word endings, called *suffixes*. These suffixes help you distinguish the words from other parts of speech and help you understand their function in a sentence. When you are unsure about a word form, check in your dictionary. Keep a record of words that are problems for you on your word forms list. (See p. 150.)

Verb	Noun	Adjective	Adverb
Special endings[14]			
-ize, -en, -ate, -(i)fy, -y	**-tion, ity, -er, -ness, -ism, -ment, -ent/ant, -ship, -age, -ery** -ence, -ics, -ure, -ing	**-al, -ent, -ive, -ous, -ate, -ful, -less, -like** -ory, -able, -ant, -ish, -ic, -ing, -ed, -y, -ly[15]	**-ly, -wise, -ward(s)**
Examples			
to expect	(an) expectation	expectant	expectantly
to evaluate	(an) evaluation	evaluative	
to educate	(an) education	educational	educationally
to satisfy	(a) satisfaction	satisfactory	satisfactorily
to believe	(a) belief	believable	believably
to memorize	(a) memory	memorable	memorably
to economize	(an) economy/economics	economic	economically
to socialize	(a) society	social	socially
	intelligence	intelligent	intelligently
to fool	a fool	foolish	foolishly
to succeed	(a) success	successful	successfully
	(an) environment	environmental	environmentally
to care	(a) care	careless, careful	carelessly, carefully
to increase	(an) increase	increasing/increased	increasingly
to beautify	(a) beauty	beautiful	beautifully
to exemplify	an example	exemplifying, exemplified	
to fail	a failure/ a failing	failing/failed	unfailingly
	fame	famous	famously
	happiness	happy	happily
	(a) business	business-like	
to price	a price	pricey, priceless	price-wise

Example sentences:

My friend *succeeded* in solving a communication problem with her roommate. *(verb)*

This *success* encouraged her to be more direct. *(noun)*

She was *successful* in realizing the nature of the problem. *(adjective)*

She *successfully* explained her point of view to her roommate. *(adverb)*

---

[13]In the chart, the article *a* indicates that the noun is a count noun; *(a)* or *(an)* indicates that the noun can be used as a count noun or a noncount noun. No article means the noun is used only as a noncount noun.

[14]In the chart, the endings in **bold** are listed according to their frequency in academic writing. Not all endings listed have examples in the chart.

[15]A few adjectives end in *-ly* (e.g., *friendly, lovely, lonely*) and do not have an adverb form. To use these qualities to describe verbs, you need to use expressions such as *in a friendly way*.

Chapter 2

REFERENCE CHART 2.1   Word Partnerships

Many words in English form close partnerships with other words. The chart below shows some different types and structures. See Reference Chart 2.2, p. 173, for additional examples of word partnerships.

Type	Examples *(from "Return to Vietnam," p. 24)*
Fixed Expressions These need to be memorized.	
a. Idioms (special meaning)	a. The tofu custard Arnett had in Hanoi was a **far cry from** the custard she remembered. (very different from)
b. Phrasal verbs (two- or three-word verbs)	b. The sights and sounds **brought back** many memories. (recalled) The tofu custard didn't **measure up to** Arnett's expectations. (meet)
c. Verb + preposition (the phrase has the meaning of the verb + the meaning of the preposition—direction, location, etc.)	c. Her mother **prayed for** a safe journey. Arnett **retreated to** her room when her mother's friends came over.
d. Past participle + preposition	d. The custard seller was very **puzzled by** her excitement. The custard was **made of** tofu.
e. Noun + preposition	e. What was the **significance of** the custard? Her **experience with** the custard showed her that things weren't exactly as she remembered them.
f. Other fixed expressions	f. **On the other hand**, many other things were familiar to her. **In spite of** her fond memories, the tofu was still a disappointment. **In conclusion**, her return to her roots contains a lesson for all of us.

Word Partnerships

Some words frequently occur together, but they are not fixed expressions. For example, several different verbs are "partners" with the noun *opportunity* in the verb + noun pattern: *have, get, find, take, seize, miss, lose*. But other verbs (e.g., *make, grasp*) with similar meanings to one of these verbs can <u>not</u> be partners with *opportunity*.

g. Verb + noun	g. have	an opportunity (to)
	find	an opportunity (to)
	visualize	a time/place
	describe	an experience
	spend	my life/money/time
	learn	a lesson (from something)
	make	a point (about something)
	feel	a connection (to something/someone)
h. Verb + adjective	h. feel	familiar
	feel	foreign
i. Adjective + noun	i. vivid	memories
	congested	market
	rapid	force
	stifling	heat
	exotic	fruits
j. Noun + verb	j. memories	fade away
	the road	leads

Note: *When your teacher gives you feedback about word partnerships that you have problems with, list the correct expressions in your word partnerships list. (See p. 150.)*

REFERENCE CHART 2.2   **Prepositions Occurring with Selected Verbs, Adjectives, and Nouns**

See Reference Chart 2.1 for categories, definitions, and additional examples of these word partnerships. Verbs in bold are especially frequent in academic writing.[16]

A. Phrasal Verbs

*Arnett **set out** to discover her roots.*

break down (break into pieces, divide into parts)	**put on** (apply, assume, impose)
bring on (cause)	set out (begin with purpose)
carry out (do, perform)	set up (establish)
cut off (isolate)	stand out (be conspicuous)
end up (be, become)	sum up (summarize)
find out (discover, learn)	**take on** (assume)
go on (happen, continue)	take over (assume control)
grow up (mature)	**take up** (introduce, begin, discuss a topic)
make up (comprise, be composed of)	**turn out** (end, end up)
pass on (convey)	write down (record)
point out (indicate, call attention to)	
point up (indicate, reveal, make more emphatic)	

B. Verb + preposition[17]

*Arnett **compared the tofu in Hanoi with** the tofu she remembered from her childhood.*

accuse *X* of	complain about/of	**fill *X* with**	prevent *X* from
account for	compete with	forgive *X* for	**refer to**
allow for	compensate for	**give *X* to**	**result in**
add to	concentrate on	hear about	**send *X* to**
agree on/with	consent to	insist on	stop *X* from
approve of	**consist of**	**lead to**	succeed in
ask for	**contribute to**	listen to	talk about
believe in	**deal with**	**look at**	think about
belong to	decide on	**look for**	**think of**
care for	**depend on**	look forward to	**use *X* as**
come from	**differ from**	object to	wait for
compare *X* with	discriminate against	**obtain *X* from**	work for
comment on	feel like	**occur in**	

The following verb + preposition combinations are listed in passive form because they are most commonly used in passive in academic writing. They can also be used in active form.

*Arnett's expectations **were based on** her childhood memories. (passive)*

*Arnett **based** her expectations **on** her childhood memories. (active)*

be accustomed to	**be composed of**	**be divided into**	be opposed to
be addicted to	be connected to	**be expressed in**	**be regarded as**
be aimed at	**be considered as**	**be included in**	be related to
be applied to	be convinced of	**be involved in**	be seen in/as
be associated with	**be defined as**	**be known as/for**	be used in
be based on	**be derived from**	be made of	

C. Adjective + preposition

*We are often **disappointed by** our expectations.*

able (unable) to	excited about	innocent of	similar to
afraid of	familiar with	interested in	sure of
angry about/with	famous for	likely to	surprised at/by
aware of	fond of	married to	thankful for
capable (incapable) of	frightened by	pleased by	tired of
certain of	guilty of	proud of	upset with
comfortable about/with	happy with	relevant to	used to
content with	in charge of	responsible for	willing to
different from	in favor of	satisfied with	worried about/by
disappointed by/with	independent of	sensitive to	

D. Noun + preposition (The article *a/an* is included to indicate that the noun is a count noun.)

*While growing up, Arnett often had a bad **reaction to** hearing Vietnamese, even though she had **respect for** her cultural background.*

access to	a comment on	faith in	relevance to
an addiction to	a concentration on	freedom from	a reaction to
admiration for	confidence in	hope of	respect for
(an) agreement on/about	a connection with	an influence over/on	a reason for
an alternative to	a contrast with	an introduction to	a remedy for
an approach to	a contribution to	an opportunity for/to	responsibility for
an argument against/for	a decision about/on	opposition to	a search for
an attachment to	a demand for	a need for	(a) similarity to
an authority on	a dependence on	patience with	a solution to
a capacity for	a doubt(s) about	a reference to	a talent for
a chance of	an effect on	a reaction against	a threat to
a charge of	an exception to	a relationship with	(a) tolerance for

Note: *Check your dictionary for words not on these lists. Put any combinations you have trouble remembering on your word partnerships list. (See p. 150.)*

---

[16]As reported in Biber, et al., 1999, *The Longman Grammar of Spoken and Written English*, pp. 410, 416-418.

[17]X = someone or something

REFERENCE CHART 2.3	**More Problem Areas for Subject-Verb Agreement**

Chart 2.2, p. 33, presents some major problem areas. This chart describes additional areas that may cause problems.

Problem Area	Rule / Tip	Examples
1. Words that are always singular: *each, every, one (of the), either, neither, someone, anyone, everyone, somebody, anybody,* etc., *no one, none*	Treat these words as third person singular, even though they may be followed by plural nouns in a phrase with *of: each of my cousins.*	**Each** of my cousins *knows* about the family reunion. **Every one** of them *has received* an invitation. **None** of them *was* forgotten.[18] Not **everyone** *is* able to arrive on the same day. **Either** arrival date *seems* good.
2. Words that can be either singular or plural, depending on the noun that follows them a. Paired coordinators: *either ... or* *neither ... nor* b. Quantifiers: *all, some, any, the rest of the, most of the, a lot of, much, many, which,* etc.	a. Agreement is with the noun that follows *or/nor.* b. Agreement is with the noun that directly follows the quantifier. As with all nouns: Use singular if the noun is singular or noncount—e.g., *father, food, dish.* Use plural if the noun is plural—e.g., *uncles, dishes, restaurants.*	a. **Either** my sisters **or** <u>my father</u> *is planning* to arrive early. **Neither** my brother **nor** <u>my uncles</u> *are going* to stay an extra day. b. **All of the food** *is* delicious. **Some of the food** *is* very cheap. **Which dish** *tastes* best? **Which dishes** *are* your favorites? **All of the information** about vegetarian restaurants *is* available on the Internet. **All of the cafes** in our neighborhood *are* reasonably priced.
3. Words that refer to groups of people (collective nouns): either singular or plural—*the class, staff, faculty, crowd, audience, jury, committee, family, group, administration, media, opposition, team,* etc.	a. Use *singular* if the focus is on the group as a unit. (most frequent usage) b. Use *plural* if the focus is on individual members of the group.	a. **The class** *is* writing about Arnett's article. b. **The class** *are* writing about *their* own *experiences* returning to a special place.
4. The + adjective (referring to a group of people): *the elderly, the poor, the young, the sick,* etc.	Use a plural verb. Don't forget *the.*	**The elderly** *are* given great respect in many cultures.
5. Nouns with misleading forms a. Singular nouns that look plural: *economics, mathematics, news,* etc. b. Plural nouns that look singular: *people, police*	Nouns that end in *-ics* that refer to a field of study: use singular. Memorize these special nouns.	a. **Linguistics** *was* her favorite course in college. Yesterday's **news** *was* surprising. b. **The people** *seem* very interested. **The police** *are investigating* the scene.

Problem Area	Rule/Tip	Examples
6. Confusion in relative clauses *(See Chapter 6 for information about relative clauses.)*	a. The verb agrees with the head noun (the noun that the relative pronoun refers to) when the relative pronoun is the subject of the clause. b. When the head noun is *one of*, writers often use a plural verb when the noun is plural. But remember to use a singular verb when *one of* ... is not modified by a relative clause. *(See 1.)*	a. I read the **article** that *describes* Arnett's experience. I would like to read other **articles** that *describe* similar return trips. b. Arnett is **one of many authors** who *have* described travels to a place of birth. **One of the sights** *surprises* her.

[18]*None* is generally singular in written English, but is used as both singular and plural in spoken English. *(None of them **has/have** responded to the invitation yet.)*

Chapter 3

REFERENCE CHART 3.1	**The Punctuation of Direct Quotations**

For additional information about quoting, refer to Strategies for Writing, p. 188.

Note: *The first example in this chart shows a line number in parentheses to refer the reader to the location of the quotation in the text. Some teachers and academic departments require different citation conventions, so you will need to check with your instructor for the appropriate conventions for your papers.*

Quoting a Full Sentence	Example	Tip
1. Reporting signal before the quote	**Khosla says**, "Americans aren't always so sensitive to foreign tastes and habits." (line 14) **According to Khosla**, "Americans aren't always so sensitive to foreign tastes and habits."	Use a comma after the reporting signal (or a colon for a long quotation). Use quotation marks around the exact words of the author, and begin the quotation with a capital letter. Put the period before the quotation mark.
2. Reporting signal after the quote *(not as common as 1 in academic writing)*	"If you are negotiating with an Israeli, don't pause," **the training organizations Charis and Meridian advise.**	Use a comma (or question mark or exclamation point as appropriate) before the closing quotation mark.
3. Reporting signal separates the quote	"In negotiating with foreign business people," **Khosla tells us,** "small things matter."	Use a comma after the first part of the quotation and a comma after the reporting signal. Don't capitalize the second part of the quotation when it is part of the original quoted sentence.

Quoting Part of a Sentence	Example	Tip
4. Reporting a phrase *(commonly done when the language of the original is especially memorable or effective)*	**Khosla says** that the trust shown by the 3M executives "made a deep and lasting impression" on the representatives from Sumitomo. **Khosla describes** the misunderstanding between the French and American HP engineers as "a cultural logjam."	The quoted material must fit grammatically into the sentence in which it is included. Put a period (or question mark or exclamation point) before the closing quotation mark if it comes at the end of the sentence.
5. Leaving out some of the author's words in the middle of a phrase or sentence	**Khosla reports** that "HP turned to Charis International Training … to help improve the relationship."	Indicate that some words are left out by using ellipses (three dots) or four dots if it is the end of a sentence. Be sure your sentence is grammatical and logical.

REFERENCE CHART 3.2   Common Reporting Verbs: Grammar and Meaning

See Chart 4.3, p. 86, for information about verb tenses and Chart 6.2A, p. 142, for more verbs and their patterns.

Verbs followed by an asterisk (*) require that the reader be mentioned. *(Khosla **tells us** that cultural misunderstandings can be avoided through training. Khosla **tells readers** to consult the Meridian website for more information. ⊘ Khosla **tells** that ….)*

If the verb is followed by a double asterisk (**), mentioning the reader is usually optional. It may be required if the verb is followed by an infinitive. *(Khosla **asks us** to consult a website for further tips.)*

Your Position	Verbs[19]	Grammar Patterns and Examples
1. Neutral *(As the writer, you neither agree nor disagree.)*	a. says, tells*, asks**, writes, states	a. + *that* clause *(all five verbs)* + infinitive: *says, tells, asks* + *wh-* clause: *tell, ask* Khosla **says** *that* good relations between 3M and Sumitomo have been built on trust. Khosla **tells us** *to consult* the website for further tips. She also **tells us** *why* so many problems occur in cross-cultural communication.
	b. According to X, … To quote X, … In the words of X, …	b. + full clause (either a direct quote or a paraphrase, as appropriate). **To quote the author**, "Americans aren't always so sensitive to foreign tastes and habits."
2. Show the author's purpose (i.e., your idea of the author's purpose)	a. advises**, argues, asserts, assures*, cautions**, claims, comments, contends, concludes, emphasizes, explains, indicates, informs*, insists, maintains, observes, predicts, proposes, recommends, remarks, reminds*, reports, requests, reveals, shows, states, stresses, suggests	a. + *that* clause The author **argues** *that* cultural training can prevent misunderstandings. The author **advises** (Americans) *that* Europeans may be insulted by the use of nametags. (*Underlined* verbs can also take + wh- *clause*) Khosla **indicates** *what* can cause problems in cross-cultural partnerships.
	b. advises*, cautions**, claims, counsels**, encourages*, instructs*, invites*, proposes, requests*, urges*	b. + to + verb *(infinitive)* Khosla **advises readers** *to consult* the Meridian and Charis websites for further information.
	c. describes, discusses, examines, explores, focuses on, talks about	c. + noun phrase or a *wh-* clause The article **discusses** *the importance of cultural sensitivity*. Khosla **describes** *how* the length of e-mails caused problems.

Your Position	Verbs	Grammar Patterns and Examples
2. Show the author's purpose (i.e., your idea of the author's purpose)	d. admits, <u>advises</u>, <u>proposes</u>, <u>recommends</u>, reports, <u>suggests</u>	d. + verb + -ing Khosla **suggests** consulting the Meridian and Charis websites for more information. *(<u>Double underlined</u> verbs can also take a that clause with simple verb form (subjunctive). See Chart 6.2A, pattern 6, p. 143.)* The CEO **suggested** that each employee take an intercultural training class.
	e. *Nouns related to reporting verbs can also be used:* advice, assertion, claim, explanation, observation, point, proposal, recommendation, statement, suggestion.	e. + that clause The author makes **the observation** that companies doing business globally can benefit from cultural training. (= The author **observes** that...) *(See Chart 6.2B, patterns 8 and 9, pp. 148–149.)*
3. Show your attitude	a. *You doubt or question the information:* claims	a. + that clause Khosla **claims** that cultural training will help avoid misunderstandings.
	b. *You agree with the author:* verbs: points out, shows, demonstrates	b. + that clause or wh- clause Khosla **shows** that cultural training will help avoid misunderstandings. Khosla **points out** how much cultural training can cost.
	expressions with <u>as</u>: (As + subject + verb) As Khosla points out/argues, demonstrates/explains/puts it/says/shows/states/suggests ...	+ complete clause **As the HP experience shows,** companies may have to spend a great deal of money for training.
4. Show that the author didn't explicitly state a point	implies	+ that clause Khosla **implies** that many employees of international companies are culturally insensitive.

[19]All verbs listed in parts 1 and 2a, 2b, and 2d of this chart, except for *encourages* and *invites*, can be followed by direct quotations as well as paraphrases.

Chapter 4

REFERENCE CHART 4.1   Passive Forms

A *be* passive verb always has a form of *be* and a past participle.
A *get* passive verb always has a form of *get* and a past participle.
The *get* passive is generally used only in the simple tenses (i.e., simple present, simple past, future) and not in the progressive or perfect tenses.

A. Verb Tenses and Modals in the Passive

	Past	*Present*	*Future*	*Modal*
Simple				
be	was/were taken	am/is/are taken	will be taken am/is/are going to be taken	might be taken
get	got taken	get/gets taken	will get taken am/is/are going to get taken	might get taken
Progressive	was/were being taken	am/is/are being taken	will be being taken *(rarely used)*	might be being taken *(rarely used)*
Perfect[20]	had been taken	have/has been taken	will have been taken	might have been taken

B. Other Passive Forms: Infinitives and Participles

	Infinitive	*Participle*
Simple/Present	to be taken to get taken	being taken
Perfect	to have been taken	having been taken

[20]The perfect progressive passive does not occur frequently in either speech or writing. The forms are: *had been being taken, has/have been being taken, will have been being taken, might have been being taken.*

REFERENCE CHART 4.2	The Passive: Additional Uses, Special Problems, Special Cases	
Problem	**Rule/Tip**	**Examples**
1. Misusing verbs that are always active	Only verbs that take objects (in the active) can be used in the passive. Pay attention to these verbs that are always active but are sometimes misused as passive verbs: *happen, occur, take place, appear, seem, arrive, fall, rise, go*	a. My friend's hard disk crashed and he lost all his files. ⊘ It **was happened** last night. *Correction:* It **happened** .... b. ⊘ When the error message **was appeared** on my screen, I asked my roommate for help. *Correction:* ... when the message **appeared** ....
2. Mistaking active for passive forms *(See Chart 4.1 for other information.)*	The auxiliary verb *have* (past, *had*) does <u>not</u> make a verb passive.	a. ⊘ I **had addicted** to computer games. *(active verb)* *Correction:* I **was addicted** .... b. ⊘ Before email, the fax machine **had used** extensively. *(active verb)* *Correction:* ... the fax machine **was used** ....
3. Misusing verbs that are usually passive	Memorize these verbs that are most frequently used in the passive: *bear, suppose*[21], *locate*	a. ⊘ My classmates **born** before the development of the Internet. *Correction:* My classmates **were born** .... b. ⊘ Today students **suppose to** get their course assignments from a website. *Correction:* Today students **are supposed** to get ... c. ⊘ My classroom **doesn't locate** near the computer lab. *Correction:* My classroom **isn't located** ....
4. Using troublesome verbs that can be both active and passive	Many verbs can be used in both active and passive, but for some verbs it is problematic to decide which form to use: e.g., *involve, affect.*	<u>Active:</u> Some serious accidents **involve** cell phones. Computers **have affected** the way we communicate. <u>Passive:</u> My classmate **was involved** in a serious accident while using his cell phone. The way we communicate **has been affected** by the availability of the Internet.
5. Correctly using *use* and *used to*	a. The verb *use* can be active or passive. b. *Used to* has two meanings: an adjective[22] meaning "accustomed to", or a semi-modal (followed by the simple form) that describes a past habitual action.	a. ⊘ Some students **are use** e-mail to ask their professors questions about assignments. *Correction:* Some students ~~are~~ **use** .... *(active verb)* Nowadays, email **is used** to ask about assignments. *(passive verb)* b. ⊘ Now students **used to** sending e-mails to their friends on a daily basis. *Correction:* Now students **are** used to .... *(active verb; the sentence needs a main verb, are.)* My parents **used to send** me e-mails everyday during my first year of college. *(active verb)*

Problem	Rule/Tip	Examples
6. Recognizing when to use the passive to make clear connections between clauses	a. When information at the end of one sentence (or clause) is repeated in the next sentence (or clause), that information should come at the <u>beginning</u> of the next sentence (or clause).	a. I couldn't send you an e-mail this morning because my e-mail system **was infected** by a virus last night. *(Here, information about <u>e-mail</u> comes at the end of the first clause. Choosing the passive allows you to put <u>my e-mail system</u> as the subject of the second clause.)*
	b. If there are several sentences about the same topic (person or thing), it is best to keep this topic consistently in the subject position. Passive allows you to do this.	b. <u>Henry</u> began an excellent job in a fast-growing software company several years ago. After three years of hard work, <u>he</u> **was informed** (by the management) that <u>he</u> was in line for a major promotion. <u>He</u> was thus finally able to buy a house for his family. *(Here, <u>Henry</u> is the topic of the three sentences. Choosing the passive allows you to put <u>he</u> as the subject of the second sentence.)*

---

[21]*be supposed to* is followed by the simple form of the verb.

[22]Like other adjective + preposition combinations (see Reference Chart 2.2, p. 173), *used + to* is followed by verb + *-ing* if a verb follows, as in the first example in 5b *(are + used + to + sending)*.

Chapter 5

REFERENCE CHART 5.1	Joining Words *so, so that, such that, that*	
Joining Word	**Tips**	**Examples**
1. **so** *(result)*	An informal coordinator; avoid overuse of *so*; use more formal joining words such as *as a result, consequently*; avoid beginning a sentence with *so*.	Parents and children do not always communicate well, **so** misunderstandings are common. *More appropriate for academic writing:* … communicate well; **as a result**, misunderstandings …

2. **so … that**, **such … that** *(result)*	a. Use *so* before:
	an adjective
	   *(so **bad** that …)*,
	an adverb
	   *(so **quickly** that …)*,
	few/many + plural
	   *(so **many problems** that …)*,
	little/much + noncount
	   *(so **much time** that …)*.
	b. Use **such** before:
	adjective + count noun
	   *(such **good relationships** that …)*,
	adjective + noncount noun
	   *(such **good communication** that …)*.
		a. My friend's relationship with her parents was **so** strained **that** they could not communicate.
		
		b. It was **such** a difficult situation **that** she decided to leave home.

3. **so that** *(purpose)*	*That* is optional, but it is preferred in academic writing. A modal occurs in the main clause. Meaning: in order to *(tells why)*	She left home **so that** she <u>would</u> be able to work out her problems. *(= She left home **in order to** work out her problems.)*
4. **that** *(relative pronoun in a relative clause)*	Use in a restrictive relative clause to refer to a person or thing. *(See Chart 6.1A.)*	Her parents didn't approve of the decision <u>**that** she made</u>.

5. **that** *(introducing a* that *clause)*	a. *That* clause used as a verb complement
	   (See Charts 3.3A and 6.2A.)
	b. *That* clause used as a noun complement
	   (See Chart 6.2B, patterns 8, 9.)
	c. *That* clause used as a noun subject
		a. They <u>knew</u> **that she would have problems being on her own**.
		b. They were not aware of <u>the fact</u> **that they were a large part of the problem**.
		c. <u>**That**</u> **she left home** surprised her friends.

Chapter 6

REFERENCE CHART 6.1	**Reduced Relative Clauses**

Chapter 6 reviews formation and use of relative clauses. (See Charts 6.1A, p. 129, and 6.1B, p. 130.) You can often streamline your writing by shortening a relative clause to a reduced relative clause.

Structure	Example	Information/Tips
Relative Clause	Environmentalists protest against companies **that are violating environmental laws.**	This relative clause can be reduced because the subject is a relative pronoun (*that*) and the verb includes a form of *be* (**are** *violating*).
Form of a Reduced Relative Clause: a. Verb + *-ing*	a. Environmentalists protest against companies ~~that are~~ **violating environmental laws**.	To reduce a relative clause, take out the subject relative pronoun and the *be* part of the verb.
b. Verb + *-ed*	b. Some activists contribute to organizations ~~which are~~ **recommended by the Nature Conservancy**. Hill's redwood tree, ~~which was~~ **eventually named Luna**, still stands in the redwood forest.	Some non-restrictive relative clauses can also be reduced. *(b, c, d)*
c. Noun (also called an appositive)	c. Julia Hill, ~~who is~~ **an environmental activist**, went to Ecuador to protest the destruction of the rainforest.	
d. Adjective	d. Julia Hill, ~~who is~~ **friendly and outgoing**, communicated with the loggers to break down the stereotypes they had of each other.	
e. Preposition[23]	e. The reporter said that the woman ~~who was~~ **in the tree** was Julia Hill	

[23]Prepositional phrases frequently follow and modify nouns. Not all of these are reductions of relative clauses; for example, the following are not reductions: *Hill's beliefs **about the environment**, scientists **from around the world**, research **on rainforest vegetation**, the logging **of redwood trees**, protests **against logging**, solutions **to problems**.*

Appendix C: Strategies for Writing

The Strategies for Writing in this appendix can guide you as you generate and develop your ideas in response to the readings and/or class discussions.

Read

Read Actively to Prepare for Writing

The more you are able to interact with a reading, the more you will understand it, and the better your writing will be. The following suggestions will help you develop active reading strategies and will help you prepare to write about the selections in this text.

Before Reading

Read and respond to the Before Reading questions. These questions are designed to prepare you to read by prompting you to think about the topic of the reading and any personal experiences you may have had that connect to the content.

After Reading

Use the After Reading questions to help you understand the reading completely and answer questions you may have. Answering the After Reading questions also prepares you to respond appropriately to the writing topics without wasting time unsuccessfully writing about content you are not sure about.

Move from Reading to Writing

Clarify an Assignment

Your teacher may ask you to choose from Topics for Writing or give you a different writing assignment. Before you start writing, make sure you understand the assignment. Ask yourself:

- What are the parts of the assignment?
- What does this assignment ask me to do?
- How much information from the reading, if any, is required?
- Do I need to explain the author's ideas?
- Do I need to state and explain my opinion about the author's ideas?
- Is personal response required?
- Which After Reading questions are related to the assignment?
- How much background information is required for the reader?
- Are there examples of student writing that I need to refer to in the chapter or on the website?

Establish a Purpose

Before you write, it is important to know what your purpose is. You may be doing one of the following or a combination:

- Explaining the main idea of a reading

  What is Deborah Tannen's point in "When You Shouldn't Tell It like It Is"? Using information and examples from the reading, discuss what you think the main idea is. *(Chapter 1)*

- Explaining your views on the author's ideas

  What is Khosla's point in the article, "You Say Tomato"? Do you agree with the ideas presented in the article? Why or why not? *(Chapter 3)*

- Giving a summary and personal response to the reading

  Compare your ideas and beliefs to those of Julia Hill. In an essay, first give a summary of the reading that focuses on Hill's purpose for her actions. Then discuss an example that is important to you: an environmental issue, a public protest, an experience with nature, or your ideas about "finding something more." In your paper, show a connection between your example and the story of Julia Hill. *(Chapter 6)*

- Writing about your experience that relates to the reading

  Explain why the four trees are important to Esperanza. Then write about something or someone who is important to you (*your* "four skinny trees"). Discuss an example from the past that shows why the person or thing is meaningful. Be sure to make a connection between your ideas and Cisneros' ideas at the end of your paper. *(Chapter 6)*

- Discussing a problem presented in the reading and possibly providing a solution

  Who or what is responsible for the separation of Sen-jo from her "soul"? Explain how the following people play a role: Chokan, Ochu, and Sen-jo. *(Chapter 5)*

- Writing creatively in response to the reading

  Imagine a world without computers. What would that world be like? Think about positive and negative outcomes. Consider how life would be different without computers at home, at school, and/or at work. *(Chapter 4)*

- Writing about a related topic and making connections to the reading

  "Return to Vietnam" illustrates points about different topics related to the human experience. Choose one of the following topics (or develop an idea of your own) and explain how the article makes a point about the topic you've chosen: expectations, disappointment, memory, change, roots. *(Chapter 2)*

About the Writing Process

Some writers write first and organize later. Others write detailed outlines and follow them closely. Some writers revise many times. Others revise minimally. Regardless of your individual process, the stages described below can help you with your writing.

Prewrite

Generate Ideas

As you participate in class discussions and do the activities in *Read, Write, Edit*, you can begin to generate ideas for writing by asking yourself some general questions:

- What is the author's point or message and why is it important?
- How does the author's point or message relate to my experience?
- What interests me most about this reading or this topic?
- What would interest my readers?
- Which of my ideas could be developed with support from the reading?

Figure Out and Focus Your Point

Use the following to guide you in finding a point that works:

- Focus on analysis (explaining and making connections), not summary. Formulate questions about the reading to help you:

  Question leading to summary: What happens to the two women in the office in "When You Shouldn't Tell It Like It Is"? *(Chapter 1)*

  Question leading to analysis: Why are the two women in "When You Shouldn't Tell It Like It Is" confused and unhappy?

- Narrow your topic so you can focus your discussion:

  Question that leads to a broad discussion: What are the problems with the Internet? *(Chapter 4)*

  Question that helps you narrow your point: What are the disadvantages connected with using the Internet for research?

- Choose a point that you can effectively develop with specific support from the reading and/or your experience. Go back to the reading and your notes on the After Reading questions and class discussions and highlight possible supporting ideas. Use the strategies described below for generating supporting ideas, including examples from your experience.

Get Started

The following techniques can help you generate and develop ideas and discover what you are interested in writing about. They can also help you narrow and focus your point. Brainstorming and mapping work especially well in groups or with partners.

Brainstorm: Brainstorming, or listing, helps you get ideas down on paper by quickly writing words or "chunks" of words in response to a question or topic. By reviewing your list you can categorize, make connections, discard some ideas, or expand on other ideas.

Map: Making a visual word map, also called clustering, generates ideas as you freely write down words associated with a topic. Begin with the topic: write it down and draw a circle around it. Write key words associated with the topic and draw circles around the key words and lines to show connections to the topic. Then add details under the key words and draw more circles and lines to connect the supporting details to the key words each detail refers to. Mapping organizes your ideas as you generate them and helps you see which ones you would like to develop and which ones to discard.

Freewrite: Freewriting helps you get ideas down on paper without worrying about form or structure. It also helps you come up with new ideas that you can use when developing a paper. Write a question about the reading and answer it by writing rapidly for several minutes without stopping to reread or thinking about grammar. (See example questions in Figure Out and Focus Your Point, p. 187.)

Loop: Using a previous freewrite, underline a word or phrase you would like to write more about. Write it on a different sheet of paper and freewrite again. Looping, or repeating this process, often results in detailed answers to your questions and specific examples from your experience that you can use to formulate and support the main point of your paper.

Write, Revise, Edit

Draft and Revise

When you write your paper, you will not necessarily write in the order presented here. Be sure to write in an order that is appropriate for your topic and your individual way of writing. Some writers like to organize before they begin. Others write first and organize as they revise. Use the suggestions below that best fit your process and purpose.

The Introduction

An effective introduction to a paper that discusses a reading should include the following:

- The title of the reading;
- The author of the reading;
- The important people or main characters discussed in the reading;
- A brief description of the situation described in the reading;
- Your main idea or point in response to a topic;
- Information—details and facts—from the reading that your reader will need to know in order to understand your main idea.

If the paper doesn't discuss a reading, make sure you make your main point clear and give important background information.

Refer to the Text

To convince your readers that your analysis and discussion of a reading is reasonable, you'll want to include references to the text that support your ideas. This evidence can be in the form of paraphrases or quotations. (The two examples below are from Chapter 2. See Reference Chart 3.1, p. 177, for additional information about quoting accurately.)

Quote: Use brief quotations when the author's language helps you clearly make your point. The writer supports his ideas about the significance of Arnett's experience with the tofu dessert with the quotation, "My roots may be here, but they were buried long ago." (lines 35–36) Notice that brackets replace words from the original with the writer's own words.

> Arnett's experience with the tofu custard makes her face the truth and think of the facts. She realizes that she no longer comfortably belongs in Vietnam even though that is the place of her birth. She understands that her "roots may be [there], but they were buried long ago."

Paraphrase: Paraphrase, or use your own words, to summarize information with some detail or explain the author's ideas without using the author's exact words or sentence structure. Here the writer paraphrases the quotation, "Though I spent most of my life in the United States, bits of Vietnamese culture still seeped into my American childhood," (lines 1–2) and adds detail from other parts of the reading.

> Because of her close connection to her Vietnamese mother while growing up in the United States, Arnett was regularly influenced by Vietnamese language, customs, and culture.

The Conclusion

A conclusion should flow smoothly and logically from the body of the paper and provide an ending that finishes the discussion. You may conclude by using some of the following techniques:

- Briefly summarize your main points.
- Refer to something you wrote in the introduction.
- Make connections. For example, explain the connection between your example or experience and the author's message or point.
- Raise a question that is closely tied to the discussion in the body of your paper for your readers to consider.

In your conclusion:

- Avoid introducing new ideas that need further development.
- Don't give a long summary.
- Don't directly address your reader with "you."
- Avoid ending too quickly.

Peer Review for Content

By closely reading the paper of a partner and giving feedback on the content, writers can help each other develop and support their ideas and opinions. This feedback can help writers evaluate their drafts and figure out how to revise their papers.

Activity 1 • Read Around—Getting Ideas from Other Writers

Form small groups with students who have written on the same topic and follow these steps:

- Pass your paper to the person next to you.
- Read through the paper which has been passed to you.
- When you are finished reading, on a separate piece of paper, take notes on ideas that you find interesting or different from what you've written in your paper, and write down any questions that you have about your partner's paper.
- Then, pass the paper you just read on to the next person.
- Repeat the process until each person has read and taken notes on all the papers.
- Discuss your responses to the papers with your group, so writers can take notes.
- As a class, discuss the ideas that each group came up with, and if time permits, put notes on the board.

Activity 2 • Peer Review—Reading and Responding to a Partner's Paper

This activity can follow Activity 1 or it can be done separately. Work with a partner who has written on the same topic. Follow the steps below, writing your responses on a separate piece of paper. This paper will be the Peer Review Sheet.

- Exchange papers. Read your partner's paper all the way through once. Write questions you have about the paper on the Peer Review Sheet.

- Does your partner include adequate background about the topic? Give comments about any background information that is missing.

- Does the writer include a point or statement of opinion about the topic? Underline what you see as the writer's main point and give comments about how the main point could be stronger.

- Does the writer support the ideas in the paper by providing adequate details and examples and explaining them clearly? Comment on the following topics on the Peer Review Sheet and on the paper.

  Strengths: What is interesting and/or well-supported?

  To work on: What is unclear and/or not supported?

- Does the writer include a conclusion that connects with the introduction and provides an "end" to the paper? Give your partner comments about the conclusion.

- Discuss your comments with your partner. Then, give your partner the Peer Review Sheet to help in revising the draft.

General Guidelines for Revising

Depending on your individual writing process, your experience writing about readings, and your skill as a writer, you may need to revise several times.

Use Partner Feedback

Refer to the Peer Review Sheet from your partner and follow the steps below:

1. Read, think about, and evaluate your partner's comments.

2. Decide which suggestions you think are most useful in helping you revise.

3. Use your partner's suggestions and your own ideas as you revise to make your main idea or opinion clear and well supported.

Revise on Your Own

Allow some time to pass between writing and revising your paper and ask yourself:

- Does the paper have a clear main point?

- Do I need to rewrite the main point to better reflect what I've written in the body?

- Does the paper move logically and smoothly from beginning to end?

- Do I provide enough support for my ideas?

- When writing about an author's ideas, do I provide enough explanation?

- Are my introduction and conclusion an effective beginning and ending?

- Will the paper interest my readers?

Edit

When you are finished revising and have a final draft, be sure to use the grammar information in the chapters, in the Editing Guides in Appendix A, and in the Reference Charts in Appendix B to help you edit and finish your paper.

Index

Items in parentheses indicate that a topic is treated in an Activity (A), a Chart (C), or a Reference Chart (RC).